P9-DVJ-352

THE CASE
of
GENERAL YAMASHITA

THE CASE *of* GENERAL YAMASHITA

A. Frank Reel

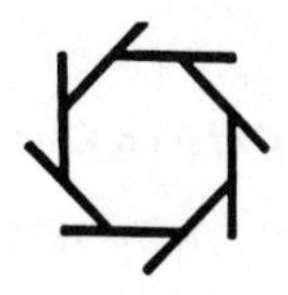

1971

OCTAGON BOOKS

New York

Reprinted 1971
by special arrangement with A. Frank Reel

OCTAGON BOOKS
A DIVISION OF FARRAR, STRAUS & GIROUX, INC.
19 Union Square West
New York, N. Y. 10003

LIBRARY OF CONGRESS CATALOG CARD NUMBER: 71-154015

ISBN 0-374-96766-0

Printed in U.S.A. by
NOBLE OFFSET PRINTERS, INC.
NEW YORK 3, N. Y.

TABLE OF CONTENTS

APPENDIX

I

RAPE, MURDER, AND A STATEMENT

"THE significance of the issue facing the Court today cannot be overemphasized. An American military commission has been established to try a fallen military commander of a conquered nation for an alleged war crime."

With these words, Mr. Justice Murphy of the United States Supreme Court opened his opinion in the case of General Yamashita.

The military commission that tried the general was entirely American; the high court that gave a ruling on the case was American; the general who approved and executed the sentence was American.

America made the decision, pronounced the law, and set the precedent. The precedent will not be lost on the world.

If the decision was right and just, it will become a precedent of justice among nations.

If the decision was wrong, it must turn into a curse upon justice among nations, unless the wrong is acknowledged to the world.

In this alone lies the importance of the case of General Yamashita. This alone is the reason for which this book has been written.

* * * * *

The girl's voice was barely audible. "Three Japanese marines . . . dragged me out. . . . I tried to resist . . . they pushed me down . . . one of them stood guard. . . ."

Another young girl stepped to the witness stand. Her age,

she said, was sixteen. Almost in a whisper she described the Japanese "marine" who had forced her to accompany him to a room in the Bay View Hotel in besieged Manila on the night of February 9, 1945. "He took ahold of my blouse and tore it open . . . he laid the bayonet on one side and the gun on the other side of me."

The witnesses' stories were addressed to five middle-aged men, generals in the United States Army. The generals watched the girls' faces, except for those moments when each would turn his gaze in the direction of the prisoner who was to be held responsible for the wrongs that the witnesses were reciting. No ordinary man could hear that testimony and fail to be moved by a desire for revenge.

Less than twenty feet from the girls, facing them, sat a man who was described by the judges and the attorneys simply as "the accused." Calm, stolid, occasionally blinking, he stared at every witness who took the stand. Even when he inclined his head the better to hear a remark of the interpreter, who sat on his right, he did not let his eyes stray from the witness.

Two short months before, this man had been a powerful military leader, a general who commanded the loyalties and the lives of more than a hundred thousand men. Now he was a dishonored prisoner, charged with the most heinous of crimes, captive of a people whose fanatical hatred for him was in direct proportion to the power he had but recently wielded. It is probable that he believed, as did every other person in the courtroom, that he was soon to meet a violent death. But he was completely stoical; no sign of emotion crossed his oriental features.

Surrounding him were his lawyers, American Army officers appointed as "defense counsel." One of them, a middle-aged colonel, leaned over and whispered to a younger captain, who sat beside him: "This testimony is terrible."

"Yes—and no," answered the captain. "In some respects it helps more than it hurts. I wish it were all like this."

Strange statement for an attorney for the defense? Perhaps not. At any rate, it was not "all like that." Rape was only part of the gruesome picture.

An elderly Chinese is on the witness stand, painting a vivid word picture of three of his countrymen kneeling in front of a ditch that Japanese soldiers had forced their captives to dig in the rugged soil of Batangas Province: "Then three Japanese soldiers with fixed bayonets advanced and thrust the bayonets into the bodies of the kneeling Chinese. When the bayonets were pushed through the victims, the soldiers kicked the bodies into the ditch. That was around ten yards away from me. Around five yards away from us I saw a Japanese officer with a big saber in his hands. He went forward and he lift his sword and cut off the head of a Chinese."

Now a Filipina woman is in the witness chair, holding an infant on her lap. She is shouting: "I have two children, one on each hand. I was holding them one on each hand. We were near the river and the Japanese was dragging my child away from me. . . . When they held me by the shoulder tightly, they were able to get my child. After they have taken my children, each one of them screamed. When I looked over at my girl child I saw that she was bayoneted right on the breast, which penetrated through the back. After I saw that my children were wounded—I was bayoneted on my back . . . five times. . . . My two children were killed." What about the child now in her arms? It was born only three months after the massacre.

Another Filipina mother tells of seeing five of her children bayoneted and cremated: "Four of my children were burned in that house, and I was carrying with me one of my children with his intestines out. The nine-months-old baby with his intestines out was the one I carried with me. . . . Yes, he died of those bayonet wounds."

For twenty days and for six or seven hours of each day, similar testimony continued. Approximately two hundred witnesses took the stand. Scores of pictures, many of them gruesome scenes depicting mutilated bodies, supported the statements. Tens of thousands of innocent people had been brutally killed, thousands more had been tortured and raped. If the testimony was true (and I believe that most of it was) and if the accused General Tomoyuki Yamashita, erstwhile commander of the Fourteenth Army Group, Imperial Japanese Army, was responsible for the atrocities, then he was indeed the vilest criminal in all the world's history. Genghis Khan and Attila the Hun must bow in humble homage before this bloody monster.

The five American Army generals who constituted the military commission that tried General Yamashita did find him guilty as a war criminal. The American commander-in-chief of the Pacific Theater confirmed that finding, saying: "This officer . . . has failed his duty to his troops, to his country, to his enemy and to mankind. He has failed utterly his soldier's faith"; his life was a "blot on the military profession."

On the twenty-third day of February, 1946, General Yamashita was stripped of his uniform and hanged in disgrace.

And yet—

II

"THE LAWS OF WAR"

THE Japanese bombing of Pearl Harbor on December 7, 1941, was followed by a similar attack and an invasion of the Philippine Islands. In the confusion of the ensuing weeks, American Army authorities in the Philippines proceeded to confiscate (or "requisition") all available property that might be useful to the American and Filipino defenders of the islands. Every automobile and truck that was capable of sustained motion, stocks of food, clothing, and hardware, communication facilities, fuel stores—all were forcibly taken from their private owners for military use in the emergency. Of course, under the extraordinary circumstances, the usual Army procurement procedure had been dispensed with. In many cases the dispossessed owners of the property were given rudely scrawled receipts; in some instances even that much formality was lacking.

Three years later American troops reoccupied the Philippine archipelago. As each area was cleared of the enemy, the officers of the victorious forces were besieged by claimants who now sought reimbursement for their losses of 1941. Accordingly, a "Claims Service" office was set up in the ruins of Manila, even before that embattled city was cleared of the enemy, and a crew of American Army lawyers and investigators waded into the factual and legal problems presented by a hundred thousand petitioners. I was one of those lawyers.

What is the connection between the settlement of claims and the defense of an accused war criminal? In my case it was a bit of accidental "muddling through" that was not untypical of Army practice. Indeed, this bit of personal history may be justified by the nostalgic reminiscences that it will undoubtedly stimulate in the minds of other ex-GI's. The truth is that I was appointed as one of General Yamashita's defense counsel because I said that I did not want the job.

The entire problem of trying captured Japanese "war criminals" in the Philippines had been assigned in the summer of 1945 to the War Crimes Division of General MacArthur's Judge Advocate Office. Dozens of well-trained men from that division labored for many months preparing the case against General Yamashita. Starting long before the Japanese surrender, able Army lawyers were roaming over the islands and provinces of the Philippine archipelago, taking statements and affidavits from aggrieved citizens who could attest to brutalities of Japanese soldiers. With them went photographers and intelligence officers. And in Washington and Manila other Army lawyers were poring over heavy texts on international law and dictating voluminous opinions to the end that the prosecuting officers might have the necessary authorities available during the eventual trial. But, with all that careful preparation, little or no thought had been given to the matter of lawyers to defend the accused. Whatever the prevalent idea as to the meaning of the familiar concept of "fair trial," it was recognized that the accused must have the right to counsel, and it is a basic fundamental of American military law that every accused has Army counsel appointed to defend him. He need not accept the services of the appointed defense counsel—he may employ lawyers of his own choice—but it was essential that the order appointing the military commission that was to try General Yamashita include not only a designation of prosecuting counsel but also the assignment of Army officers on the defense. This order was scheduled for publication by October 1, 1945—less than one month after the surrender.

Although the prosecution staff numbered scores of lawyers and assistants, it was planned to have the function of trial and presentation of evidence restricted to six officers. Accordingly, six more lawyer officers were desired for the defense. Where could they be found?

General MacArthur had delegated the function of conducting the trial to Lieutenant General Wilhelm D. Styer, the commander of AFWESPAC (the letters stand for "Army Forces, Western Pacific," the subechelon that had been given jurisdiction over military installations in the Philippine Islands). General Styer, in turn, referred the matter of defense counsel to his staff judge advocate, Colonel "Bud" Young. Young's force was small and overworked. He could spare but one man, Lieutenant Colonel James G. Feldhaus, a lawyer who had been a taxation expert in South Dakota. Young also drafted Colonel Harry E. Clarke, of Altoona, Pennsylvania, from his job as head of the Adjutant General's Correction Division, a position that entailed responsibility for the operation of the disciplinary barracks and rehabilitation center for convicted American soldiers in the Philippines. Young then obtained the Army officer who was legal adviser to the military police command in Manila, Lieutenant Colonel Walter C. Hendrix, a practitioner from Atlanta, Georgia.

Three more men were needed. Claims Service had most of the lawyers in AFWESPAC, so, on a day late in September, Young telephoned the claims office and asked to speak to Colonel Myatt, the chief of claims. Colonel Myatt was absent, confined to the hospital with a mild ailment; hence, in accordance with military custom, Young spoke to Myatt's executive officer, Lieutenant Colonel Egner, the acting chief. Young told Egner that three officers who were lawyers were needed at once for the Yamashita defense; that they might be any three that Egner or Myatt might name; that he, Young, was well acquainted with two claims men, Lieutenant Colonel Leigh Clark and Major George Guy; that he would be pleased to have those two men plus another one; but that, in any event, three names were to be given to the top personnel officer, one Major General Sturtevant, no later than the following day.

Rumor spreads rapidly in any Army installation, and within an hour the officers in the Claims Service knew of the impending draft. That night at dinner I discussed the possibilities with Bill Ruddock, an officer who was attached to General MacArthur's Judge Advocate section. Ruddock had seen the document that had been prepared as the basis for the Yamashita trial. Called the "charge" in Army parlance, it was a short statement of the offense that the prosecution was to prove against the surrendered Japanese general.

Ruddock expressed himself in strong words about the charge. "Yamashita is being charged as a war criminal because his men violated the laws of war," he said. "They have nothing on him at all. They're trying to establish a new theory—that a commanding officer is responsible if his troops violate the laws of war, regardless of whether he ordered the violations or even knew of them. Under such a principle, I suppose even MacArthur should be tried. It is bad law. I wish I had the opportunity of taking a crack at it. I wish I could be defense counsel. Why don't you volunteer for it?"

I was a mere captain. Aside from the two men from Claims Service whose names had been suggested by Young, I did not know the already appointed personnel of the defense. I did, however, know that they were superior to me in rank, and I had had enough experience with the Army to realize that, if an officer wishes to stand on rank, those who serve under him are helpless. Also, in civilian practice I had learned that it can be very unpleasant to be "sitting in" at the trial of a case that is conducted by another lawyer. No matter how well the other lawyer does the job, the observer who is constrained to silence will believe he could do it better, and the nervous strain attendant upon such a position did not appear attractive to me. With my modest rank, I would probably be lost under a blanket of colonels.

The following morning upon leaving my tent I met Lieutenant Colonel Egner. "Don't put me on that case," I said to Egner. "It isn't that I object to defending a Japanese war criminal. As a matter of fact, I would like that, but I know you have one full colonel, four lieutenant colonels, and a major already on the case, and I'm only a captain and I'll be darned if I want to carry anybody's briefcase for the next six weeks."

"O.K., I'll remember that. I don't blame you," answered Egner.

Later that day Egner went to the hospital to see Colonel Myatt, our chief. After discussing affairs of the office, Egner told Myatt that AFWESPAC wanted three officers from Claims Service who were lawyers to be assigned as defense counsel in the Yamashita trial. Colonel Myatt sat up in bed, his eyes blazing. To take three officers from a division head who is trying to build an empire and to accomplish a difficult task is like attempting to take three cubs from a mother-bear.

"They can't have them," said Myatt. "We need all our men. We are shorthanded now. You know how few lawyers we have and how many more we need. Washington just turned down our requisition for more officers. How are we going to get our claims settled if they start raiding our personnel?"

Then the colonel became a man of action. Pointing a finger at his bewildered assistant, he ordered: "You go to see General Sturtevant right away. You tell him we can't spare the men."

An obedient soldier, Egner did as he was bid. Later that day he walked into General Sturtevant's office and informed the general that Colonel Myatt had told him to report that he was sorry but that he could not furnish any officers for the forthcoming trial. Elderly, bald General Sturtevant was very polite. "Why not?" he asked quietly.

"Well," explained Egner, "we haven't enough officers now. We need all we have to do our job as it is."

"Anything else?" asked the general.

"Yes, Washington has just turned down our request for additional officers and we're shorthanded."

"Anything else?"

"Yes, we have a backlog of over ten thousand claims, and General MacArthur wants these claims settled, and we just can't do it if we have to give up any lawyers."

"Anything else?"

"No," said Egner, "I guess that's all."

"Well, Colonel Egner," said the general, his voice suddenly becoming loud and his manner stern, "I have a piece of paper here. On it are two names. I want a third *and I want it right now!*" With that, General Sturtevant pushed a piece of paper across the desk to Egner, thrust a pencil into his hand, and, as Egner said in describing his predicament to me later: "I had to write down a name right then and there, and all I could think of at the moment was that you had said something to me about the goddamned case that morning so I wrote down your name."

As it turned out, my fear of subordination was not justified. I found Colonel Clarke, who was senior counsel, to be a man of rare understanding and courage. He did not stand on rank at all; and, as a matter of fact, during the trial of the case the two junior officers, Captain Milton Sandberg and I, did the bulk of the cross-examining of the witnesses. Sandberg's assignment as defense counsel came about in as unorthodox a manner as did mine. Lieutenant Colonel Leigh Clark, who had been one of the members of Claims Service originally appointed as defense counsel, was extremely upset and angered by it. He was a judge in Birmingham, Alabama, and expressed the fear that if he served as lawyer for a Japanese general it would be impossible for him ever to be re-elected to the bench. The inevitable publicity resulting from the case would, he said, be utilized by his political opponents, who would certainly see to it that he became identified in the public mind with his unpopular client. That night, in his tent, the Alabaman gave voice to his opinions before some fellow-officers, all but one of whom agreed that his fears were justified. Sandberg, who was present, was the lone exception, and he ventured the opinion that the good judge might be exaggerating slightly and that he did not believe the publicity would be quite so damaging as the others thought. The following day, Leigh Clark conferred with Colonel Young, and, as a result, a new order was issued removing the judge's name from the list of defense counsel and substituting that of Sandberg.

III

THE WAR THROUGH THE ENEMY'S EYES

AUGUST, 1945. On the sixth day of that explosive month an atomic bomb was dropped on the Japanese city of Hiroshima. Two days later, Russia declared war on Japan; and on the day after that a second atomic bomb was loosed, this time on Nagasaki. Twenty-four hours later the Tokyo radio announced that the Japanese government was prepared to meet Allied demands for "unconditional surrender," and by August 14 the holocaust was at an end. The emperor of Japan broadcast an "imperial rescript," ordering his troops to give themselves up and to co-operate with the victors; and preparations were made to execute formal surrender documents before the month had faded into history.

At his ambulatory headquarters, high in the mountains of northern Luzon, General Tomoyuki Yamashita, commander of all Japanese troops in the Philippine Islands, heard the radio broadcast of his emperor's rescript. But he waited until September 2, the day of formal surrender, to pass through his defense lines, descend from the hills, and present his sword to the American conquerors.

As the end of the war approached, Americans had said much about bringing enemy "war criminals" to trial. Preparation for any criminal trial is likely to take time, and in Europe, although the "cease-fire" order had been effective for many months, the projected war-crimes trial at Nuremberg was not yet under way. Indeed, it was not destined to commence until more than half a year after the capture of the culprits. In the Pacific Theater of Operations, however, there was no such delay. The military commission that was to try General Yamashita, as well as his defense counsel, were both appointed on October 1, 1945, less than one month after his surrender.

The defense met together for the first time on October 4, decided that our first task was to acquaint ourselves with our "client," and arranged a conference to take place the following day.

At that time General Yamashita was interned with other Japanese prisoners of war at New Bilibid Prison, which was located about thirty miles south of Manila. Upon arrival at the prison camp, the defense staff was ushered into the chapel, the only room available for a conference. We asked to have the general, his chief-of-staff, his assistant chief-of-staff, and his interpreter brought in. The prison officer grinned. "So you're the guys that have to defend these monkeys, are you?" he asked.

As we waited, we wondered what these "monkeys" would be like. None of us had ever been well acquainted with any Japanese. Was the common belief that they were likely to be "tricky," evasive, and unreliable merely propaganda? Whatever they were, we would be on guard. No polite and clever explanations would fool us. We were as skeptical as only lawyers can be.

That conference was the first of approximately seventy similar meetings. From then until General Yamashita was sentenced, more than two months later, he, Lieutenant General Muto (his chief-of-staff), Major General Utsunomiya (his assistant chief-of-staff), and his interpreter, Masakatsu Hamamoto, were inseparable, and we saw them daily.

The fact that Hamamoto was Yamashita's interpreter proved to be the greatest stroke of good fortune that we were to have during the trial. When we heard the young man speak flawless English, we asked him where he had learned the language.

"Harvard," he said proudly, "class of '27."

For me that was an unexpected shock. Could it be that this most foreign of enemies was a man with whom I shared some of my most cherished loyalties? I looked at him closely. And then I remembered the oriental student who had been in the class ahead of me and whom I had often seen running through the Yard in Cambridge, dressed in tennis clothes. Before the interrogation of General Yamashita could start, I had to describe for a Japanese prisoner of war the full details of the Harvard Tercentenary celebration of 1936, explain what had become of "Copey" and Kittredge and Bliss Perry, and tell of the fate of our football team during the years since Pearl Harbor.

After graduation Hamamoto had returned to Japan, where he had gone to work for General Motors Corporation. He had started as a factory laborer, he told us, and had worked his way up to a responsible executive position when the war came in December, 1941. Then he went into the Japanese military service as a civilian interpreter and secretary attached to the army. During the latter part of the Japanese occupation of the Philippine Islands he acted as an unofficial liaison officer between the army and the "puppet" government that the Japanese had sponsored in the archipelago. When General Yamashita took over the army command, Hamamoto became his personal secretary and interpreter, and he had remained by the general's side throughout that last disastrous year.

Hamamoto was our indispensable man. We were soon to learn that interpretation can be a most exasperating problem during a trial. Translation of Japanese into English and the reverse are most difficult, for the languages do not have the common roots found in European tongues, nor can the social and military customs to which the words necessarily refer be readily transposed. But Hamamoto's greatest value lay in his grasp of those customs and of Japanese and American thought and psychology. Even his knowledge of American slang proved useful. At one point during that initial conference, mention was made of certain Japanese generals. I asked Hamamoto what their function was. "Oh," he said airily, "they're Pentagon boys." And later he told us gleefully of how he had acted as interpreter for a conversation between an American soldier and an English "Tommy."

Because of Hamamoto's quickness and wit, defense counsel were never quite sure that all General Yamashita's statements (all spoken through his interpreter) were genuinely his. We occasionally accused Hamamoto of being the author of some of the general's more convincing and analytical discussions—accusations which Hamamoto insistently denied. It was the cause of much banter between us. But at the end of the trial, while Yamashita was being cross-examined on the witness stand for eleven hours by the chief prosecutor and was answering rapid-fire, unexpected, cleverly phrased catch questions with his own straightforward, emphatic, and at times even poetic brilliance (the answers now being interpreted, not by Hamamoto, but by the painstaking, bumbling "official court interpreters") we were forced to admit the error of our overcautious skepticism.

The initial interview with General Yamashita revealed a man of dignity and poise. We explained to him that he had been charged with being a war criminal and that we had been appointed by the American Army to defend him. He was entitled to any lawyers he wanted, we said—he might even send to Japan for counsel if he did not wish to avail himself of our services. Yamashita smiled. "I am very grateful to the United States government for furnishing me counsel," he replied. "I appreciate your giving up time from what must be pressing duties to defend me."

Yamashita had received a Japanese translation of the charge. It recited that he had violated the laws of war in that he had failed to discharge his duty as a commander to control his troops, permitting them to commit brutal atrocities. Could he not be informed further as to what those atrocities were, when and where they were committed, and who the perpetrators were? We said that we had already decided to move that the charge be made "more definite and certain," and we understood that the prosecution was ready to furnish us with a "bill of particulars" that would give details of the crimes which they were prepared to prove. We could, however, tell the general that we had heard of many horrible atrocities that were probably typical of what his accusers had in mind. There was murder, torture, rape, pillage, the destruction of Manila, mistreatment of civilian internees and prisoners, the cold-blooded killing of approximately one hundred and fifty American prisoners of war on Palawan Island—Major Guy had recently been on Palawan and had been shown the place where the murders occurred. Didn't the general know about any of these things?

Yamashita was emphatic. He had heard of none of these occurrences. And if such crimes had been committed—.

We cut him short. There was no doubt about it. The atrocities could certainly be proved. What we were concerned about was the question of any connection that the general might have had with them. What we wanted to know, first, was how in the world so many brutalities could be committed and he not know about them.

The answer turned out to be a complete history of the Japanese side of the Philippine campaign. It was Yamashita at his best, for he was essentially a strategist, most happy when he was drawing military diagrams and maps and explaining the disposition and movement of troops. Aided by General Muto, whose prodigious memory produced a wealth of detail, the American defense counsel heard the inside story of our reconquest of the Philippine archipelago from the lips of the fabled "Tiger of Malaya." Aside from any connection with the impending trial, it was a thrilling experience for American officers, who had been engaged in making war on the Japanese but one short month before, to hear the story of enemy reaction to our Army's efforts. Literally, it was "something to write home about."

But the narrative was more than a history of military maneuvers. It proved to be the essential basis of General Yamashita's defense in the war-crimes trial; for it was the story of a man with a mission to perform, a man who was beset by overwhelming difficulties and harassed by overpowering forces, a man who was entirely unable to carry out the ordinary functions of a "desk" commander in a rear echelon, whose ability to communicate with his troops was destroyed, and who was finally isolated and crushed by the superior power of his opponents.

Yamashita, we learned, first saw the Philippine Islands when he arrived there on October 7, 1944, to assume command of the Japanese Fourteenth Army Group. That was the first notice that some of us had that, contrary to popular impression, he had not been connected with the "Bataan death march" of 1942. At the time of the "death march," Yamashita had been in command of the Japanese Malayan campaign, from which post he was sent to northern Manchuria. He had remained in Manchuria until September 27, 1944, on which date he was suddenly recalled to Tokyo and thence dispatched to the now precarious Philippines. He had remained in Tokyo just long enough to exchange his heavy uniforms for tropical clothing. He had received no orders other than those instructing him to take over the command of the Fourteenth Army Group from Lieutenant General Kuroda, a task that encompassed the military mission of defending the Philippine archipelago against the expected American attack. Yamashita's position was to be subordinate to the supreme southern commander, Field Marshal Terauchi, whose headquarters were at that time in Manila and who, jointly with the Japanese ambassador, was to retain control over all political and economic affairs.

Yamashita found himself in an impossible situation. The haphazard defense plan that had been prepared by his predecessor was useless and had to be scrapped. Supplies were meager, especially of the all-important commodities, rice and petroleum, and had been unsystematically scattered over the islands. Command functions were badly divided. Of the approximately three hundred thousand Japanese troops on Luzon, Yamashita found that his chain of command encompassed only one hundred and twenty thousand, or less than half. He had been given no control over the air force, over the maritime command, over the naval troops, or over some thirty thousand men who were attached directly to the supreme southern command. Those soldiers that were assigned to him were poorly trained and of low morale, largely as a result of the fact that they had served overlong in the tropics and because a considerable number of them were casuals who had suffered the discouraging experience of having had transport ships sunk from under them. A few weeks before Yamashita's arrival, American planes had established control of the air over southern Luzon, and the general soon learned that he could not even venture from his headquarters except on cloudy days or at night.

Of General Kuroda's staff officers, only three men were left to orient Yamashita to his task. The chief-of-staff was ill and had to be evacuated to Japan. His place was filled by Lieutenant General Muto, who was rushed to Manila from Sumatra, where he had been in command of the Japanese occupation forces. Muto was a brilliant administrator but, like Yamashita's other staff officers, was completely unfamiliar with Philippine problems and Philippine geography. He arrived in Manila on October 20, 1944, to assume his new duties and was immediately informed that American troops had landed at Leyte two days before. "Very interesting," he said, "but where is Leyte?"

Before General Yamashita could even learn of his problems, preparatory to formulation of a plan to deal with them, the Leyte landing engrossed his energies. The Japanese had expected an American landing attempt in one of the southern islands, but they did not know that it would occur so soon as it did. Yamashita's orders were that the projected battle would be a Japanese navy and air force "show," and his army troops would merely "co-operate" with those other branches. The Japanese army maintained one division on the island of Leyte, and this, together with regiments stationed on other near-by islands of the Visayan group, had been considered sufficient to handle the situation. In typical Japanese military fashion, the orders from imperial headquarters in Tokyo had simply said: "The navy and air force will engage the Americans and will win a decisive victory."

Of course, the initial victory went to the United States forces, a fact which apparently struck the Tokyo leaders with some impact four days after the first landing. At any rate, on October 22, Yamashita's orders were suddenly changed, and he was directed to send "the greatest possible troop strength" to Leyte forthwith. Entirely unprepared for this revolutionary shift, Yamashita tried his best to carry it out. He managed to gather together fifty thousand soldiers and accompanying supplies of food and ammunition from areas widely dispersed throughout Luzon. He fought to get ships from the maritime command and protection for those ships from the Japanese navy and air force, and, by dint of herculean work, he managed to get an expeditionary force under way. It was not his fault that the activity of American submarines and airplanes was such that only half those men got to Leyte alive. I believe that Yamashita used soldierly restraint when he described his problem to us in the following language:

"I was naturally unprepared for the sudden change in our

over-all defense plans and experienced tremendous difficulty in the successful execution of this new order. The problem of assembling the widely dispersed units originally intended for the defense of Luzon, the drawing-up and execution of new disposition of troops, the reconcentration and rearrangement of war-material depots, the mobilization of transport facilities, the consultation and arrangement with the navy and the air force command for convoy and aerial protection, and other complex problems connected with having to organize and transfer a large army composed of units under diversified command to a new battlefield were multifarious and difficult to solve, and, in spite of my anxiety for quick action, progress was slow and far from meeting requirements. The transports which were massed through admirable efforts on the part of my subordinates were, with a few exceptions, practically all sunk or damaged by the American air force en route, and it was my misfortune to receive discouraging reports of these disasters day after day. However, my orders were such that I was obliged to draw up new shipping plans to meet the critical situation in Leyte. I was so occupied with these difficult problems that I had hardly time to turn my attention to other business."

Yamashita realized that the battle for Leyte was lost when the Americans accomplished their landing at Ormoc Bay on December 7. But his superiors at the imperial headquarters did not see it that way and insisted that there be further troop movements and continued defensive activity in Leyte. Accordingly, the general ordered the Japanese to counterattack by landing in force at Carigara Bay, and he was again compelled to bring troops and supplies to the Luzon harbors for this purpose. It was not until the Americans moved into the island of Mindoro that the Tokyo authorities agreed that Leyte was lost and Yamashita was permitted to abandon the Carigara project.

Thus mid-December had arrived before Yamashita could

turn his attention to the defense of threatened Luzon. The draining-off of picked troops for the Leyte debacle had so weakened the Japanese garrison that the general stated that had MacArthur's men landed on Luzon early in December, they could have overrun that vital island within a very short time. Yamashita saw his immediate problem as twofold: first, to rebuild his troop strength and, second, to unify his command. To accomplish the first objective, he requested Count Terauchi to get reinforcements. Three fresh divisions were dispatched from Japan, but again the American airplanes and submarines interfered. Only from one-third to one-half of the new men arrived on Luzon. He was more successful in the unification of command, albeit the process was slow. In December, Yamashita was given control over the thirty thousand miscellaneous troops that had been attached to the southern command—on January 1 he became head of the air forces—and gradually, over a period of time that covered January and the first half of February, he succeeded to the command of the various units of the maritime force. An extremely limited "tactical" control over the naval forces "when engaged in land operations" was given to Yamashita early in January.

Yamashita saw that the defense of Luzon presented a difficult strategic problem. The Americans were free to select any of numerous landing points, and the Japanese general was convinced that, aided by our superior naval and air forces, our army could successfully carry out any of the landing operations "with absolute certainty." Once the landing had been made, the strength and mobility of our fire power was such that Yamashita saw that he could not meet us on flat land and that his only chance to delay our advance was to take to the hills. Later, on the witness stand, Yamashita described this problem in vigorous language:

"In view of the Leyte operations I realized that a decisive battle was impossible. Therefore, I decided on a delaying action to divert American forces in Luzon so as to keep them from attacking Japan as long as possible. In my experience with the Leyte operations I realized that the American air forces and navy were exceedingly superior to ours and also the fire power of the ground forces was superior and very mobile. Therefore, I knew that I could not conduct warfare on flat land. So I decided to employ a delaying action in the mountains."

Where did the city of Manila fit into this picture? "I decided to put Manila outside the battle area," said Yamashita. "I ordered my troops out of Manila. I decided to abandon it without a battle. There were three reasons for this decision. First, the population of Manila is approximately one million; therefore, it is impossible to feed them. The second reason is that the buildings are very inflammable. The third reason is that because it is flat land it requires tremendous strength to defend it."

But Manila now lay in ruins. The area on the south side of the Pasig River had been the scene of one of the bloodiest battles of the war. Apparently the Japanese army had stayed in the city after all?

"No," answered Yamashita, "the Japanese army had moved out. There were only fifteen or sixteen hundred army troops left in the city, and their essential mission was to guard those military supplies that had not yet been removed. But there were approximately twenty thousand Japanese naval troops who did not move out, and they were the ones who fought the Americans." The story that followed seemed fantastic, but we were to learn later from the testimony of witnesses who were called by both sides during the trial and also from captured Japanese documents that were in the possession of American intelligence officers, that it was amply supported and that it was true.

Briefly the facts are these: Yamashita's order to his army to evacuate the city of Manila was issued in the middle of December, 1944, and was carried out during the following six weeks. Late in December, Yamashita moved his headquarters from Fort McKinley (near Manila) to Baguio, a city high in the mountains of northern Luzon. The move was coincidental with the activation of a new army group known as the "Shimbu army" that was placed under the command of Lieutenant General Yokoyama. The mission of the new unit was to complete the evacuation of the city of Manila and to carry on defensive warfare against the Americans from the hills east and south of the city. At the time of these events the Japanese navy was operating independently of the army, but a few weeks later a limited command function over the naval forces when they were engaged in land operations was transferred to the Shimbu army. Inasmuch as the Shimbu army had been ordered by Yamashita to get out of the city and since the sailors who were engaged in land operations were now tactically part of the Shimbu army, the evacuation order applied to them as well as to the soldiers. But Admiral Iwabuchi, who was in immediate command of the naval forces, refused to take his men out of Manila. The Americans effected the successful landing at Lingayen Gulf on the eighth of January, 1945, and almost immediately all land communication between Manila and the Yamashita headquarters at Baguio was cut off. Although the Americans entered the northern part of Manila on February 4, it was not until February 13 that General Yamashita learned that the navy men were still in the city. He immediately got in touch with General Yokoyama, who was at the Shimbu army headquarters in the hills east of the city, and ordered him to get the sailors out of Manila "in accordance with our original plan." It was too late. American forces had already surrounded and trapped the naval troops. General Yokoyama's attempted rescue mission of February 14 and 15 was repulsed, and the bloody fighting in the southern part of the city was under way.

Why did Admiral Iwabuchi refuse to take his twenty thousand men out of Manila? He and his men were dead; hence General Yamashita could not give us a definitive answer. The later testimony and the captured documents, however, tell a convincing circumstantial story. Before he was directed to subject himself and his men to army command, Admiral Iwabuchi had received a previous naval order, an order to destroy the valuable harbor facilities of the finest seaport in the Orient, the docks and the naval storehouses. Faced with such a dilemma, Admiral Iwabuchi apparently did what one might expect an admiral to do under the circumstances—he stayed to carry out the directions of the Naval Ministry. But all that General Yamashita could tell us was: "It was entirely contrary to my plans for Manila."

After the conquest of Manila, American power fanned out over Luzon. The Japanese troops in accordance with Yamashita's plan were intrenched in the hills and mountains, with certain strong elements of the Shimbu army holding the Batangas peninsula; but the activities of the American Army and Air Forces, aided by the ubiquitous guerrilla bands, severed all land communications between the various echelons of Yamashita's army and reduced them to a number of isolated units. As General Marshall later reported to the secretary of war, Yamashita "was forced into a piecemeal commitment of his troops." Yamashita personally was compelled, almost monthly, to move ever farther north, ever higher into the mountains.

Thus we saw revealed the picture of Yamashita's insurmountable difficulties upon his arrival in the islands, the blueprint of a situation that began with such a welter of impossible tasks that there simply was no time for training procedures or even inspection trips and that ended with the general's virtual isolation from the diverse elements of a scattered command. The state of his communications was such that he could not know of atrocities which we said Japanese troops had committed, in Manila and Batangas and in other islands of the archipelago. "If those crimes were committed," Yamashita insisted, "I positively and categorically affirm that they were against my wishes and in direct contradiction to all my expressed orders, and, further, if they were committed, they occurred at a place and a time of which I had no knowledge whatsoever." And, he added, had he suspected that they were going to be committed, he would have taken steps to prevent them, and had he learned of them later, he would have punished the perpetrators.

Before the conference was over, Yamashita's lawyers had a few more questions to ask. There was, of course, the question lawyers always pose: Have you talked to anyone about this case? Have you told this story to investigators from the prosecution staff?

"Yes, of course—many times." Not only the general but his staff officers had often talked of their experiences. They had freely answered all questions. They had unhesitatingly signed and sworn to the truth of affidavits. Each had given many statements. Why not?

No one had told them that they did not have to talk. Such a concept was new to them and most difficult to understand. In Japan one who was accused of crime had to give all the facts to the prosecution as soon as he was apprehended. That investigation was the basic feature of the entire Japanese "trial," and the prisoner had to talk. He had no "rights." The state had all the rights.

The misgivings that we as lawyers may have had as a result of this disclosure were soon dissipated. It made no difference. The information that was given to the prosecution was the same as that given to us and was identical with that which would later be presented to the military commission. There were no secrets, no discrepancies, no loopholes. For over two months we were to discuss this narrative and explore into hundreds of ramifications and details. Never once would we find that these men had lied, concealed, or invented. Yamashita and his staff officers were telling the truth.

Another question: "Was the general a 'samurai,' and, if so, what were the implications of that status?" Yamashita smiled; he was not a member of the samurai class. He was a commoner. In Japan there were three classes—the peers, the samurai, the commoners. His father and brother had been doctors. He might have been a doctor, too, had he made higher grades in elementary school. But he was sent to cadet school, where he did much better. He had risen from the ranks.

He was a Shintoist. Shinto is a religion, he pointed out, and it cannot be explained in a short time. Nor was he so pious a man as to be able to explain its philosophy easily and in a few words. Basically it is a religion founded on the premise that there is a divinity which watches over all things and dictates that we humans must be true to a path of righteousness—or to our consciousness of being right—which is the way of heaven. As to the divine origin of the emperor, that is a doctrine that had been taught him as a child, but today the old man of sixty years had his doubts as to the mythology. It must be remembered, however, that the governing theory of many old countries was posited on some connection between the rulers and divinity.

One further question: "When surrender was unavoidable, why hadn't the general committed suicide?" The answer was simple. That would have been a violation of the emperor's orders. The command was to surrender, to co-operate with the Americans. Yamashita had done so.

But only a few days before, General Tojo, the former premier, had attempted harakiri. Was that a violation of the orders?

Yamashita answered grimly: "Yes, Tojo disobeyed the order of his emperor."

We, too, were soldiers. And so we could understand the note of scorn in the old warrior's voice.

IV

STAGE SETTING

THE arraignment of General Yamashita took place on the eighth day of October, 1945. On the day before, a Sunday, the president of the military commission, Major General Russel B. Reynolds, ordered a rehearsal, or "dry run," as it is called in the Army. The rehearsal was quite in order, for the entire trial was to be in the nature of a drama, with the world as audience.

The ornate reception hall of the high commissioner's residence in Manila had been converted into a courtroom. On the floor were seats for three hundred spectators. In the balconies were moving-picture cameramen and radio commentators. The front of the large room was semicircular, with seven French doors that looked out onto Manila Bay. This part of the room was the stage. Before the middle window, on a slightly raised platform, was the judges' bench. It consisted of a long, boxlike table, behind which were five leather swivel chairs. Directly back of the center chair, which was to be occupied by the president of the commission, stood crossed flagstaffs bearing the emblems of the United States of America and the Philippine Commonwealth. In front of the bench were two desks, one for the stenotype reporters and another for the official interpreters. To the commission's right and to the front was a long table for the accused and his counsel. A similar table for the prosecution staff was on the commission's left. And in the space between the prosecution's table and the end of the judges' bench was the witness chair, also on a platform. There were microphones for the commission, the defense, the prosecution, the interpreters, and the witness. Loudspeakers were suspended from the ceiling and were placed at strategic points along the walls. On either side, in the "wings," were spotlights, and overhead were strung six powerful klieg lights. These were lighted frequently during the trial, on signal from the moving-picture cameramen, and they helped the tropical sun produce an uncomfortably torrid temperature.

The first two rows of audience seats on the left were reserved for "generals and important guests." The front rows on the right were held for newspaper correspondents and photographers, who were permitted to flash camera bulbs at any time during the proceedings. The rest of the seats were filled by persons who waited in long lines outside the building and who were admitted on a "first-come, first-served" basis. For the entire six weeks we played to a full house.

At the "dry run," arrangements were made as to where the accused and his counsel were to sit and where they were to stand at various times during the performance. Cameramen stationed themselves and their spotlights to the utmost advantage.

The actual trial did not begin until the morning of October 29. This time there was no rehearsal, but the parties were given copies of a "script" on the preceding day. The script detailed various statements that the president of the commission and the chief prosecutor would make, oaths that would be administered, and other similar formalities that would be necessary to get the trial under way. The final lines of the prepared script were grimly amusing. During the three-week period that had elapsed between the arraignment and the opening of the trial, defense counsel had filed with the military commission a motion to dismiss the action. This motion and its import will be described in more detail later. Suffice it to say here that the motion went to the root of the charge against General Yamashita and that we had decided to present it to the commission well in advance of trial; for, as we said in a memorandum that was given to the commission with the motion, if our position was correct, the commission might rule with us, avoid a trial entirely, and thus "prevent what may be a needless and embarrassing expenditure of time, personnel, and money." The motion was filed on October 19, but the president of the commission informed us that it would not be acted on until the body formally reconvened on October 29. Accordingly, the prepared script dealt with the matter. The following is a copy of the last part of that illuminating document.

"Presiding Officer: 'There has been filed with the Commission by Chief Defense Counsel a Motion to Dismiss dated 19 October 1945. The Defense will now be heard in regard to this Motion.'

"(*Defense counsel will argue Motion*)

"Presiding Officer: 'The Prosecution will now be heard in regard to the Motion to Dismiss.'

"(*Prosecutor will argue Motion*)

"Presiding Officer: 'Does the Defense have anything further to offer in rebuttal?'

"Presiding Officer: 'Does the Prosecution desire to offer anything further in regard to this Motion?'

"Presiding Officer: 'The Commission will consider the Motion in Chambers.'

"Presiding Officer: 'Subject to objection by any member of the Commission, the motion is——.'

"(*Thereupon Presiding Officer will rule on Motion*)

"Presiding Officer: 'The Prosecution will make its opening Statement.'

"Presiding Officer: 'Is the Prosecution ready to proceed?'

"Prosecutor: 'We are.' "

The revelation of the script was reminiscent of a similar incident that occurred in the famous trial in 1925 of a man named Scopes, who had violated the Tennessee law prohibiting the teaching of evolution in the public schools. Clarence Darrow, the defendant's attorney, had filed a motion to quash the indictment against his client. The trial judge had taken the motion under advisement over the week end, announcing that he would give his decision in court on the following Monday morning. He was immediately besieged by newspaper reporters who wanted to know what disposition he was going to make of the motion. The old judge, of course, refused to commit himself. One bright journalist asked him whether he expected to hear evidence on Monday. The jurist answered, "Yes." And then he wondered why the next editions of the newspapers announced with confidence that the indictment would not be quashed.

V
THE ARRAIGNMENT

AT THE rehearsal of the arraignment the question had arisen as to just what persons were to be allowed inside the bar inclosure. Defense counsel informed the commission that, in addition to his interpreter, General Yamashita wanted to have Generals Muto and Utsunomiya, his chief-of-staff and assistant chief-of-staff, at his side. It was explained that we had already learned that General Yamashita relied heavily on Muto, and to a lesser extent on Utsunomiya, for matters of detail that were important in re-creating the picture of past events. Major Kerr, the chief prosecuting officer, protested. Such a thing was unheard of. Why those men might be charged as war criminals themselves. He would certainly object to having them in the courtroom. It was General Reynolds who suggested a way out of the difficulty. The accused could have any *defense counsel* he chose. Why not let him request Muto and Utsunomiya as "associate defense counsel" in addition to the regularly appointed lawyers? In that way, they might sit at the defense table.

Nevertheless, on the following day, after General Yamashita had told the commission that he accepted the duly appointed defense counsel and that he felt "highly honored to have been given such distinguished persons" to represent him, and after he had added: "I should like to have my chief-of-staff, Lieutenant General Muto, and my assistant or deputy chief-of-staff, Major General Utsunomiya, as additional counsel—there are a number of records and facts with which they alone are conversant—I need their advice and assistance," Major Kerr again protested. He pointed out that the two men might become witnesses for the defense, and it was objectionable to have anyone dubbed "counsel" take the witness stand. Kerr again warned that these very men might themselves later face charges as war criminals, but he failed to explain how that might disqualify them as assistants for the accused. Growing more and more excited, the prosecutor wound up: "The prosecution does not and will not recognize the men named as chief-of-staff or as deputy or assistant chief-of-staff. We maintain, sir, that the day when Yamashita had his chief-of-staff or assistant chief-of-staff is over!"

No one felt disposed to argue so obvious and irrelevant a truth. The president of the commission spoke sharply. "The request of the defense is granted," he said.

The newspapers hailed this "victory for the defense." Well might we cherish it. It was the only victory of any real importance that we were to gain.

Before allowing General Yamashita to plead "not guilty," the defense asked that the charge be made "more definite and certain." After all, a man must know what he is pleading to. The charge as served read simply:

"Tomoyuki Yamashita, General Imperial Japanese Army, between 9 October 1944 and 2 September 1945, at Manila and at other places in the Philippine Islands, while commander of armed forces of Japan at war with the United States of America and its allies, unlawfully disregarded and failed to discharge his duty as commander to control the operations of the members of his command, permitting them to commit brutal atrocities and other high crimes against the people of the United States and of its allies and dependencies, particularly the Philippines, and he, General Tomoyuki Yamashita, thereby violated the laws of war."

We knew that the prosecution was now prepared to serve us with a "bill of particulars," a document that would describe in more detail the crimes of Japanese troops. But what, specifically, had the *accused* done? The charge said that he "failed to discharge a duty." When? Where? Dates and places? It said that there was a "permitting" of troops to commit atrocities. Did that mean that he actually gave a permission? Or was the participle used to connote the automatic result of the failure to discharge a duty—as when we say that release of a lever "permits" wheels to turn? If the former, when was any such "permission" given? Where? To whom? To do what? Some four months later a justice of the Supreme Court of the United States was to describe the language of the charge as "vagueness, if not vacuity"; but it all seemed clear enough to the commission and the prosecution. Major Kerr "definitely" objected to our motion. He would have no such thing. It might be "appropriate in a court of law, but certainly not in this proceeding." He had prepared a bill of particulars. It mentioned General Yamashita's name only in the preamble, but it listed sixty-four sets of crimes that Japanese troops had committed in various places in the archipelago. And if Major Kerr was assured by the commission that he might file some supplementary particulars later, he would condescend to give us this bill now. That was enough.

The commission agreed.

Three weeks were allotted for preparation, and with a bang of General Reynolds' gavel, the trial was adjourned until October 29.

VI
DRAMATIS PERSONAE

WHEN the curtain rose on Yamashita's arraignment, on either side of the stage could be seen six uniformed lawyers—respectively, the gentlemen of the prosecution and of the defense. Chief of the prosecution staff was Major Robert Kerr, infantry officer, who had been a lawyer in Portland, Oregon. He was tall, debonair, and wore a small, black mustache. Kerr was proud of his infantry insignia; he frequently belittled himself as a "mere soldier" to be distinguished from the members of the Judge Advocate's Department who were on his staff as well as on ours. He appeared to enjoy his job. After Yamashita had been sentenced to hang, a newspaper reporter quoted Kerr as saying that he had come to the Pacific expecting to shoot Japs on the beaches rather than hang them, but it was all the same to him. He seemed to me to be an able lawyer, but most observers believed that he was eclipsed by the four captains who were his assistants and who shared the burden of examination of witnesses. Captains Hill, Webster, Calyer, and Pace had all been district attorneys in civilian life. They all showed that they were trial lawyers of broad experience—I never want to meet any better prosecutors.

The sixth member of the prosecution staff was a Filipino attorney, Major Glicerio Opinión. His name had been added to the roster shortly before the trial, for it was believed wise to give the Filipino people some real representation in the conviction of the man who was charged with responsibility for their sufferings. Opinión was an amiable chap who was addicted to long, direct examinations of his witnesses and whose frequent redundancies and repetitions were the cause of some merriment in the courtroom. He had the habit of repeating the witness's last words before putting his next question. On one occasion, Opinión inquired as to the sex of a child that a Filipina witness stated she had held in her arms.

"Male," she answered.

"Male," repeated the major. "And was it your son or your daughter?" Another time, after ascertaining that a witness was a widow, the spectators were surprised to hear Opinión say: "I see, a widow. And where is your husband?"

On the defense side the six counsel were soon reduced to four. Before the trial began, Lieutenant Colonel Feldhaus, the Dakota tax expert, became sick and was hospitalized for an operation. We did not see him for over a month. He returned to the courtroom in time to help out with the summation and closing arguments. Major George Guy, a lawyer from Cheyenne, Wyoming, was the only member of the staff who was not in the Judge Advocate General's Department. He wore the crossed swords of a cavalry officer and had served through most of the Pacific campaign with the colorful First Cavalry Division. Like Sandberg and me, he had been with Claims Service when he was appointed to the Yamashita case. He was a hearty, flamboyant sort of man who possessed in an extreme degree the enviable ability to get to the most exciting part of the Pacific Theater when dramatic action was imminent. He had "been around." I believe that there was not another officer in all the area between Tokyo and Sydney who knew so many "important people" by their first names. And they all called him "George." Consequently, when it developed during the course of our preparation that General Yamashita had an interesting background of opposition to the Japanese "war party" in general and ex-premier Tojo in particular and that he was held in high esteem as a "moderate" in Japan and that these possibly helpful facts might be proved by "character witnesses" (certain Japanese gentlemen who stood well with the MacArthur occupation forces in Tokyo), George Guy was the obvious choice to fly to Japan to interview them and arrange to bring them to Manila. He left before the trial began and was gone for about a month. When George returned, he brought along affidavits from the potential witnesses, gifts for his fellow-counsel, and fascinating stories of life in newly occupied Tokyo. Later, when the character witnesses arrived in Manila, George Guy arranged for housing and feeding them (they had to be secluded and guarded from the possibly violent reactions of Filipinos who were viciously anti-Japanese), and he also acted as trial counsel in the presentation of their testimony to the commission.

Lieutenant Colonel Walter Hendrix had been a prosperous lawyer in Atlanta, Georgia. He was a big man, rotund even with his six feet of height. He had strong features, strong convictions, and a strong conscience. When the defense attorneys first met, Hendrix let it be known that he was not pleased by his appointment to defend Yamashita and that he would have been much happier had he been assigned to the prosecution. But, as he learned to know our client and to understand his position, his misgivings vanished, and he became the most fiery and reckless of defenders. After the trial began, Hendrix' enthusiasm ripened into near fanaticism. He was outraged by what he considered the commission's patent bias, as demonstrated by its summary disposition of our objections to evidence that he as a lawyer knew would generally be regarded as inadmissible. Hendrix' reaction was much more violent than mine. I had been a labor lawyer before entering the Army, and in the course of my practice I had defended many strikers who had been accused of various misdemeanors and minor offenses while on picket lines and whose treatment at the hands of local judges in small New England towns had been somewhat less than fair. So I was not unused to the highhanded tactics of the military commission, which was composed of men who, after all, were generals and not attorneys and whose consciousness of power would necessarily be matched only by their ignorance of law. But Hendrix had not had that kind of civilian practice. He could not take it, and, after he had been squirming in his seat while court was in session, his emotions would explode during a recess. "No damn general is going to push me around!" was his not infrequent comment.

Hendrix had been judge advocate and legal adviser for the military police command in Manila. In that capacity, he had had occasion to appear in the local courts. He was the only one of Yamashita's defense counsel who was a member of the bar of the Supreme Court of the Philippine Islands; hence, when it became apparent that our road to the United States Supreme Court led through the Philippine Supreme Court, Hendrix was intrusted with the function of preparing and arguing the original appeal. That task took him away from the trial chamber. It also resulted in a memorable incident when he appeared before the Philippine court, later referred to by the rest of us as "the time when Hendrix blew his top"—when all Hendrix' pent-up antipathy to the military hierarchy and its method of administering "justice" burst forth in an impassioned speech that almost resulted in his court-martial. The incident will be described in due course.

Clarke, Sandberg, and I were therefore left to handle the greater part of the trial. Captain Milton Sandberg was a young lawyer from New York City. After graduating from Columbia Law School in 1937, he had worked on tax matters in the New York comptroller's office. Like myself, he had entered the Army as an enlisted man, had attended the Judge Advocate General's Officer Candidate School at Ann Arbor, Michigan, and had been assigned to Claims Service in Manila. He displayed a fluorescent wit and a steady, analytical mind. His ability to think ahead and his innate fighting spirit made him an ideal man for this case. Although Sandberg's trial experience had been necessarily limited, he was well versed in appellate procedures, and his part of the eventual argument before the United States Supreme Court can only be described as brilliant. He and I seldom disagreed as to strategy, tactics, and phraseology, and, considering the difficulties that confronted us, I believe we operated as a reasonably balanced team. At least, the score of newspapermen who sat through the six weeks of trial thought so.

Colonel Harry E. Clarke, of Altoona, Pennsylvania, was senior defense counsel—senior in rank, age, and maturity. He was a soldier who enjoyed being a soldier. He had served in the first World War and had been active in the Pennsylvania National Guard between the wars. Long before Pearl Harbor, Clarke had entered active service with his beloved Twenty-eighth Division. He had been overseas for forty months, serving in Australia and New Guinea before coming to the Philippines, where he had been put in charge of the Army's correctional institutions. He had lived through the Pacific campaigns with the top men. He knew the generals, the other colonels, the regular Army men, and they knew him. The Army was his life. And it was that fact that made his uncompromising position during the trial so important and so courageous; for, although, as I have indicated, the bulk of the actual fighting was done by Sandberg and me, the battle would have been impossible had not Clarke backed us up. Rank meant nothing to him—he judged his staff on their ability as lawyers—but it meant a great deal to the generals who constituted the military commission. Clarke was content to let his two captains examine witnesses, argue with the commission over their right to examine, battle the commission over objections to testimony and affidavits and moving-picture films. But it was the colonel who was called into the commission's chambers and upbraided because the defense counsel were not adhering to the quiet role that had been expected of them. To Army generals the fact that he was senior in rank meant that he was responsible for what was going on. Why, this continual insistence on the right of cross-examination was wasting valuable time! It amounted to insubordination! It verged on contempt of the commission! It almost looked like grounds for court-martial! But Colonel Harry Clarke never wavered. He would accept responsibility. Maybe we were going pretty far, perhaps further than he would have gone were he alone on the defense, but we had a job to do—we knew what we were doing—we were right. Court-martial and be damned.

To be sure, the defense counsel had some internal arguments. In most of them, Colonel Clarke would be found on the side of caution. Very often, as the result of his objections, harsh statements would be softened or doubtful courses abandoned; but, as I look back on it, in practically all cases his conservatism was justified by eventual results. In all our important decisions we were unanimous. Clarke was well aware of the hierarchy's aversion to our attempts to bring the case before civilian courts. Had he at any time refused to co-operate in our various legal moves, we should have been stymied. It was easy enough for Sandberg and me to take advantage of our unique position as lawyers appointed to defend an unpopular man and respectfully but firmly to attack intrenched authority. We did not intend to stay in the Army any longer than we had to. The war was over, we wanted neither promotion nor favor, we looked forward to resuming civilian status. But Clarke's position was quite different. He had something to lose in incurring the displeasure of superior officers whose friendship he liked and needed. And that is why his consistent stand against what he believed to be injustice reveals a courageous liberal in the finest American tradition.

VII

THE MILITARY COMMISSION

THE military commission consisted of three major generals and two brigadier generals. They were all members of the regular Army, professional soldiers, who could, therefore, not be expected to offer serious resistance to the desires of General MacArthur or of any other superior officer on whose favor their future well-being might depend. That was bad to begin with, but we expected it. Therein lies the most serious defect in our system of military justice, whether it be trial by court-martial or by military commission. The judges are supposed to make a decision based on the evidence, but it is next to impossible to find a military court that, under the Army system, can feel free to act independently of the wishes of the appointing authority, even though the latter does not have the advantage of hearing the witnesses.

Two other facts about the five generals caused the defense counsel more concern. First, none of them was a combat man; they had all been appointed to the commission from "desk" jobs. We believed that General Yamashita's difficulties would be more readily and sympathetically understood by men who might have faced similar problems. General Reynolds, for example, had but recently come to the Philippine Islands from Chicago, where he had been commanding general of the Sixth Service Command, an area comprising the states of Illinois, Wisconsin, and Michigan. We did not doubt that the command functions in Chicago were well outlined in daily written reports and orders and that the commanding general there might well know of all the activities of his subordinates in that district. There were neither hostile air forces nor guerrillas operating in the Middle West.

We were most concerned, however, by the fact that not one of the five generals was a lawyer or had ever had legal experience. The rules governing the appointment of the commission stipulated: "If feasible, one or more members of a commission should have had legal training." Apparently the appointing authority had found it not "feasible." Nevertheless, General Reynolds was designated "law member" as well as "president."

One may justifiably be impatient with lawyers who think that only fellow-members of their profession have any brains. It is no more true that all lawyers are intelligent than it is that all lawyers are crooks. But it was far too much to expect laymen without legal assistance on the bench to understand the trial of a case of this type, a case that was to make fundamentally new law and that would necessarily involve hundreds of legal decisions on matters of evidence, international law, the construction of congressional statutes, and the interpretation of treaties.

Many laymen profess to believe that lawyers, especially trial lawyers defending an accused criminal, are pettifogging technicians. If only *they* had the chance, if only *they* were judges, they would put a quick stop to all that nonsense! And Army generals, who have become accustomed to dictatorial power, are prone to share that view. The sad truth of the matter is, however, that all those safeguards of the rights of an accused that defense counsel were to plead for so strenuously are not just "technicalities." They are the product of man's struggle against oppression and tyranny over a span of a thousand years. They may have become incrusted with refinements and exceptions and checks and balances, but they are vitally real, and to thrust them aside as mere "lawyers' tricks" is to return to the days of trial by fagot.

The difficulty of trying to argue evidentiary questions with laymen was to become apparent before the trial was an hour old.

Why was there objection to the admission of an affidavit into evidence? It was "hearsay"? Congress had legislated against it? Perhaps, but General MacArthur's rules specifically allowed the admission of affidavits! And who are we to question the validity of any of the acts of the very man who authorized our existence! As a matter of fact, we shall caution you later in chambers not to mention General MacArthur's name again in this courtroom. When an affidavit is considered, you say that we do not have the witness before us; we cannot see whether he appears to be truthful, we cannot cross-examine him to ascertain whether he may be lying or to bring out facts not mentioned in the affidavit, facts which the man who took the written statement may have been careful to omit? But affidavits save time. The objection is not sustained. And now we have the written report of a member of the war crimes commission—there is objection to that, too? Why? It is "opinion"? We do not have the officer who signed the report here so that we might learn whether he is qualified to give an opinion or even to find out upon what facts, if any, he based the opinion? Objection not sustained. The commission recesses into chambers and calls in senior defense counsel. What do those insubordinate whippersnappers mean by all that objecting? Once the commission has made a ruling, why do they repeat the objection? Doesn't that verge on contempt of the commission?

Of course, the objections were not the same. And even if they had been, defense counsel would have not only the right but the duty to repeat the objection. General Reynolds and his confreres, not being lawyers, could not comprehend that. It was not their fault.

Two brigadier generals and three major generals. To a soldier at any Army post, brigadier generals are extremely important men. But, when one saw them daily in a unit with three superior officers, they appeared like office boys. They walked in last, sat down last, got up last, and walked out last. They had nothing to say in the courtroom during the trial. Brigadier General Bullene, who sat at the end of the bench nearest the witness chair, watched the witnesses carefully. Brigadier General Handwerk, who sat at the opposite end of the bench, just gazed out into space. One newspaper correspondent joked: "Someone will have to tell Handwerk when the trial's over, or he'll just keep on coming in every day and won't know the difference." During one noon recess, another newspaperman put a copy of *Time* magazine on the table in front of General Handwerk's seat—"just to see what would happen." When the court reconvened, the general took his seat and stared straight ahead. About fifteen minutes later he glanced down, noticed the magazine, and idly turned its pages as the testimony rolled on. The incident was noticed only by the initiates.

As president of the commission, Major General Russel B. Reynolds was its spokesman. He ruled on questions of evidence and read the frequent statements and formal announcements of the commission. He often interrogated the witnesses, and he displayed a lively interest in all the proceedings. Bald and austere, he looked the part of a judge. He had the knack of appearing to understand everything that was said, which was sometimes misleading to counsel. Although Reynolds made it a point to appear judicious and impartial while on the bench, it soon became evident to defense counsel by the questions which he put to witnesses and by his directions to the prosecution as to lines of inquiry he wanted them to pursue that he conceived one of his functions to be that of trying to find some solid evidence on which to base an eventual conviction.

On General Reynolds' right sat Major General Leo Donovan. I always believed that he was our only possible friend on the court. Surely, a man with the name of Donovan must have his share of the fire of humanity in his bones. In him, if in anybody, we might find a latent sympathy for the underdog—for the "tiger," if you will, brought to bay. Occasionally he would ask questions. And he essayed the only humor that emanated from the bench. Since the ballot of the commission on its finding and sentence was secret, I have no idea of how any of the generals voted. A two-thirds majority was necessary for conviction. But I dare say that if, in the deliberations of that body, any one of the judges ever had an inclination to modify the drastic penalty, it was General Donovan. I may be quite mistaken.

The remaining member of the commission was Major General James A. Lester. He had but recently been head of the military police command. From the moment the trial began, Lester made it clear that he was antagonistic to the accused and impatient with what he considered delays caused by the accused's counsel. Newspaper reporters and radio men referred to Lester as "the hanging judge." Ordinarily this attitude was evidenced only by gestures, facial expressions, and exaggerated mannerisms, but on one occasion his pent-up bile boiled over.

Counsel for both sides had experienced considerable aggravation in the matter of language interpretation. Long before any Japanese witnesses took the stand, posing the most difficult of translation problems, interpreters had been required for witnesses who spoke Chinese, Spanish, and Tagalog. There are many dialects extant in various parts of the Philippine Islands, but the most prevalent one in the Manila area of Luzon is called "Tagalog." At numerous times during the presentation of the prosecution's case recourse had been had to Tagalog interpreters. Apparently they were somewhat less than letter perfect (a fact explained by the niggardly sums the government was prepared to pay for civilian interpreters) because, during recesses, Tagalog-speaking spectators in the courtroom had told one or more members of the defense staff of mistakes that had been made. We had said nothing in open court about the matter. On a number of occasions, Major Opinión of the prosecution staff, who spoke Tagalog, had corrected his interpreter, and once had insisted on the production of a substitute.

Tantalizing difficulty was experienced one day while Sandberg was attempting to cross-examine a Tagalog-speaking witness. Long conversations in the native dialect were held between the interpreter and the witness which were never translated by the interpreter for the benefit of those of us who could understand only English. At length Sandberg stopped his examination and asked the interpreter to translate for the commission the substance of an extended colloquy that the interpreter had just had with the witness. The interpreter explained that he was trying to get the witness to understand his use of Tagalog, that the man on the stand was from Batangas Province and thus spoke a different type of Tagalog than did the translator. Sandberg then addressed the military commission. "If the commission please," he said, "if this interpreter can't translate our questions properly in the dialect of this witness, we ask that another interpreter be gotten. We think it is most improper—and, incidentally, this has been going on for some time—for the interpreter to engage in colloquies with the witness."

At this point, General Lester whispered in General Reynolds' ear, and Reynolds announced that the commission would not get a new interpreter but "suggests that you phrase your questions with just as few words as possible."

The long, mysterious conversations between the witness and the interpreter continued, and in my cross-examination of the next witness the same difficulties were encountered. Then the commission adjourned for a ten-minute recess. During the recess a number of Filipino newspaper reporters told Sandberg that the actual interpretation had been worse than usual, that numerous serious errors had been made, and that the interpreter had actually reported that one witness went "east" when the witness had testified that he went "west."

As soon as the commission reassembled, Sandberg rose to his feet and addressed General Reynolds: "The defense has been informed during the recess that the translations, interpretations by the Tagalog interpreter, were false in a number of respects, in a manner that amounts to being scandalous."

When he heard the word "scandalous," General Lester turned red and grasped the arms of his chair. "We are at a disadvantage," continued Sandberg, "the defense is, in that we do not have any Tagalog interpreter. We would like to move at this time that the last interpreter be permanently disqualified from interpreting hereafter."

Once more General Lester leaned over and spoke hurriedly and heatedly to General Reynolds. "That is a very serious charge against a sworn interpreter," said the commission president. "Before the court could take such drastic action . . . we would certainly have to sustain this charge against him."

"We don't mean to infer in any respect that the interpreter acted in anything other than good faith," replied Sandberg, "but apparently the interpretation has not been correct, and in a capital case of this sort, we urge most strenuously that there must be accuracy."

If Sandberg thought he was extending the olive branch, the offer was spurned by General Reynolds. "We will have to have tangible evidence that inaccurate statements were submitted," said the General. "The commission asks that counsel disclose in court the source of the allegations, so that we may weigh this most unusual and most serious charge."

In this difficult position, Sandberg was compelled to inform the commission that his informants had been Philippine newspaper reporters and that he did not know their names. Immediately two young Filipinos arose from the press section, stated that they had given the information, and volunteered to take the stand. General Lester grinned and grabbed for the microphone that was on the bench in front of General Reynolds. "General Lester, a member of the commission, will interrogate the witness," said General Reynolds.

Major Kerr first ascertained the witness's qualifications. The lad on the stand did not appear to be over twenty years of age. He said that his name was Armando Malay, that he was a graduate of the University of the Philippines, that he had on at least two occasions translated Tagalog into English in court proceedings, and that he was familiar with the phraseology used in Batangas Province.

Now General Lester took over. With his voice trembling with anger, he turned on the witness: "Do you understand that any question posed by this commission to you which tends to degrade and incriminate you, you are at liberty not to answer? Do you understand that?"

"Yes, sir," answered the boy.

"In answering any questions that might tend to incriminate you, you understand that you might be subject to *punishment by a court of law,* if subsequent to this case legal remedies for other persons were involved?" asked Lester, raising his voice as he went along.

The young Filipino stood his ground. He was not to be intimidated. "Yes, sir," was the answer.

Lester tried again: "Knowing that, you are willing to testify?"

"Yes, sir," repeated the boy, "because I want the defense and the prosecution to get the full benefit of the testimony, and not—"

General Lester refused to let the witness finish his answer. "Are you the source of information to the counsel for the defense?" he interrupted.

The witness acknowledged that he was, and, after referring to notes that he had made at the time of the disputed testimony, he stated that the man whom Sandberg had cross-examined had testified that he went to a village or *barrio* that was "east of his own *barrio*, but the translation that the commission got from the interpreter was 'west,' which is the opposite direction."

Lester's hands and lips trembled, and he shouted three questions in quick succession at the astonished newspaperman: "Well, what bearing did that have on the issue at stake? Did it have any material bearing whether the witness went east or west? In what way did it invalidate the testimony?"

Of course, the questions were improper, even had the witness been given an opportunity to answer them. It is not for a spectator in the courtroom to pass judgment on the materiality of testimony. But, nothing bothered, the lad on the stand replied: "If a person—if a witness says he went east, and the translator says he went west, I think the whole testimony becomes wrong, sir. A direction is a very important matter."

Unwilling to acknowledge his defeat, General Lester barged ahead. He argued with the witness. "It might be in some case," he growled, "but in this case what bearing did it have what the direction was?"

"It has a very important bearing in my mind, sir," answered the Filipino, "because if a man goes west, says he went west, and he testifies on events that happened in the direction which is west, but the commission hears that he went east, and it subsequently turns out that there was nothing that happened in the east, don't you think, sir, that the whole testimony would be jumbled?"

General Lester did not answer. The witness then described another example of erroneous translation that was so flagrant that it caused General Donovan to exclaim that he had received an entirely wrong impression of the disputed testimony. And the second Filipino reporter, who voluntarily took the stand, did as well as the first.

Fuming and frustrated, General Lester relinquished the microphone. At this point Hendrix, who before the trial had been Lester's judge advocate in the military police command, whispered to Hamamoto: "Tell General Yamashita that Lester is *my* general." The message was translated to General Yamashita, who looked at Hendrix, chuckled, and whispered back in Japanese. "The old man says I should extend to you his most profound condolences," said Hamamoto.

VIII
THE LEADING MAN

ON THE night before the arraignment Colonel Clarke instructed General Yamashita to appear in court dressed in his best available clothing, complete with all possible decorations. Obediently, the general wore his least shabby green uniform, high cavalry boots and spurs, and four rows of campaign ribbons.

Shortly after the arraignment we had a call from fiery little Lieutenant Colonel Meek, chief of the prosecution branch of the local war-crimes office. "Damn it," he said, "it makes me mad. If I had my way I wouldn't let Yamashita come into court all decked out in a uniform. Why, goddamit, he stole the show! He dominated that courtroom! If I had my way, I'd put him in prison overalls and put chains on him. It made me so mad I wanted to punch him and all of you in the face."

I could not help laughing, for I knew that, even in overalls and chains, Yamashita would steal the show and would dominate the courtroom. What Meek could not know, or would not see, was that in this instance clothes did not make the man. Whatever else might be thought of him, General Yamashita personified dignity and serenity. Victor or vanquished, commander or captive, he carried himself like a man.

Yamashita looked his sixty years. He was large for a Japanese, a full head taller than his fellow-prisoners. American and Filipino news reporters variously described him as "bull-necked," "pot-bellied," or "potato-faced." Those flamboyant adjectives were not inaccurate. His large head was supported by an equally large neck, his girth was ample, and his face did bear some resemblance to an Aroostook County tuber. But his eyes were deep and thoughtful—the eyes of a man who had seen life, who understood life, and who was not afraid to die.

Some newspapermen said that he looked "cruel," but they were men who had never had the opportunity of talking to him and of looking into those eyes as they did so. I have never run across an American soldier who had had a chance to know Yamashita who was not attracted to him personally. This includes the military police and prison personnel who had guarded him, as well as the chaplain who had merely noticed Yamashita at New Bilibid Prison and who wrote in the letter column of the *Chicago Sun:* "He did not look like a vicious killer."

It may be pointed out that Americans are naturally friendly and that we tend to like anyone. But bear in mind that almost all the Americans to whom this reference is made were soldiers who had been taught to hate all Japanese, who traditionally described them as "dirty yellow bastards," and whose initial reaction to the inscrutable Japanese face, especially when it belonged to a "notoriously cruel" enemy general, would be somewhat less than favorable.

Yamashita was the consistent stoic. Although a witticism would produce a smile or a hearty laugh, especially when it was at his own expense, his features never betrayed emotion. Throughout the trial I was asked: "How is Yamashita taking it?" I had to say truthfully: "I don't know." I felt that he surely knew of the stupendous odds that were stacked against him. He could not listen to the mounting evidence of bloodcurdling Japanese atrocities every day for four weeks and not realize to what it must inevitably lead. Obviously, the thought of death did not bother him, although the idea of dying as a dishonored war criminal was abhorrent. Before the trial began, Yamashita told a newspaper interviewer that he had "full faith in the American idea of fair play." But after the sentence of death had been pronounced, General Muto confessed that his chief had never expected any other result. In fact, according to Muto, the only feature of the proceedings that proved completely surprising to the Japanese was the vigorousness of their defense counsel. I think Sandberg was right when he pointed out that we were at fault if Yamashita was ever led to hope for a less disastrous result. Not that we ever said anything to indicate the possibility of a favorable verdict, but it might have been difficult for the Nipponese mind to comprehend why the American officers would put up such a fight if they did not think they might win. I believe I gave Muto the correct answer: "One either is a lawyer, or one isn't a lawyer."

Yet General Yamashita appeared to be the oriental sphinx. Whatever the thoughts and emotions he experienced, they were not reflected in his features, speech, or actions. When he was sentenced to hang, he seemed to be the least affected man in the courtroom. And the report is that he maintained that calm on the scaffold.

IX

HOW THE TIGER GOT HIS STRIPES

EARLY in the war Yamashita had electrified the world when he led his troops down the hitherto "impassable" Malay Peninsula and conquered the supposedly impregnable bastion of Singapore from the rear. Many were the legends that grew out of that campaign—stories of British surprise; the big guns pointing out to sea that could not be turned around; the English officer who maintained to the last that "the bloody Japs must attack from the water; they wouldn't come down from the north because—well, because *we* wouldn't do it that way"; and the legend of Yamashita, the "brilliant" conqueror, the "Tiger of Malaya."

Yamashita was no tiger. Whatever his virtues or vices, ferocity was not one of them. And *he* did not believe that the conquest of Singapore had been brilliant. "It was a bluff," he said, "a bluff that worked." Yamashita's story was that he had been sent down the Malay Peninsula with only about thirty thousand troops, as a diversionary movement. The Japanese did not anticipate a successful attack on Singapore; like us, they believed the fortress to be "impregnable." Progress down the Malayan shore was accelerated by the use of small boats in nighttime operations, successively by-passing and isolating the defending soldiers. When the outskirts of Singapore were reached, most of Yamashita's force was still intact, but British troops in the city outnumbered his, three to one.

Within a few days Yamashita was able to mass his men outside the city. The show of strength resulted in the now famous surrender conference between the Japanese commander and British General Percival, who headed the Allied defenders. The meeting took place in the cashier's cage of a Singapore bank; outside the wire inclosure stood newspaper reporters and observers, watching the procedure. The generals met in the early afternoon. As Yamashita described the situation, he knew that the British had over one hundred thousand armed men in Singapore, as opposed to his thirty-odd thousand, but he also knew that the British were not aware of his comparative weakness. His chief concern was that they should not find it out. "I felt that if we had to fight in the city," he said, "we would be beaten. I offered surrender terms to spare the city, but, first of all, the surrender had to be *at once*. I insisted that the 'cease fire' order be effective at six o'clock that very evening." General Percival demurred: he wanted the "cease fire" order to be given at eight o'clock the following morning. Yamashita was truly frightened, for he believed that during the night the British would have the opportunity to discover his numerical weakness and that then he would be forced into disastrous city fighting. He instructed his interpreter to tell General Percival that he must know whether the British would agree to cease firing by six o'clock—it was a simple question that could be simply answered, either "Yes" or "No."

Unfortunately, the interpreter was not Hamamoto, who at this time was languishing in a Japanese army reception center, awaiting assignment that would not be forthcoming for three months. General Yamashita's interpreter at the Singapore conference was a harried Japanese soldier whose English was apparently terrible. At any rate, after Yamashita's relatively plain instruction, the interpreter engaged in a long and seemingly complicated discourse with General Percival in what was meant to be the English tongue. As the minutes rolled on, Yamashita became restive. He looked at his watch—five minutes, then ten minutes—still the interpreter and

General Percival talked on in an incomprehensible language. Finally, Yamashita interrupted. Raising his voice and shaking his finger at his interpreter, he said: "There's no need for all this talk. It is a simple question and I want a simple answer: 'Yes' or 'No.' "

Outside the cage the newspapermen watched. They saw Yamashita shaking his finger. They could not understand Japanese, but they caught the "Yes or No." The answer was "Yes." The ferocious conqueror, backed by overwhelming power, was laying down terms to a beaten adversary! The "Tiger of Malaya"! A phrase was coined, and a myth was born.

Not long after I heard it, I told this story to one of my Filipino friends. He laughed and insinuated that I must be extremely gullible. "You don't really believe that the Japs took Singapore with thirty thousand troops if the British had one hundred thousand, do you?" he asked. "That's preposterous. Of course Yamashita now wants to appear modest. And of course he wants to appear to be mild—he can't afford to be the ferocious conqueror today. The shoe's on the other foot. Outnumbered three to one? And the great military achievement just a bluff? That's a hot one!"

Corroboration came from an unexpected source. Some three months after General Yamashita talked to me of Singapore, *Life* magazine published the hitherto unrevealed text of a secret speech that Prime Minister Winston Churchill had delivered to the English House of Commons on April 23, 1942. "Singapore, with a force of 100,000 men, surrendered to 30,000 Japanese," Churchill admitted. He cautioned against an investigation of the "debacle" at that time, because it would "hamper the prosecution of the war."

I sent a copy of *Life* to my Filipino friend.

X

YAMASHITA—BY MUTO

OUR picture of General Yamashita is illuminated from two sources, the first a short biography that was written for defense counsel by owlish General Muto, his chief-of-staff, who had known him intimately since childhood, and the second the stenographic notes of an exhaustive interview with Yamashita that was undertaken by a pair of American Army psychiatrists.

Muto's narrative covers much of the same ground as the psychiatrists' questions, but it makes better reading. As translated by Hamamoto, it begins:

"Tomoyuki Yamashita was born a commoner on November 8, 1885, the son of a simple country doctor in a small village in Shikoku. The village is located on the upper streams of the Yoshino River cradled in the rugged mountains that run through the center of that Island, forming the backbone, as it were, of Shikoku or the 'Island of Four Provinces.'

"The child is the father of the man, and the place of birth and early childhood had much to do with the formation of the personality and character of the future general. Nestled in the quiet isolation of this mountainous district, cut off as it was from the hustle and bustle of modern civilization, the boy Tomoyuki grew up to be a natural, healthy, peace-loving youth—clean-cut, open, upright, industrious, and straightforward, qualities which form the foundation of his character today. The surrounding hills were covered with thick verdant foliage, traversed by countless clear, sparkling streams and rivulets. The villagers were naïve, kindhearted, and contented people, free from the cunning and scheming of their worldly-wise and money-ambitious city brothers. It was in this environment of natural beauty and harmony, in the midst of peace and contentment, that Tomoyuki spent his most formative years.

"As a boy, Tomoyuki Yamashita was carefree, healthy, and mentally as well as physically alert. He was fond of spending his time out in the open, roaming the hills and fields he loved best, which caused some concern to his parents and teachers—especially the latter."

The reader who might guess at this stage of Muto's biography that there would follow an incident of Yamashita's childhood that would serve to illustrate an admirable trait of character—something akin to the George Washington "cherry-tree" story—is not to be disappointed:

"His grandfather was fond of growing prize chrysanthemums, and every year, at the proper season, made cuttings of the best specimens and carefully planted them in well-prepared beds. It was the practice of the aged man to water these cuttings personally every morning, watching over them with meticulous care. One year, the usual cuttings were made and planted, but no buds came out—the cuttings mysteriously died, one after the other. Perplexed, the veteran chrysanthemum grower went out early one morning and caught his grandson in the forbidden plot, pulling out the remaining cuttings, one by one, and, after examining the roots, replanting them. The astonished grandsire stopped his grandson and severely reprimanded him for this act of vandalism, only to receive the following reply: 'Grandfather said that watering the plants made the roots appear. I have been watching for the roots every morning.' The grandfather looked into the clear, steady eyes of his grandson and giving him some cuttings from his choicest specimens quietly let this son of nature carry on his own experiment. Such open-mindedness and intellectual curiosity have always marked him from his colleagues and would-be competitors."

The tortured and mutilated victims of Japanese brutalities in the Philippines were blaming Yamashita for their broken lives and decimated families. This happy little boy with the inquiring mind had become the commander of cruel and barbarous soldiers. He had become a general of the Imperial Japanese Army. How had that happened? Muto tells us:

"Although young Tomoyuki learned to love nature and in return nature taught him much, his inattention to studies did not improve his grades in the village elementary school. His gentle mother was very much concerned, and his grandmother called the little boy into her room for long disciplinary talks time and time again. No results were forthcoming, and, although Tomoyuki did not repeat any grade, he did not win any prize for scholarship.

"However, when the country lad was sent to the city high school, forty kilometers from his home, his scholastic records suddenly began to improve, and when the young scholar came home at the end of the year he wore on his cap the proud medal of first honors in studies. His mother was greatly relieved; the grandmother welcomed her favorite grandson with tears of happiness.

"The following year, Tomoyuki left for Hiroshima to matriculate in the Hiroshima District Military Preparatory School, destined to become an army officer. Once, when questioned why he, the son of a doctor, whose elder brother followed his father's profession and whose two remaining younger sisters all married into families of physicians, picked a military career, General Yamashita quietly replied, 'It was perhaps my destiny. I did not choose this career. My father suggested the idea perhaps because I was big and healthy and my mother did not seriously object because she believed, bless her soul, that I would never pass the highly competitive entrance examination. I went to Hiroshima, took the competitive examination, passed it, and found myself in school headed for the Cadet's Academy.' Thus almost accidentally began the military career of one of our greatest living generals.

"After passing the Central Military Preparatory School in Tokyo and the Cadet's Academy, both with high honors, Tomoyuki Yamashita was commissioned second lieutenant of the infantry in the Japanese army in 1908—three years after the end of the Russo-Japanese War of 1904–5. In school he was both popular and respected by his classmates because of his simplicity, kindheartedness, and industry. He never strove for leadership, nor was he ever a member of any faction or clique. He was always the mediator in the usual arguments that boys, being boys, always got into. Even the hotheaded among his classmates respected the calm, open-minded fairness of the country-bred youth and abided by his fair, impartial judgment."

Yamashita made an excellent record as a young officer. He showed himself to be industrious and popular with both his superiors and his subordinates. In 1911 he was appointed to the staff of the infantry school, and between 1914 and 1917 he attended the army staff college. There followed two years with the general staff and then he was transferred to the War Ministry. He remained with the War Ministry for eighteen years, except for special assignments in America and Europe, including a short period as military attaché in Austria. The significance of this experience in the War Ministry, in so far as pre-1945 Japan was concerned, is explained by Muto:

"Among the high-ranking officers of the Japanese army, the generalization can be made that they belong to one or the other of two distinct schools of thought and action, depending on their locale of service—the General Staff or the War Ministry. Those belonging to the former group, being primarily responsible for military operations and questions of high command, have the winning of war uppermost in their minds and, since they have little or no direct contact with the general public, are prone to place primordial importance on armament and military preparedness. Opposed to this school of thought, we have the group belonging to the War Ministry, whose responsibility is to put into effect the plans of the General Staff. In the course of their work, the officers of the War Ministry have to negotiate with the government, and, before any action can be taken to increase personnel or equipment, approval of the Diet must be first obtained. This brings them into direct contact with popular opinion, and the rights and privileges as well as the desires of the general public must be constantly kept in mind. Consequently, the War Ministry group are, from the nature of their work, more sympathetic and subservient to the will of the people than the General Staff group, and we find them opposed to the latter on most questions. This is especially true of those officers who have to do with mobilization and budgeting.

"Tomoyuki Yamashita served as member of the war affairs section, which had to do with mobilization and budget, from the time he was captain to the time he became chief of that section with the rank of full colonel. During his term of office he drew up a drastic program of disarmament which has, to this day, brought severe criticism on his head from the preparedness-first group, when, in 1929, the unheard-of reduction of personnel and armament in the Japanese army was put into effect."

We later learned that Muto here referred to the "Ugaki plan." General Kazushige Ugaki was Japanese war minister in 1929, and under his aegis Yamashita drafted a scheme for reduction of a number of divisions from the Japanese army, to bring it to a strength "adequate for defensive purposes only." The plan was pushed through the Diet, much to the army's distress. General Ugaki was later appointed premier of Japan, but the curt refusal of the army to name a war minister to his cabinet made it impossible for him to serve. Ugaki went into retirement, from which he emerged after a decade, and he had again become a prominent figure by the time of the American occupation of Japan in September, 1945. Now a very old man in failing health, he was unable to come to Manila to appear as a character witness for General Yamashita, but he sent an affidavit in which he described the accused as "a strong character, clean and honest and of a kindly and gentle disposition . . . well thought of by the people, and the type of man needed for the future of the country."

In 1936, Yamashita, then a major general, left the War Ministry to assume command of an infantry brigade in Korea. From there he was sent to inactive stations in North China and Manchuria, where he remained until he was recalled to Tokyo in 1940 to head the important command of inspector general of the air service.

"He remained at this post for only a short time," Muto says, "for he was soon sent abroad by the then minister of war, Lieutenant General Tojo, on a six months' inspection tour of Europe. This action on the part of General Tojo was widely criticized by many who believed that for some unknown reasons General Tojo did not particularly desire having General Yamashita in Tokyo."

This antipathy on the part of the powerful Tojo was to follow Yamashita throughout the war. Its origin is mysterious, unless it was a holdover from the army's resentment at Yamashita's authorship of the Ugaki disarmament plan. Yamashita himself would not talk about it. "I have nothing against General Tojo. Apparently he has something against me," was all that he would say.

Yamashita's European trip took him to the Axis countries. The Germans and the Italians were to show him all their weapons, and he assumed that they had done so. "I later discovered that they had held out on me," he told us as though it was a fine joke. But he did see enough so that, when he returned to Japan in June, 1941, he reported that, unless the Japanese army carried out immediate and far-reaching improvements in its air force, tanks and mechanized armaments, signal and communication service, engineering and chemical warfare departments, it could not meet the requirements of modern war. The report was not well received by Tojo, and when American power in the Pacific later moved into action, it became readily apparent that little or no attention had been paid to Yamashita's recommendations.

It was while homeward bound on this trip—crossing Siberia by train—that Yamashita first heard of the German attack on Russia. The other members of the military mission were of the common opinion that the Russians could not stop the Wehrmacht, but Yamashita prophesied that, although Germany would be initially successful, the front was too broad for her, the fight would be protracted, Germany could not hold out, and the Soviets must eventually win. It was at this time that he expressed the view, as described by Muto, that "judging from the national strength and condition of armament of the Japanese nation, it was imperative that Japan should bring the China incident to an immediate close and place the relations with America and Great Britain on a peaceful basis. His opinion won acceptance among some quarters, but he was suddenly transferred in September, 1941, to the comparatively unimportant post of defense commander of the Kwantung army and sent to Manchukuo."

The Japanese, according to Muto, considered that war between their country and the United States became "inevitable" late in November, 1941. It was at this time that Yamashita was placed in command of the Japanese Twenty-fifth Army, and when the war started, this army moved into the Malayan campaign. Singapore was captured by February 15, 1942, and overnight Yamashita became a national hero in Japan. But once again Premier Tojo stepped into Yamashita's path. The hero was not to be permitted to receive the applause of the crowds or to make his report to the emperor. "The new assignment awaiting the victorious general was another unimportant command in far-away Manchukuo," says Muto. "His marching orders even stipulated that he was not to stop over at Tokyo on his way to Manchukuo."

And so it happened that during the greater part of the war, General Yamashita drilled troops thousands of miles away from the scene of any action. More than two and a half years were to pass before changing events were to end the exile and bring General Yamashita into the situation that was responsible for his present unhappy position. Muto's sketch completes the story:

"In July, 1944, Saipan fell. The Tojo cabinet resigned en bloc. Peliliu was lost to the American forces in September, and all eyes now turned to the Philippines, whose defense was precarious and growing worse day by day. It was under this critical circumstance that, in October, General Yamashita was suddenly recalled from his Manchukuo post to command the Fourteenth Army Group in the Philippines. He arrived at Manila on the seventh of October, after spending only four days in Tokyo on his hurried trip to his new assignment.

"Upon arrival, he found the defense of the Philippines in a sorry state. With hardly any breathing spell he pitched into his new assignment with his usual vigor and worked to correct the weakness with almost superhuman efforts, but only ten days after his arrival the American landing in Leyte took place. In the Malay campaign he consistently took the offensive, but in the Philippines he was handicapped from the very outset and was forced to take the defensive from beginning to end. In spite of his efforts and the courageous fighting of his men, he was forced to retreat into the mountains of northern Luzon, where he received his final orders to surrender from Imperial General Headquarters on September 3, 1945. He issued orders for unconditional surrender to his entire army. This was the last order he issued. His career as a military man was ended."

This is not quite all. Muto adds some generalizations about his friend's character which may tend to be ecstatic but which illustrate, among other things, the loyalty and devotion that Yamashita inspired in his subordinates.

"The personality and character of General Yamashita are the combined products of his natural traits, his education and training, and his subsequent career as a soldier. In analyzing the character of General Yamashita, one must not overlook the influence of Harmony and Order which are the fundamental laws of nature herself and which were so manifest in the hills and streams and forest of his childhood days and youth. Strife and greed and ugliness are qualities which the general detests most in man, and there are few among his compatriots who are so natural, so unassuming, so little given to worldly ambition. . . . An inherent trust in fellow-beings is a quality found only in souls which are themselves pure and good, and by anyone who has been fortunate enough to come into contact with the big heart and upright character of this man this truth is quickly found out."

XI

THE PSYCHIATRISTS' EXAMINATION

ON OCTOBER 13, 1945, five days after the arraignment, Colonel Clarke permitted two Army officers who were psychiatrists to conduct a day-long examination of General Yamashita. Questions were put through Hamamoto, who obtained the general's answer and then told the gist of it in the third person. The psychiatrists obtained much the same information about Yamashita's childhood and home life that Muto had furnished, but they went about it in their own scientific way. For example, the stenographic record of the interview reveals this typical exchange:

"Q: Has he always enjoyed good health?
"A: Yes, he has always enjoyed good health.
"Q: Did he develop normally from babyhood?
"A: Yes.
"Q: Did he eat and sleep well?
"A: Yes.
"Q: Did he have any fears?
"A: No.
"Q: Any night terrors or nightmares?
"A: No.
"Q: Did he bite his fingernails or wet the bed?
"A: No.
"Q: He was just a happy, carefree youngster with no fears at all?
"A: Yes."

And again:

"Q: How did he reconcile his childhood nature of being a happy, carefree type of child with the decision to go into military life, where he had to be harsh and cruel?

"A: There is a wide breach in the psychology of the Eastern and Western mind on this point. He did not feel any inconsistency at heart because of the viewpoint or the conception of the role of a soldier in Japan, and that is that they do not consider a soldier or a career in the army a more or less harsh and cold-blooded profession or calling, although it is true that when fighting each other gun to gun they fight very hard, but beyond inflicting death to the other party where both are fully armed and on the battlefield, the soldier does not do any harm to any other person, and so to the general at that time the military calling was not considered a cold-blooded profession and he did not feel any inconsistency."

How about his marriage? Psychiatrists have a penchant for the details:

"Q: When did the general get married?

"A: 28 years ago. He was 31.

"Q: Does he give any reason for not getting married earlier?

"A: No particular reason why he married at 31. No particular reason for not marrying earlier. That is the average for marrying.

"Q: How long a courtship did he have?

"A: About a year and a half.

"Q: Were his parents pleased about his marriage?

"A: Both parents were dead at that time.

"Q: Was he happily married?

"A: Thank you, very happy.

"Q: Does he have a family?

"A: Unfortunately, he has no children.

"Q: Did that upset or disappoint him?

"A: Yes, he had medical consultation, but nothing could be done.

"Q: Is his wife still living?

"A: Yes.

"Q: Were they in comfortable circumstances?

"A: Ordinary—in other words, not very poor or very rich.

"Q: What did he and his wife especially enjoy doing together?

"A: Gardening, taking walks together in the mountains, fishing.

"Q: Did they like music or dancing?

"A: Music but not dancing. He himself is no musician, but he enjoys listening to music."

The interviewers were anxious to discover Yamashita's reactions to Japanese atrocities. There was much fruitless discussion of the Shinto religion, of Bushido, and the so-called "samurai code," and then the question:

"Q: How does Shintoism make atrocities, murder, rape, etc., possible?

"A: Such atrocities are not condoned and should be punished if they do occur.

"Q: When they do occur is it because men run wild so to speak?

"A: He can say very emphatically that a true believer in Shintoism will not commit such things. Those in a position to command are responsible for seeing that such occurrences are prevented and if they once are aware of it to punish it under military laws such as we have in our army.

"Q: Atrocities are explained on the basis of their perpetrators being under the bad god, Susano. Could the general discuss that?

"A: Not being a Shinto priest he cannot go into the theology of the matter, but there are two guiding spirits which control the action of a human being—the Nigitama, meaning a gentle spirit, and the Aratama, which represents the rough spirit. This the general believes represents the positive and negative, as we say in scientific discussion.

"Q: How is it possible to behead a prisoner of war? Is it compatible with Shintoism?

"A: There is no relation whatever with this act of maltreating a prisoner of war and the teachings of the Shinto religion. He doesn't know why they were beheaded, but there is no direct connection with Shintoism."

The most significant information gleaned from the psychiatric interview is found in the answers to questions pertaining to Yamashita's views on the war. They are quoted in full:

"Q: What made him fight the way he did fight? What is his reaction to war in general?

"A: As to war in general, from his study of the history of war he has concluded that in the old days a war was fought for the whim and fancy of a local lord, sometimes for more legitimate reasons, but always in the interest of a particular individual. In modern times he believes that the cause of war is fundamentally economic, an attempt to solve economic needs and allied matters on the part of a nation as a whole—in other words to fulfil the economic requirements of the people as a whole.

"Q: What about this war?

"A: He believes that the cause of this war is fundamentally economic. In other words, Japan 50 years ago was more or less self-sufficient—the people could more or less live off the land. In that 50 years the population increased to about double, so that Japan had to rely on outside sources for a food supply and other economic requirements. In her effort to fulfil the new and increased economic requirements which were fundamentally that of feeding the people, she felt it necessary to expand her economic activities outside as well as inside her borders. In order to buy or import her commodities, she had to pay for it ultimately in commodities. This effort on her part was prevented for one reason or another by other countries. Japan made attempts to solve the misunderstandings through peaceful methods, but, when all her efforts were either thwarted or negated, in order to sustain the livelihood of her people she felt it necessary to engage in open warfare.

"Q: Did all the people in Japan want this war?

"A: The general gives an answer straight from the shoulder like the frank and honest person he is. He says that he has been away from Tokyo for a long time and was not there when this war broke out, but to the best of his knowledge he believes that there were many people not in complete accord with having open hostilities. He never believed in this war and thought in his mind every effort should have been continued to solve this problem peacefully even to the extent of reducing armament expenses and diverting this fund to industrial development, since the economic well-being of the people was the fundamental question.

"Q: If he were not thoroughly sold on this war it is amazing that he would be placed in this command. It is not consistent.

"A: There would be an inconsistency had he volunteered for any particular command. In his case the command came from above; this was his duty to assume this position and as he was brought up as a soldier he had to be true to his responsibility. He sees no inconsistency in having fulfilled the particular military mission that he was given from above.

"Q: How does the general feel about the sneak attack on Pearl Harbor and the American idea of fair play?

"A: He was not in Tokyo at the time and was not following the developments that led to the war, and naturally he is in no position to judge the Pearl Harbor attack as a sneak attack or as legitimate tactics, but, generalizing, he would say he doesn't approve of any sneak attacks but that even war should be open.

"Q: Would the general state his opinion regarding the possible prevention of war from now on?

"A: He has no master-plan, naturally offhand, of saving the world for peace. He realizes the seriousness of the problem. All he can say at this time is that any plan to insure peace must have as a foundation, first, a practical way in which all the peoples of the world can survive on the principles of equality, and, second, we must have a common conception of what is wrong and adopt practical ways and means of disseminating this moral concept."

As the interview drew to a close, the psychiatrists asked a question that revealed a complex common to many Americans at this time. In discussing the trial with American soldiers and civilians during the autumn of 1945 and early winter of 1946, I was bothered by the prevalent fear that we would be considered "soft" by other nations if we gave free play to our natural instincts for justice in the treatment of a fallen enemy.

"Do you look on the American spirit of fair play as a weakness?" was the revealing question that the officers asked.

Hamamoto paraphrased Yamashita's Japanese: "He believes that the American spirit of fair play is the core or the motivating cause for the future expansion of America into a greater nation."

Sometime later I was allowed to see the report of the interview that the two interrogating officers had prepared. To one who believes that honest analysis depends on unprejudiced objectivity, it was most disappointing. The psychiatrists acknowledged that they were surprised to find that General Yamashita had answered their questions honestly and frankly, that they were convinced of his sincerity. "The general appears more as a benign, aging Japanese officer than the formidable 'Tiger of Malaya,' " they said. "He was, throughout the interview, alert, interested, courteous, and cooperative. One was, against one's will or better judgment, inclined to credit him as being sincere in his answers."

Why "against their will"? What preconceptions did these supposedly objective investigators bring to their task? "If we did not have positive knowledge of the many instances of documented cruelties and inhumanities practiced by his soldiers," the report continued, "one would be inclined to believe his protestations of kindliness and good sportsmanship. In this connection, one is strongly reminded of the neurotic character in confinement, who appears to believe that his conduct is in accordance with his convincingly recited ideals. In other words, the interview revealed a lofty, benign code of ethics and behavior quite the antithesis of actual practice as far as is known. It would seem difficult to credit the assertion that he had no knowledge of any atrocities or cruelties practiced by soldiers of his command on the persons of American soldiers and Filipinos. The courteous manner and cooperative attitude are also characteristic of the neurotic character under detention who is surprisingly facile in presenting a façade of normality and in convincingly presenting self-serving or defensive material."

The impropriety of using extraneous "facts" to destroy the clear implications of an objective interview is heightened by the realization that the "facts" were nothing more than a reflection of the hysterical prejudice and wild gossip that were rife in the Philippine Islands at the moment. This is evidenced by the report's succeeding statement: "The humiliating, brutal treatment of Generals Percival and Wainwright by the Japanese gives the lie to General Yamashita's statement as to his treatment of them." Of course, General Yamashita gave no statement as to "his treatment" of General Wainwright. General Wainwright's name was not mentioned in the interview, and General Yamashita had not seen or had any connection with him during the war. Had these eager scientists asked about Wainwright, Yamashita might have informed them that not he, but General Homma, had accepted Wainwright's surrender at Corregidor, and that this had occurred more than two years before Yamashita ever saw the Philippine Islands. Nor had the interviewers asked about General Percival. In answer to a question as to how he felt about his confinement, General Yamashita had remarked that when he received the British commander's surrender at Singapore, he had given orders that "General Percival was to be given complete choice as to whether he wanted to live in his headquarters or in a house with freedom of movement within a wide territory"—a statement that was apparently entirely accurate.

In short, these two scientific American officers admitted that, contrary to their own preconceptions, Yamashita appeared to be a man who had done no wrong and that, if it had not been for certain misnamed "facts" which they assumed to exist, they would have been objectively convinced of his innocence. As it was, they could only analyze and reason that his sincerity and apparent truthfulness was the evidence of a psychosis resulting from confinement. In other words, had Yamashita's answers betrayed a harsh and cruel nature, he would have been branded a criminal type. Since his answers revealed humanitarian instincts and a clear conscience, he was still branded a criminal.

These were the officers who talked to a defeated enemy general about the American spirit of fair play.

XII

A QUESTION AND AN INTERVIEW

GENERAL YAMASHITA often spoke of his admiration for the ubiquitous sense of humor of the American soldiers. After commenting about it during a lull in our preparation of the case, he asked me: "What has happened to America in the last twenty-five years? I notice a change in these boys from the American soldiers that I saw in Germany and in Paris after the last war. They were happy-go-lucky then, too, but they seemed to carry a chip on their shoulder, and all they seemed to care about was money. They had the attitude: 'Our country makes more automobiles—or has more railroads—than any other country. Our country can do anything. Do you want to make something of it?' Or I would go into an art museum, and, if American doughboys came in, all they'd say about a beautiful picture was: 'I wonder how much it costs?' Today I notice a difference. American soldiers are still carefree, but they're not so brash. There's some humility and politeness and appreciation, and they don't talk about dollars all the time. What has happened in the United States to cause that change?"

I told him of the depression and of breadlines and Hoovervilles and *The Grapes of Wrath.* I tried to explain what apparently Japanese as well as Europeans have difficulty in understanding, that in America we, too, had had hunger and misery. I told him of "poverty in the midst of plenty" and of unemployment, and I ventured the opinion that Americans had found some problems that even they could not easily solve and that had not yet been completely solved. The war had been a temporary palliative, but our boys were no longer uncompromising optimists as to their own economic futures. And I added that, partly because of that and partly because of the results of the last war, our attitude now was not the same as in 1917. There were no catchy war songs, no parades, no cocksure certainty that we could make the whole world "safe for democracy."

Yamashita nodded: "There will be no trouble in occupying Japan," he said prophetically. "The Japanese admire the Americans. The Japanese will like the Americans."

"Even after the atomic bombs?" I asked.

Yamashita smiled. "Even after the atomic bombs," he said.

Interviewing of witnesses and preparation of the defense case prior to trial took place in a vacant dwelling in the outskirts of Manila that the Army made available to us. The use of the house obviated the necessity of daily trips to the prison camp, and it was so located that Japanese captives could be brought in from the camp in a closed ambulance without attracting the attention of a hostile populace. It was in a room on the second floor of this building, the night before the opening of the trial, that General Yamashita was interviewed by a young American sergeant, reporter for *Yank*, the Army men's weekly magazine. The report of the interview was never published, for *Yank* passed out of existence a few weeks later.

The reporter said he wanted "human interest stuff." "What kind of a car do you drive?" he asked. Car? The general had never had an automobile. While working in the War Ministry in Tokyo he had commuted from his suburban home by train or trolley.

"How big is your home?"

The general waved his arm. "About as big as this," he said.

"As big as this house?" asked the reporter.

Yamashita laughed heartily. "No, no," he said, "as big as this *room*."

The interviewer's final question was: "What do you think of your defense counsel?"

Yamashita became serious; his voice lowered and seemed to tremble slightly, apparently betraying deeply felt emotion. "At the arraignment I told the military commission that I felt honored and grateful that the United States has given me such able men to represent me. Today I would repeat that, but I would add more. For three weeks now I have watched them work on the preparation of this case. They have worked hard every day and every evening, and they have given up their Sundays. For them to do that for me, who, after all, has but recently been their enemy, touches me very deeply."

XIII
SPEED

IN THE Pacific Theater of Operations, General Douglas MacArthur was the fountainhead of all authority. His sense of complete personal responsibility cast him in the role of a dictator; delegations of power were extremely limited. By the time General Yamashita came to trial, General MacArthur was in Tokyo, one thousand miles away. But the decision to try Yamashita, the very charge on which he was to be tried, the rules of evidence (such as they were) that would guide the military commission in the conduct of the case, all came from the commander-in-chief. And so did the order for speed.

Speed was the keynote of the trial. General Yamashita came down from the hills and surrendered to the American forces on September 3, 1945. On September 25 he was charged with being a war criminal. Two weeks later he was arraigned and served with a bill of sixty-four particulars. Trial was set for October 29.

The three weeks that intervened between the arraignment and the trial were used by General Yamashita's lawyers in an attempt to build a defense to the sixty-four particulars. The bill alleged murder, massacre, rape, and pillage of innocent noncombatant civilians, both in Manila and in the provinces; mistreatment, starvation, and murder of American prisoners of war and civilian internees; wanton devastation and destruction of public, private, and religious property. We knew that to make even a pretense of investigation of these crimes, involving thousands of people and hundreds of miles of territory, would take many months. All we could do was to go over each of the particulars with Yamashita and his staff officers, learn from them who among the Japanese prisoners of war might be in a position to know what had happened, interview those prisoners, satisfy ourselves that the general did not know of the occurrences, that his communications at the time and place involved were such that he could not know of them, perhaps that the troops that were at the particular location at the moment were not then under his command. We acquainted ourselves with the Japanese military network, their chain of command, their line of communications. We studied the Japanese court-martial system to ascertain what steps were taken within the Japanese army to punish criminals. We delved into ramifications of the enemy's food problem to find out why prisoners of war were underfed. We discovered why General Yamashita had had to depend on his subordinates for information, who those subordinates were, their weaknesses, their blind spots, their problems. As General Yamashita had told the *Yank* reporter, we worked every day, every Sunday, every evening.

As the Monday that had been set for the opening of the trial approached, defense counsel felt that, although they had not been able to prepare witnesess for an affirmative defense, they at least were ready to deal with the prosecution's case as outlined in the bill of sixty-four particulars. But late on the final Friday evening, a messenger arrived with a new bill of particulars, a "supplemental" bill. It contained fifty-nine new items. We were dumbfounded. We had expected that perhaps one or two or three new items might be added; but here we were, just two days before trial, and the charges that we would have to meet were almost doubled—from sixty-four to one hundred and twenty-three, and practically all of them involving new places, new persons, new witnesses.

Of course, we would ask for a continuance, and it was agreed that I would make the motion. I knew that the commission would feel impelled to go on with the trial; publicity had set the stage, the prosecution witnesses would be ready, the power behind the commission was in a hurry. But after we had worked day and night for three weeks on sixty-four items of a bill of particulars, the commission simply could not refuse us some time to prepare for fifty-nine new ones.

Accordingly, on Monday morning the prosecution was permitted to file its "supplemental" bill. I immediately requested a continuance, and in my argument referred to General MacArthur's directive that set forth the rules of procedure for the military commission. Deriving what aid I could from the weight I knew that his name carried with his subordinates, I quoted General MacArthur: "The accused shall be entitled to have *in advance of trial* a copy of the charges and specifications, so worded as clearly to apprise the accused of each offense charged." And then I added:

"In advance of trial, I suppose technically could mean thirty seconds in advance of trial, but that is not what is intended. This phrase obviously means sufficiently in advance of trial to allow the defense to prepare itself."

The world was watching this trial. Could the five generals afford to appear to be unfair? I concluded:

"We earnestly state that we must have this time in order to prepare a defense adequately. I might add, sir, we think that this is important to the accused, but far more important than any rights of this accused, we believe, is the proposition that this commission should not deviate from a fundamental American concept of fairness, decency, and justice, which dictates that an accused has a right to defend himself."

The commission retired to chambers for deliberation. A few minutes later the generals returned to the bench. The president, General Reynolds, announced the decision:

"The motion of defense counsel for a continuance is not sustained. If, however, at the end of the presentation by the prosecution of evidence concerning the bill of particulars, dated 1 October 1945, as presented during the arraignment, defense counsel believe they require additional time to prepare their case, the commission will consider such a motion at that time."

That was not entirely unsatisfactory. It is true that General Reynolds did not guarantee a future continuance—he merely said that an eventual motion would be "considered." But that same afternoon the promise did become definite. The prosecution put a witness on the stand who was to testify as to a crime in one of the items of the supplemental bill of particulars. General Reynolds interrupted Major Kerr and announced that no evidence would be permitted on any of the items of the new bill "until the defense has had time to prepare its case." The chief prosecutor then asked:

"How long will that be, sir? Because we have to make arrangements, if the commission please, so that we may rearrange the presentation or the order of the presentation of our case; and if I may know how long that 'armistice' is to apply, I may then arrange accordingly."

"General Reynolds: Has the defense any comment to make?

"Captain Reel: If the court please, we understood this morning that, after the prosecution's case was in on the sixty-four particulars, we would be given some time to prepare on that.

"General Reynolds: That is correct.

"Captain Reel: Then I believe, based on our experience with the first sixty-four particulars, that we will require two weeks to prepare ourselves on the fifty-nine new ones."

General Reynolds then stated that there was nothing more to say. With this assurance, we proceeded through the trial. At least we would eventually have time to prepare our affirmative defense. Ten days later the subject came up again. There had been no continuance, and the prosecution wanted to know when we would be ready to meet certain items of the new bill. "Frankly," said Major Kerr, "it took the war crimes commission some three months to investigate these matters, and I cannot conceive of the defense undertaking a similar investigation with any less period of time." In answer General Reynolds said: "It is our determination to give [the defense] the time they require." And addressing us, he added: "We will see to it that you get time to prepare your defense."

The commission sat all day, six days a week. Occasionally there were night sessions. But at the commission's request we attempted to acquaint ourselves with items of the supplemental bill of particulars on Sundays and during our "free" evenings. Colonel Clarke explained to General Reynolds in chambers that the colossal task of this preparation, as well as the daily handling of the trial, had fallen on the shoulders of three men, Captains Sandberg and Reel and Colonel Clarke himself. Lieutenant Colonel Feldhaus had gone to the hospital for an urgent and serious operation before the trial began; he would probably be lost to us for its duration. Major Guy had been sent to Tokyo to interview character witnesses, and when he returned he would be kept busy taking care of them. Lieutenant Colonel Hendrix was occupied with legal research involving our attempt to get this matter before the courts, at this time specifically the Philippine Supreme Court. At the commission's request we were announcing day by day in open court that we were ready to meet prosecution evidence on various items of the supplemental bill, but we were depending on a continuance after all the prosecution's evidence was in, so that we might prepare our affirmative case.

General Reynolds answered Colonel Clarke by proposing additional defense counsel, adding that he would recommend the granting of any reasonable request for new men that we might make.

It was impossible to throw green men into that situation

and expect them to be able to assume any major share of the burden. We had been working on the case for five or six weeks and to acquaint new men, even able lawyers, with the factual and psychological background while the trial was drawing to a close would have taken time we could not afford to spare. Nevertheless, two second lieutenants were assigned to help us when the trial had progressed about three weeks. Neither was a lawyer. One fell ill the day after his appointment and was hospitalized until the proceedings were over. The other, Lieutenant Haig Kantarian, proved to be of great assistance—he did the "leg work" that is the bane of every trial lawyer's life. Later on, another second lieutenant was designated to take the place of the sick officer, but it was then too late for the harassed defense counsel to take time out to educate a new man.

On November 12, the commission again called senior defense counsel into chambers. The judges had always appeared to be in a hurry to finish the trial, but apparently something had happened to cause even a further acceleration. The commission, said General Reynolds, would not look kindly on *any* request for a recess, and later on the same day he made the formal announcement from the bench: "The commission will grant a continuance only for the most urgent and unavoidable reasons."

Why? What had happened since November 8, just four days before, when the general had reiterated his promise to give the defense "the time they require"? Something had caused this change of position. Later we discovered what it was.

General Reynolds' prepared statement made his new position quite clear:

"The commission will grant a continuance only for the most urgent and unavoidable reasons. The trial has now consumed two weeks of time. The prosecution indicates that this week will be required to finish its presentation. Early in the trial the commission invited senior defense counsel to apply for additional assistants in such numbers as necessary to avoid the necessity for a continuance. The offer has been extended from time to time throughout the trial. The commission is still willing to ask that additional counsel be provided, for we do not wish to entertain a request for a continuance."

General Reynolds paused for a moment and directed his gaze at the three defense lawyers who had been present all through the trial—Clarke, Sandberg, and me. He continued:

"The commission questions either the necessity or desirability for all members of counsel being present during all the presentation of the case of the prosecution. We feel that one or two members of the defense staff in the courtroom is adequate and that the remaining member or members should be out of the courtroom performing specific missions for senior counsel."

Sandberg and I had been cross-examining the prosecution witnesses. We had been objecting to inadmissible evidence. We had been carrying on the fight against the prejudicial effect of unsound hearsay and opinion and gossip. As one news correspondent put it, we were the "ball carriers" for "Quarterback Clarke." Not only would the trial move faster, but the commission's life would be considerably more pleasant were we both not in the room. But we had been appointed to defend a man on trial for his life. And we were not only subordinate officers, we were lawyers. We stayed.

General Reynolds concluded his statement. "The commission," he said, "directs both prosecution and the defense so to organize and direct the preparation and presentation of their case including the use of assistants, to the end that the need to request a continuance may not arise."

Of course, the prosecution was not interested in a continuance. The warning was directed to the defense, but we could not crowd more hours into a day. The commission had not stated that it would not grant a continuance, but it had indicated that "urgent and unavoidable reasons" would be required. We felt we had them.

Eight days later, on November 20, shortly before noon, the prosecution rested its case. Colonel Clarke arose and addressed the five generals:

"If the commission please, on the 29th of October, defense requested a continuance at that time, in order to prepare on the additional bill of particulars and an affirmative defense. At that time the court said that at the end of the presentation of the prosecution's evidence concerning the bill of particulars dated 1 October 1945, presented during the arraignment, the commission would consider such a motion.

"In the afternoon session, at the time that the prosecution proposed to establish one of the particulars in the new bill of particulars, there was a question as to whether or not it would be taken up, and the court asked the defense whether they had any comment to make.

"At that time, Captain Reel told the court that he understood that morning, after prosecution's case was in on the sixty-four particulars, that consideration would then be given to time to prepare on the other bill and on the affirmative defense, and the court answered, 'That is correct.' At that time we requested a two-week continuance.

"At the present time, defense moves the court for a reasonable continuance, in which time we may properly prepare an affirmative defense. During the time this court has been in session, the defense has been working day and night to keep up with that new bill of particulars. We have had no time whatsoever to prepare any affirmative defense."

The senior defense counsel hesitated. We needed time. But the commission was in a frightful hurry. Should he ask for a week—just one week? He would leave it up to them. "We therefore request the court to grant the defense a reasonable continuance," Clarke concluded.

General Reynolds frowned. "The commission will withdraw for deliberation," he said.

Approximately fifteen minutes later the commission resumed its session. General Reynolds read another prepared statement. It recited that, after the arraignment on October 8, there had been a three weeks' adjournment to provide time for preparation by both prosecution and defense, that the supplemental bill of particulars had been furnished the defense on October 26, that trial had started on October 29, and that a total of forty-two days had elapsed since the arraignment. General Reynolds then re-read his pronouncement of November 12. He concluded:

"In view of this simple narration of time and events, the commission feels that ample time has been provided counsel to prepare its defense. The request of defense counsel for a continuance to enable it further to prepare its case is denied."

There followed a short colloquy which is worthy of reproduction from the official record:

"Colonel Clarke: If the Commission please, the continuance having been denied we request the court to grant us a short recess of a day.

"General Reynolds: The Commission would be more willing to grant a recess until 1:30 this afternoon. Would that suffice?

"Colonel Clarke: It will not suffice, sir.

"General Reynolds: The Commission feels that the Defense should be prepared at least on its opening statement.

"Colonel Clarke: We haven't had time to do that, sir.

"General Reynolds: In view of the statement of Counsel that they are completely unready to make their opening statement and to proceed, the Commission will recess until 8:30 tomorrow morning."

Two months later, Mr. Justice Rutledge, of the United States Supreme Court, was to comment on this unseemly haste:

"Obviously the burden placed upon the defense, in the short time allowed for preparation on the original bill, was not only 'tremendous.' In view of all the facts, it was an impossible one. . . . But the grosser vice was later when the burden was more than doubled by service of the supplemental bill on the eve of trial, a procedure which, taken in connection with the consistent denials of continuance and the commission's later reversal of its rulings favorable to the defense, was wholly arbitrary, cutting off the last vestige of adequate chance to prepare defense and imposing a burden the most able counsel could not bear. This sort of thing has no place in our system of justice, civil or military. Without more, this wide departure from the most elementary principles of fairness vitiated the proceeding. When added to the other denials of fundamental right . . . it deprived the proceeding of any semblance of trial as we know that institution."

Mr. Justice Rutledge was not aware of the reason for the commission's "reversal of its ruling favorable to the defense." He could not know what mysterious voice had whispered to the five generals between November 8 and November 12. But defense counsel had quite accidentally discovered that between those two dates a radiogram had been dispatched from General MacArthur's headquarters in Tokyo to the representative of that headquarters in Manila. General MacArthur was "disturbed," said the wire, at "reports of a possible continuance" in the Yamashita case; General MacArthur "doubted" the "need of defense for more time"; General MacArthur "urged" haste.

Of course, five regular Army generals would not disobey any expressed desires of their five-star commander-in-chief that might be brought to their attention. Nor was it for them to question how someone in Tokyo could know of the "need for time" of subordinates in Manila, one thousand miles away. Read in the light of that radiogram, the commission's ukase of November 12 makes sense—to an Army man.

Why was General MacArthur in such a hurry? After the commission made its findings and pronounced its sentence, the entire record of the trial would have to be reviewed, first by General Styer's judge advocate and then by General MacArthur's judge advocate, before the sentence could be executed. We knew that a copy of the record was being furnished to both of those judge advocate officers day by day, that in each office lawyers had been assigned to the review, and that the necessary summaries were in preparation as the case went along. It had been rumored that General Styer's judge advocate had been ordered to complete his opinion within forty-eight hours after the anticipated sentence and that General MacArthur's judge advocate was to have his ready shortly thereafter. We did not know whether those astounding rumors were true, but we did know that, as the matter was being handled, it was not impossible that such a result could be accomplished. And it was the fear of just such haste that prompted us to take some of the rather unusual steps to which we resorted in laying our case before the Supreme Court. In short, we knew that General MacArthur was extremely impatient. But why? Why the rush?

I can only guess. The public's picture of a strong man must be painted in sharp colors. He is one who does not brook the law's delay. If he has promised the Philippine people retribution for their wrongs, he makes good on that promise before they have a chance to forget it. If he has brought a heinous war criminal to bay, he hangs him without bothering over dilatory details. "Avoid Court interference—take all necessary steps"—it is consistent. In Europe the war had been over for six months, yet only now was Justice Jackson getting around to the Nuremberg trials. But the German trials were coming. Within a matter of weeks or even days, Nuremberg and not Manila would command the headlines in American newspapers.

I may be doing General MacArthur an injustice. I repeat, I do not know his motives. But the plain fact of the record shows the clear pattern of what Mr. Justice Murphy was to describe as "needless and unseemly haste." The record speaks for itself—and with an uncomfortable eloquence.

XIV
LEGAL ETHICS

"IN THE opinion of probably every correspondent covering the trial, the military commission came into the courtroom the first day with the decision already in its collective pocket," commented *Newsweek* after the trial was over. Nevertheless, it was also immediately obvious to observers that the lawyers for the defense were intent on fighting for whatever modicum of justice might be available for their man. They objected to evidence that they considered improper; they vainly insisted on the right to cross-examine witnesses; they attempted to invoke the safeguards accorded to an accused by congressional statutes, by international treaties, and by Anglo-Saxon judicial tradition. The members of the military commission were confused and irked. The only safe thing for the generals to do appeared to be to resolve all doubts against the defense. Still Yamashita's counsel persisted, and, although they were rarely rewarded by any favorable rulings, they seemed to derive satisfaction from making certain that the stenographic record of the proceedings showed their arguments and defeats in full detail.

All this added up to a somewhat unpleasant interference with an otherwise well-planned drama. Newspapermen and radio commentators were sending thousands of words every day to all parts of the earth, describing this performance. What would they say about its conduct? They were not lawyers, to be sure, but neither were the commission, and most, if not all, of the correspondents had had more experience in a courtroom than had the generals. Suppose the journalists were to agree with those plausible arguments of the defense?

What would happen to the whole plan of showing the world that we were giving this criminal a "fair trial"?

The commission attempted to remedy the situation. Before the trial was two or three days old, both prosecution and defense counsel were called into chambers. General Reynolds spoke for the commission: "You men aren't knights in armor jousting with one another," he said "you are officers of the Army and of this court, and you are detailed to help us find the facts here—that's all."

General Reynolds was obviously unaware of the historical tradition underlying Anglo-Saxon trial practice. The theory of the common law is that counsel for each side involved in a case are to present all possible arguments in their own behalf, and the judges and juries, having the benefit of the opposing presentations, are to find the true facts from the whole mass of evidence thus laid before them. In a sense, trial counsel are and should be "jousting knights." And yet General Reynolds was not entirely wrong. After all, this was not a civil trial. We were officers of the United States Army appointed by the Army, and we did owe a peculiar duty to the military commission. There were times when that obligation appeared to conflict with the duty that we felt we owed to Yamashita as his lawyers, and we were often concerned with the unusual dual position in which we found ourselves. For example, in a civil trial a lawyer does not ordinarily consider himself bound to present to the court evidence which would be damaging to his client. In our case we were forced to conduct our own investigations, and on two occasions we uncovered information that might have turned out to be harmful. (Actually, the material did not prove to be damaging to our cause in either instance, although we could not have been completely aware of that fact at the time that we obtained it.) On both occasions, after thoroughly discussing the ethics of the situation among ourselves, we voluntarily turned the evidence over to the commission in chambers in the presence of the chief prosecutor.

One difficulty which we faced was that this open-handedness did not work both ways. The war-crimes investigators may well have discovered considerable evidence that was favorable to Yamashita, but neither the commission nor we would ever get the benefit of it. The staff of investigators that furnished material for the prosecution was so large that it maintained separate offices under separate executives, and Major Kerr was thus enabled to say, probably truthfully, that if the investigators had uncovered evidence favorable to the defense, he would not know about it.

The defense counsel believed, however, that, aside from a duty to lay all evidence in their possession before the commission, their task was essentially that of lawyers for an accused man. We consistently refused to weaken our resolve to fight for every right to which we believed General Yamashita was entitled, and, indeed, we had served warning on the commission before the trial began that that was to be our position. In the memorandum attached to our motion to dismiss the action that was filed on October 19, 1945, we had written:

"As officers of the United States Army, and as lawyers appointed to defend the accused, defense counsel are charged with a duty to the accused, to the Army, and to the people of the United States to pursue all proper legal remedies open to the defense, including, if warranted, recourse to the Federal Courts, and more particularly, the Supreme Court of the United States."

Had General Reynolds remembered that language, he would probably have realized that we would continue to "joust."

Before the chambers conference was concluded, General Reynolds addressed the other four generals, his brethren on the commission: "After this trial is over," he said, "you fellows will be assigned to other commissions to try some more of these war-crimes cases. I suggest that you do what we should have done in this case—that is, before the trial, conduct an 'orientation course' for the counsel." More and better rehearsals!

As we were leaving the room General Reynolds stopped the defense lawyers. "You fellows," he said with a kindly smile, "should talk to *us*, not to the record. You'll get along better." "Thank you, sir," I said. And we continued to talk to both.

XV
DOUBTS

THE greater part of the prosecution's evidence consisted of witnesses and documents testifying to atrocities committed by Japanese troops during the previous year. As summarized in the eventual findings of the military commission, the crimes "may be grouped in three categories: First, starvation, execution or massacre without trial, and maladministration generally of civilian internees and prisoners of war; Secondly, torture, rape, murder, and mass execution of very large number of residents of the Philippines, including women and children and members of religious orders, by starvation, beheading, bayoneting, clubbing, hanging, burning alive, and destruction by explosives; and, finally, burning and demolition without adequate military necessity of large numbers of homes, places of business, places of religious worship, hospitals, public buildings, and educational institutions. In point of time, the offenses extended throughout the period accused was in command of Japanese troops in the Philippine Archipelago, although by far the most of the incredible acts occurred on Luzon."

Small children described how they had seen their parents bayoneted, mothers wept as they recalled the death of their babies, men who had hidden themselves told of watching others being decapitated. Day after day, tales of bestiality and horror were recounted by Filipinos, Chinese, and occasionally Americans, until the listener wondered whether he was living on this green earth or in a bloody gash on the corpse of hell. There *had* to be revenge. Not vengeance by flame-thrower, block-buster, or atomic bomb—such devices were impersonal, that retribution was past, those victims were not to be seen here in the Manila courtroom. There had to be a personal vengeance, somehow—*on someone*. And here he was in this chamber for all to see, an individual, a creature, a man, not only a Japanese soldier but *the* Japanese soldier, the *top* Japanese soldier. But was he the "top"? He had had superiors, too. There was Marshal Terauchi, the supreme southern commander, there was the imperial headquarters in Tokyo, there was the emperor himself. But they were not here, and this man was. To be sure, no witness had seen Yamashita—not one of the many eyewitnesses to Japanese crimes spoke his name. But he must be the victim, for is he not in the courtroom—not thirty feet away from that chair where the stories are being told and the tears are being shed? Small wonder that the guard who searched all witnesses and spectators discovered that one woman carried rocks in her handbag that she was prepared to throw at the defendant upon completion of her testimony. Nor was it remarkable that another feminine witness, after describing the bayoneting of her children, shook her fist at General Yamashita as she rose to leave the witness stand, and shouted: "Tandaan mo! Yamashita!" ("Remember it! Yamashita!").

There were some in the courtroom who could sublimate sensation to thought. And as the days wore on and emotions became hardened to the barbaric facts of a brutal war, there were more and more men who were able to think. Just what was going on here? The trial of Yamashita—but was it a trial? And what was Yamashita's connection? Why *Yamashita* and not the men who had perpetrated the acts? Or why not a subordinate commander? Or why not the emperor? And might not the defense lawyers be right in protesting against rumor and gossip and hearsay and guess? "My *reaction* was"; "He told me he was not sure, but he believed"; "*I heard* from some military policeman"; "I guess"; "I think"—was this the sort of evidence on which to hang a man?

Doubts. And, as the testimony mounted, the doubts increased. Already at the close of the second day of trial, correspondent Keyes of the *London Daily Express* sent a dispatch to his paper, here quoted exactly as it went over the teletype:

"Yamashita trial continued today—but it isn't a trial. I doubt that it is even a hearing. Yesterday his name was mentioned once. Today it wasn't brought up at all. The Military Commission sitting in judgment continued to act as if it wasn't bound by any law or rules of evidence. I hold no brief for any Jap but in no British court of law would accused have received such rough and ready treatment as Yamashita. The Yamashita trial has been hailed as the most important of the Pacific, not because it is the first, but because the present Commission is supposed to be setting precedents for all future war criminal trials. The trial is supposed to establish that a military commander is responsible for any acts of any of his troops. At the same time, under British law, anyway, he's supposed to have rights. The present Commission pleads saving of time and money, but facts are so far Yamashita's American counsel haven't had a hearing.

"This afternoon, Captain Reel, one of the defense counsel, tendered the last of many objections to the admission of affidavits as evidence in a criminal case. He repeated previous defense claims that under laws of U.S. Congress such affidavits are inadmissible. Of one such affidavit he said: 'This only goes to prove the common sense and intelligence behind the reasoning prohibiting admission of such "evidence." We haven't had an opportunity to see what kind of evidence this is, no opportunity to examine the witnesses nor question them in any way.' One question and answer in one affidavit he described as not only double hearsay, but hearsay based on conjecture. It was extremely prejudicial, put in for prejudicial reasons by the prosecution."

Most of the American newspaper reporters emphasized

the sensational details of the atrocity testimony in their dispatches. Descriptions and pictures of the thirteen-year-old Filipina girl, who lifted her dress on the witness stand to display some of the twenty-six scars left on her body by Japanese bayonets; of the man who turned his back on the commission to let the generals see the gash on his neck where the blow of a Japanese sword had narrowly failed of its mission of decapitation; of the girls who told of rape and abuse as the buildings of Manila were crumbling about them—these became the morbidly fascinating breakfast fare of readers. But as the pattern of atrocity stories steadied to a regularity that approached monotony, a new note crept into the newspaper reports. Was this the trial of Yamashita or of the Japanese army? If the latter, why was the inevitable punishment to be meted out to just one member of that army, neither the highest nor the lowest in command, whose connection with the sensational crimes had not yet been shown? And what kind of a proceeding was it where the spectators, ordinary laymen and American soldiers, were, in the language of the American magazine *Newsweek*, "scandalized" by the "break with Anglo-Saxon Justice" epitomized by the commission's permission of "almost anything . . . even third hand hearsay" as "evidence"?

Perhaps in a quieter place and at a calmer time men would think differently about the trial of a Japanese general. Perhaps it was the ability to turn aside the passions of the moment and to look into the future that caused one observer to leave the courtroom, return to his barracks, and put his reactions into verse. We are indebted to Captain James A. Shackford, of High Point, North Carolina, for the following:

Come to the courtroom where a little man
    Sits unsmilingly, alone, at bay
Before the accusers, hemmed about by wan
    Cluster of counsel. One brief aisle away
Plots prosecution. And to judge the show

DOUBTS

Like God-made critics, Generals hold sway,
Gaze at the curious, who gaze back below—
All see one man on trial on one day.

That is what they come for, what they see.
Hollywood has come to have a look,
Blazing its photoflashic eye in glee
At what will read well in a picture book.
And out through seven windows is the bay—
The whole wide ocean in one little cove!
And all the ships that sailed in hate away
Caress the harbor now with sudden love!

Americans, nay all who have a stake
In earthly life, or life beyond this earth,
Come sit with me beside this crucial wake
And witness death—and die, or find rebirth.
Here are the wronged, with holes in hands and feet;
For all mankind let Doubting Thomas feel.
Here are tears not quenchable, nor sweet
(Looking, I see no judge nor witness kneel);

Behold the scars, charred corpses, hands in cords,
Heads off, or half whacked off. Here babes were tossed
High in the air and caught on tempered swords,
Beautiful swords, hand-wrought, and hand embossed!
Here is what life had done to life; and yet
Judge sits in judgment, the accused in chains:
Life is a game, the players place a bet—
The sinner loses what the righteous gains!

As if one man is here on trial alone,
As if one nation sinned, and sinned again;
("Oh, hideous are the crimes these men have done!
Thank God that we are not as other men!"
We of flame-thrower and atom bomb!) Man's hate,
His lust, his sightless eyes before broad day,
His ignorance which love can not penetrate—
Your heart and mine are culprits! Judge away!

Here judge we our own souls, and know it not.
Through blindness our one hope is dying fast;
We ride Damascus road, and at the spot
Where Saul fell groveling, we push calmly past.

One hope: to find the blinding light and fall
Into the dust in agony and shame,
Crying, "O God, of sinful creatures all,
We are most sinful! Ours the accursed name!

"Death we deserve, and everlasting death!
Wreak thy vengeance on us. We have seen
The blackness of our hearts. Our very breath
Itself, beseeching judgment, is unclean.
Ours, O Lord, ours the unpitiable wrong!
Ours was the crime! Oh smite us with Thy might!
In Thy great bounty to us we grew strong
And stood between Thy children and Thy light!"

One hope! And yet our hearts will never move.
The wage of sin is death. We stand accused.
("Jerusalem! Jerusalem! With love
How oft I would have saved you! You refused!")
So let us judge him. For his guilt is clear,
Since to the victors go the spoils of war—
Most blind of fools! An angry God does here
Arraign us all, and swift his judgments are.

XVI

"A FURTHER MEANS OF SAVING TIME"

YAMASHITA'S defense counsel could not meet the atrocity evidence factually. We could—and did—oppose the admission of testimony and documents founded on hearsay, conjecture, and wishful thinking, unavailing though our protests were, for the most part. But when an eyewitness said that he had seen hundreds of Filipinos killed by Japanese troops, we had to listen helplessly. The witness might well have been exaggerating; he may even have been lying or telling only part of the truth; most often he had been so excited and emotionally upset at the time of the occurrence he was describing that he could not possibly have the accurate recollection of detail, especially as to numbers of persons involved, that he professed. But we were unable to make any investigation of the circumstances of the crimes, and we never knew from day to day or from witness to witness what type of narrative was coming next.

Often we sought to exploit weaknesses in witness's stories by means of cross-examination, but the commission frowned on this procedure as a "waste of time." This most vital of the rights of an accused, the very essence of the distinction between a trial and an inquisition, was sacrificed on the altar of speed. The members of the military commission had, throughout the trial, displayed impatience with the defense attempts to cross-question witnesses, usually interrupting counsel to require him to "state the purpose of his line of inquiry" (thus putting the wary witness on guard to cover his inconsistencies and misstatements), or summarily ordering: "further cross-examination of this witness will be discontinued." On November 12, 1945, as part of the formal statement of the commission announcing that it would "grant a continuance only for the most urgent and unavoidable reasons," General Reynolds added the following ukase:

"As a further means of saving time . . . cross-examination must be limited to essentials, and avoid useless repetition of questions and answers already before the commission. [When a witness's inconsistencies indicate that he is lying, there is often no way to demonstrate that fact other than by repetition on cross-examination of questions asked in the direct examination, utilizing the device of juxtaposition.] We are not interested in trivialities or minutiae of events or opinions. [The commission had displayed an extremely broad and inclusive concept of what constituted 'trivialities or minutiae' of the narratives of mass crimes, responsibility for which was charged to a man now on trial for his life. Often it is only by showing inconsistency in 'trivialities or minutiae' that the basic unreliability of a witness can be demonstrated.] Except in unusual or extremely important matters, the commission will itself determine the credibility of witnesses."

That final statement well illustrates how painfully ill-fitted the military commission was for its task. Before issuing this remarkable decree, General Reynolds had frequently interrupted a line of cross-questioning to inquire its purpose, and, when told that it "went to the credibility of the witness"—which is the lawyer's way of saying that its purpose was to raise a doubt in the minds of the judges as to whether the witness was to be believed—Reynolds had ordered the interrogation either to be limited to a specific number of inquiries or to be discontinued altogether. The plain and simple fact of the matter is that, of course, in *all* cases, *including* "unusual or extremely important matters," credibility of the witnesses must be determined by the commission. No one else *can* do it. Counsel's sole function in that respect is to produce evidence on which the commission, and only the commission, is to base a judgment.

One instance of infringement of our right to cross-examination was productive of distressing amusement. On Batanes Island, the northernmost spot in the Philippine archipelago, three American fliers who had parachuted from a damaged bomber were executed. A Filipino resident of Batanes testified that a Japanese captain had told him that the admiral in command of the island had, in turn, informed the Japanese captain that he, the admiral, had received a telegram from General Yamashita ordering all prisoners of war to be killed. I protested the admission of this "third-degree hearsay," but, of course, the commission quickly overruled the objection. The witness testified that the captain spoke in Japanese and that he understood the language. Later, when the official court interpreter translated the purported Japanese statement, it appeared that it had contained nothing about "prisoners of war" and that it was not phrased in a manner that would indicate that any Japanese had ever spoken it. This, coupled with the fact that there were no prisoner-of-war camps on Batanes Island and that thousands of American prisoners of war throughout the Philippines were released without incident upon the arrival of the liberating forces, effectively dissipated any weight that the testimony might have carried. However, when I began my cross-examination, those facts were not yet before the commission, and, inasmuch as this was one of the few times that General Yamashita's name had been uttered on the witness stand, I was anxious to erase any possible damage that might have been done.

The obvious first step was to check carefully into the alleged conversation between the witness and the Japanese captain. Were there any other persons present when the captain made his remarkable statement? Yes, the witness's sister, his niece, and "two other relatives." I had the witness spell out the names of his sister and niece, and then I asked for the names of the other two relatives. As the witness was about to divulge the names of one of the two persons, General Reynolds interrupted.

"What is the purpose of all this?" he asked.

I explained that we might wish to check the accuracy of this testimony by interviewing the persons who were supposedly present during the alleged conversation and that we might even subpoena them to appear before the commission. The commission president frowned. "You may finish the one name that the witness was giving at the time we interrupted him," he ordered.

"Sir," I replied, "I believe he said that there were *two* relatives and I was asking him the names of the two of them."

General Reynolds was firm. "You may finish the one name," he said.

XVII

THE GUERRILLAS

IT IS readily apparent that, because of inability to meet the testimony of Japanese crimes with any previously obtained information about those crimes, the defense lawyers were, for the most part, forced to rely on what we called "affirmative defenses." Thus the charge against General Yamashita recited that brutal atrocities had been committed by "troops under his command." If we could show that the Japanese perpetrators of a crime were not under his command at the time of its commission, presumably the charge would fall in so far as that item of the bill of particulars was concerned. Or, if we could prove that the circumstances surrounding an atrocity were such as to show so extreme a provocation as to indicate that the soldiers involved were unrestrainable and had "run amuck," we felt we might soften any inclination to hold General Yamashita responsible, especially when he was far removed in the chain of command from the actual offenders.

For these purposes, the one hundred and twenty-three items of the two bills of particulars divided themselves into three major groups: atrocities in Manila, including brutalities committed by the "Kempeitai," Japanese military police; atrocities outside of Manila, particularly in the Province of Batangas; and charges of mistreatment of American prisoners of war and civilian internees.

Our defense to the long list of bloodcurdling incidents that occurred in Manila was based on General Yamashita's decision not to defend that city, as originally detailed to us at our first conference. We knew that we could prove that he had ordered the Japanese army to abandon Manila; that, by the time the atrocities occurred, all but some sixteen hundred army troops had been evacuated; that these remaining men, the so-called "Noguchi detachment," stayed behind to guard supplies that were also in the process of removal. We knew also that Manila (at least that part of the city that lay south of the Pasig River and that contained the scene of the protracted siege and destruction) was defended by approximately twenty thousand naval troops who had failed to leave the city. The prosecution witnesses, for the most part, testified that the Japanese who committed the Manila atrocities "had anchors on their caps," indicating that they were members of the naval forces and not of the army. Although apparently all the Japanese defenders of the city were killed, it developed during the course of the trial that Yamashita's conjecture had been correct—that the naval forces had failed to leave Manila because of a standing naval order, with which Yamashita had had no connection, to destroy the harbor, docks, and naval warehouses. When, at his headquarters in Baguio, one hundred and fifty miles to the north, General Yamashita learned that these naval troops were still in Manila, he again ordered their immediate evacuation; but by that time they were surrounded by the American Army, and an attempted rescue mission failed.

Practically all the Manila atrocities occurred in February, 1945, shortly before the city fell. The prosecution relied on a Tokyo order, effective January 8, 1945, which put General Yamashita in command of all naval troops in the Philippines "when engaged in land operations." The prosecution overlooked the fact, however, that these troops were put under Yamashita's command "for *tactical* purposes only"; that he had no "administrative" control over them, which meant, among other things, that he had no power to discipline them; and that when their admiral was faced with two conflicting orders—Yamashita's order to withdraw and an older naval order to stay and carry out a vital naval mission—the admiral quite naturally chose to ignore Yamashita and obey the navy's decree. To describe these sailors as troops under General Yamashita's "command" was a distortion. To hold him criminally liable because they committed rape and murder as their final gestures on this earth was, we felt, improper even under the prosecution's theory of "command responsibility."

The Manila atrocities were studded with rape. The Manila Hotel and the Bay View Hotel, both in the besieged area south of the Pasig River, were the scenes of violent sex orgies, much of which was under duress on the part of Filipina participants on the three or four nights preceding the city's final demise. Despite the plea of the American attackers, which had been broadcast by loudspeakers set up on the north shore of the Pasig, urging the "officers and men of the Imperial Japanese Navy" to surrender "and live to serve the new Japan when the war is over," the Japanese chose to stay and fight—to "hold out a few hours and be blown to dust," as the Americans had described the alternative. But during those "few hours," all civilizing restraints were shed. One pretty Filipina witness told a revealing story that was typical of many others. Her attacker, she said, took her to a window in the hotel room. "He pointed to the other side of the river, and he told me that there were Americans on the other side of the river, but me and him wouldn't see them; we would all be dead." It was plainly a case of men who were about to die, who feared no punishment, and who completely reverted to the animal.

That explains the remark I made to Colonel Clarke that is quoted at the beginning of this work. I found it difficult to see how anyone could believe that General Yamashita would order his men to commit rape or that he would condone such deeds if he found out about them. Not only is there no military advantage to be gained from rape, but it is the sort of thing that every commander fears and abhors because of its disastrous effect on the morale and discipline of his men.

The allegations of crime in the outlying provinces of the Philippines, particularly in Batangas, caused us more concern. In Batangas there appeared to be a pattern of calculated, cold-blooded murder, including what was evidently the planned elimination of entire villages. There were no allegations of rape in Batangas. Colonel Masatoshi Fujishige, commander of the Japanese regiment that had occupied that area and a man who prided himself on being a strict disciplinarian, called attention to that omission as a tribute to his effectiveness. But defense counsel were neither impressed nor pleased.

There is no doubt that most of the murders that were committed by the Japanese in the Philippine provinces (and also some in Manila) were deliberate forays that were planned and directed. They were not ordered by General Yamashita or even by army or divisional group commanders who were immediately subordinate to him in the chain of command, but they were decreed and at times even supervised by officers of locally garrisoned echelons. Their purpose was to stamp out guerrilla activities.

Although these bloody mass executions and "punitive expeditions" were not ordered by General Yamashita, it would be error to minimize the responsibility that may adhere to him as a commander who recognized a serious military problem and whose duty it was to find a solution. The legitimate question posed in trying Yamashita for these offenses was basically this: What moral guilt shall adhere to an army leader whose subordinates execute a military mission with such fanatical thoroughness and ferocity? This involves further judgment of the actions of the troops themselves, which, in turn, requires consideration of their immediate problem, their provocation, and what they considered the "realistic" military tradition in which they had been trained. Such indeed were some of the concepts which the defense counsel tried, with obviously small success, to bring to the military commission's attention.

It is impossible to comprehend the speedy reconquest of the Philippines by the United States forces without an understanding of the part played behind the lines by the guerrillas. Throughout the archipelago, groups of Filipinos had banded together, sometimes under the leadership of American soldiers who had escaped from Bataan, more often under colorful native organizers. The units varied in size from a dozen men to a thousand men. During the Japanese occupation their activities ranged from furnishing intelligence to the American Army in Australia or New Guinea by means of portable radio stations, to "vigilante" or even bandit activity among their own people. For the most part, the guerrillas were rabidly anti-Japanese, and, as the time for American reinvasion of the islands approached, internecine quarrels were patched and preparations made to disrupt Japanese communications from the rear while the invaders hammered on the front. Arms and ammunition came to the guerrillas from the Americans by submarine and parachute in ever increasing quantities, and formal recognition of their co-belligerent status was granted by General MacArthur's headquarters to specifically named units.

The landing of American troops at Leyte and later at Lingayen signaled the emergence of guerrilla units from the "underground." Bridges were destroyed, wires were cut, military vehicles were wrecked. Japanese night patrols would fail to return to their bases—the soldiers would eventually be found dead, their heads and other important organs removed by bolo knives. Ambush, demolition, assassination, occasionally open combat, became the nocturnal activity of over a hundred thousand men who had secreted themselves in the hills and mountain slopes and who were supplied with food and information by other more loosely organized groups of men, women, and even children in the villages below.

It is little wonder that Japanese soldiers felt that practically the entire population of provincial areas had sprung to arms against them, that the placid Filipino "civilians," who smiled at them by day, were treacherously murdering them by night.

Now it became evident, especially on Luzon, that only a small minority of the Filipinos had been sincere collaborators with the Japanese and that most of the people were loyal to the United States. General Muto, who had been the Japanese military commander in Sumatra, is authority for the statement that in all other colonial areas occupied by the Japanese during the war the conquerors found the native populations to be acquiescent, if not co-operative. Only in the Philippines did they encounter fanatical resistance, despite the Japanese device of setting up an "independent" government of the islands, which government had formally declared war on the United States. One may well wonder whether the object lesson in colonial administration will continue to be ignored by the British and the French and the Dutch.

Immediately upon his arrival in the Philippine Islands, General Yamashita was made aware of the guerrilla problem. He could not plan to meet the imminent American invasion and, at the same time, ignore this serious threat to his rear. On October 11, 1944, he issued a written order to his subordinates, the only document in which he dealt with the matter. He directed the "subjugation" of "*armed* guerrillas." The adjective is important, for, according to the very "Rules of Land Warfare" for violation of which Yamashita was being tried, the Japanese had a right to execute armed guerrillas. General Wainwright's capitulation to Japanese General Homma on May 6, 1942, had been complete. Unit commanders of American and Philippine army forces had been directed to surrender all troops, munitions, weapons, supplies, and equipment to the Japanese, who were already in occupation of most of the archipelago; and, from that time, military resistance and sabotage were illegal. In any event, armed combat by men who wear neither uniforms nor distinctive emblems and who operate secretly in civilian guise is outlawed by the "rules." We Americans quite properly regard the guerrillas as heroes, but international law brands them as "war criminals"—a paradox that seems to furnish further evidence of the stupidity inherent in formulating legal precepts for what should be an illegal pastime. But, if the "Rules of Land Warfare" were to be invoked to hang Yamashita, they might be invoked for his defense.

Although guerrillas were not, therefore, entitled to the privileges accorded to prisoners of war, there could be no legal justification for the mass execution of groups of men, women, and children. A civilian combatant may be put to death, but first it should be ascertained that he is a combatant—that is, he is entitled to some sort of a "trial." The rules are silent as to what kind of a trial he must have; it is only clear that it need not be the formal procedure which a prisoner of war is accorded. However, the fact of belligerency should be established before execution, and this the Japanese did not bother to do. The usual procedure followed one of a number of patterns. Most often the inhabitants of a village or *barrio* in a guerrilla-infested area were herded into a church or similar large building. Then they would be ordered to leave through one exit, where the village mayor or some other Filipino collaborator, often wearing a mask to hide his identity, would play the part of informer and point out to the Japanese those persons who were engaged directly in guerrilla activity or who were suspected of aiding guerrillas. Japanese soldiers would then execute these victims, ordinarily using the bayonet or sword because of a shortage of ammunition. Sometimes entire families, including infants, were killed. Frequently mass executions took place in dwelling houses which were then set afire to dispose of the bodies. There were also instances when the Japanese did not even conduct this much investigation, and "punitive raids" on towns in strong guerrilla areas would result in indiscriminate slaughter of large groups of civilians picked at random.

The picture was sickening, even to men who had become inured to war's brutality. American soldiers who had been through the Pacific campaign have told of instances when they or their fellow-"GI's" killed or mistreated Japanese prisoners. Surely rape was not unknown among our troops. And yet it is extremely difficult to conceive of American soldiers bayoneting or shooting civilians, including women and children, in cold blood. The aviator who drops bombs on a city produces the same result, but he cannot see what he does, and to the Western mind the existence or nonexistence of personal contact has much importance. Perhaps we are right when we say that the Japanese soldier is a barbarian, congenitally cruel and trained in brutality. Or perhaps he would be right if he answered that we are hypocritical.

Are we so sure that we would abide by our boasted "American idea of fair play" even in the direct, personal treatment of helpless men, women, and babies if we were subjected to the provocation and the fearsome odds that the Japanese faced? This is not an attempt to justify lynchings and massacres, but merely an inquiry whether such brutality toward noncombatants is a special attribute of the yellow race. An honest reading of United States history must give us pause. The charges of brutality by Americans toward Americans that were leveled by both the North and the South after the Civil War do not make pleasant reading. Our callous extermination of American Indian women and children by flame and shot, often preceded by unconscionable betrayal, is part of an ugly picture. But probably the most telling analogy is to be found in American activity in these same Philippine Islands in the early part of the twentieth century. During the bloody "Philippine insurrection," methods of torture were devised and used by Americans in the "pacification" of the Filipinos that demonstrate that the cruel Japanese Kempeitai were essentially clever imitators.

In 1901, Americans in the Philippine war were harried by guerrilla activity that was similar in nature, if not equal in power and scope, to that faced by General Yamashita. How did our generals meet the problem? We know of what happened in Samar, one of the Visayan group of the Philippine archipelago. Extensive guerrilla activity there was countered by a "punitive expedition" of American forces commanded by one Brigadier General Jacob H. Smith. In autumn, 1901, General Smith ordered a Major L. W. T. Waller of the Marine Corps to conduct the raid on Samar, saying in so many words: "I want no prisoners. I wish you to kill and burn; the more you kill and burn, the better you will please me. . . .The interior of Samar must be made a howling wilderness." As reported by Mr. John Bassett Moore (in his *Digest of International Law*), General Smith "wanted all persons killed who were capable of bearing arms." Major Waller was a precise soldier who, understandably, wanted precise directions. He asked the general what he was to consider the age limit in carrying out his order for extermination—in other words, how young would a child have to be to escape the massacre? "Ten years of age," was the reply.

Because he gave this order, Brigadier General Smith was court-martialed in the spring of 1902. He was charged with "conduct to the prejudice of good order and military discipline." He was found guilty, and he was sentenced to be admonished by his superior.

General Yamashita gave no such order. On the contrary, after decreeing the subjugation of "armed guerrillas," he called a meeting of the chiefs-of-staffs of the various subordinate units and cautioned them to "handle the Filipinos carefully, to co-operate with them," for the obvious purpose of gaining their assistance and of minimizing the native opposition to his forces that had been created before his arrival in the Islands.

Most of the Japanese atrocities were committed during the latter part of February and March, 1945, in Batangas Province by troops commanded by Colonel Fujishige. Called as a prosecution witness, Fujishige's testimony was direct, emphatic, and loud. He readily admitted that he had given orders to kill all persons who opposed the Japanese, including "even women and children." "There were many instances where women bearing arms inflicted considerable damage to my forces," explained the colonel. "When I was riding in an automobile, a child threw a hand grenade at me. . . . I told my troops that if they were attacked by armed women and children, that of necessity, . . . they must be combated."

Fujishige stoutly denied that he had received any orders from any of his superiors in the chain of command relative to women and children, and he was emphatic in stating that he had never received instructions to kill noncombatants, nor had he ever reported any such killings to his superiors.

During the trial the defense lawyers were frequently asked by acquaintances who were curious about the "inside story": "Didn't Yamashita *really* know about these crimes?" He did not know about the actual atrocities. The state of his communications at the time of the occurrences was such that it would have been impossible for him to know of them. For example, when the Batangas killings and burnings took place, his headquarters was more than two hundred miles away, and all land communications had long since been cut. Nevertheless, he knew that the troops were engaged in a campaign against the guerrillas. The guerrilla menace constituted one of his major problems, and he had, indeed, ordered its suppression. It is true that he had been careful to specify "armed" guerrillas and that he had cautioned the divisional staff officers to co-operate with ordinary civilians. But

Yamashita was intelligent enough to know that guerrillas do not march in parades and carry flags, that they are usually persons who masquerade as noncombatants during the day, and that to carry out an order to suppress armed guerrillas without harming innocent people was so unlikely as to be virtually impossible.

The "guilt" involved in such "knowledge" is something else. Suppression of guerrillas in the Philippine campaign was certainly as proper a military objective as the destruction of a munitions factory in a Japanese city. The American leaders who ordered the atomic bombing of Hiroshima and Nagasaki "must have known" that not thousands but hundreds of thousands of innocent noncombatant civilians, including women and children, would be killed or worse than killed in the resulting operation. But we have not yet tried those men. Perhaps Yamashita's real crime was that he was on the losing side.

XVIII

THE PALAWAN INCIDENT

A THIRD group of misdeeds charged to General Yamashita was maltreatment of prisoners of war and civilian internees. The substance of the indictment was that these persons, most of whom were American nationals, had not been properly fed while suffering internment and that this constituted a violation of the Geneva Convention of 1929 respecting treatment of prisoners of war. There is no doubt that the prisoners and internees in most of the Philippine camps received insufficient food during the three or four months prior to their liberation. Nor is there any doubt that General Yamashita knew about it and was helpless to remedy the situation. The Geneva treaty provides that prisoners of war be issued the same food rations as the captor's own soldiers, and our evidence was to show that this had been done. It is not unlikely that in a number of the camps the Japanese guards appropriated food that had been issued to the internees. Certainly, it is true that in areas where the issued ration could be supplemented by foraging in the countryside or by making purchases in public markets, the Japanese soldiers managed to obtain a better diet than did prisoners. But it is also the fact that where such extraneous sources of food were unavailable, Japanese troops were undernourished, and many of them actually starved.

Shortage of produce with which to feed his two hundred and fifty thousand armed men and ten thousand prisoners of war and internees was one of General Yamashita's most serious problems. Rice was the staple, but so effective was the American submarine and air blockade of the Philippines that only one shipment arrived safely during the entire period between October, 1944, and the surrender in September, 1945. As plaintively described by General Muto on the witness stand: "Although in the latter part of December, Manila Bay had been rendered impossible of access and egress of Japanese vessels, Marshal Terauchi had arranged to send to San Fernando [the harbor at Lingayen Gulf] approximately ten thousand tons of rice and ten or more thousands of drums of gasoline, and we were awaiting these supplies with much joy. However, instead of the rice coming ashore, the American Army came ashore."

Considerable rice is grown on the Island of Luzon, but not in areas immediately accessible to the internment camps and the cities. Transportation was essential, but not only did the activities of the guerrillas and of our Air Forces make use of the roads difficult, but shortage of fuel rendered Japanese trucks useless. The same American submarines and airplanes that sank rice ships also torpedoed oil tankers. The result was that large quantities of native rice benefited nobody but guerrilla raiding parties.

And so, as we cross-examined the prosecution witnesses who had been internees in Santo Tomás and other camps and who testified that they had been underfed, had subsisted on a ration of as low as 150 grams of rice per day, and had been denied fresh fruits and vegetables, it became apparent that our defense to these charges would be that the Japanese soldiers generally had fared no better. General Lester made it plain that he did not believe us. When an American soldier named Sakakida had completed his testimony on an extraneous subject, Lester thought he had found a fine opportunity to prove that we were wrong. Sakakida was a Nisei, a technical sergeant in the American Army who had surrendered to the Japanese on Bataan in early 1942. Having been told that the Japanese would execute any Nisei discovered in an American uniform, Sakakida assumed citizen's garb before giving himself up, and his captors were told that he was a civilian who had been employed by the Americans. The Japanese tried him for treason; but, when they discovered that it was impossible to prove that he was a Japanese citizen, he was found not guilty and was released. They then put him to work as an interpreter to assist in the trial of court-martial cases, and he was attached to the headquarters of the Fourteenth Army Group, the command later assumed by General Yamashita. When Yamashita moved his headquarters north into the hills, Sakakida went with him. After the Japanese surrender, Sakakida rejoined the American forces, with whom he was now serving as a master sergeant. After his testimony, which had to do with certain Japanese court-martial practices and records, was completed, General Lester took over the questioning. Here was a loyal American soldier, an excellent prosecution witness, and a man who had messed in General Yamashita's own headquarters—a dining hall where one would surely find the Japanese troops getting the best available food.

"While you served with the Japanese army as an interpreter from October until the time of your liberation, did you receive ample food?" asked the General.

"Not as much as I am fed by the American Army, sir," was the answer.

"Did you lose weight during that time?"

"Yes, sir."

Obviously discomfited by these undesired answers, General Lester tried again. "What was the nature of your ration as to its balance? Did you have vegetables and fruits?" he asked.

"It consisted of rice, soup, meat, fish, and a little green vegetable, sir," replied Sakakida, listing a diet that sounded strangely like that about which the recently liberated internees had complained.

"Any fruits?"

"Very seldom, sir."

"Was the ration better or worse as you went to Baguio from Manila?"

"It became worse."

"It became worse?" Lester asked increduously.

"Yes, sir," replied the witness. The examination was finished.

In addition to the charges of mistreatment, there were also two or three specifications involving isolated executions of prisoners of war or civilian internees who had been accused of attempting to escape or of aiding the guerrillas, and one item that recited the mass execution of one hundred and forty-two captive American soldiers. This was the infamous "Palawan incident," as monstrous a crime as any to be found in the entire history of World War II. In December, 1944, one hundred and fifty-one American prisoners of war were being used by the Japanese as construction laborers on an airfield on Palawan Island. On December 14, after a number of American planes had been seen overhead, the Japanese ordered all their prisoners into air-raid shelters. They then poured gasoline into the shelters, which they ignited by means of torches. Some of the trapped men were burned to death, and those who dashed out into the open ran into a hail of machine-gun bullets. Only nine Americans survived the massacre, escaping over the rocks and swimming five miles to another island.

We never saw any of the eyewitnesses to this atrocity, either Japanese or American, but, by fitting fragmentary captured diaries and statements together, it appeared that what happened here was the result of unreasoning and fanatical fear on the part of the Japanese garrison commander. The Nipponese and the American prisoners knew that our forces had consolidated their conquest of near-by Leyte. The almost constant presence of unopposed United States aircraft indicated that a landing of American troops in overwhelming force on Palawan was imminent. The small Japanese company barely outnumbered the prisoners, and the local commander apparently believed that the prisoners would render active aid to the attackers at the most strategic moment. There had already been reports that a powerful American convoy was approaching Palawan—alarms which proved to be false but which attest to the jittery state of the defenders' nerves. Apparently, this pathological atmosphere of fear caused the Japanese commander to order the massacre in what his tortured brain conceived to be a defensive move.

There was no link between General Yamashita and the Palawan atrocity. The Japanese soldiers who committed the crime were members of the air force, and at the time that the massacre occurred—December 14, 1944—no part of the Japanese air force was under General Yamashita's command. It was not transferred to him until January 1, 1945, eighteen days later. The evidence was uncontroverted; the defense was airtight.

The Palawan incident and the attention given to it in Yamashita's trial shed a light that shows the fallacy of the theory of "command responsibility" in bold relief. Here there could be no such responsibility; and yet, had the massacre occurred three weeks later (at which time General Yamashita would have known no more about it then he did now or, if he had found out about it, would have been as unable to punish the offenders as he was now), it would have had the same "legal" standing as the other atrocities. The damaging evidence was now before the commission and before the world. These were not Filipinos who had been slaughtered—these were American soldiers, sons and husbands of grief-stricken citizens of Ohio or Indiana or California or New York. The Japanese had done this deed, and now vengeance will be ours. Is the accident of date—the slight difference of a few weeks in the issuance of an order, the mere chance of time—to deprive us of retribution?

That this was the real question was implicitly acknowledged by the prosecution in its closing summation. Major Kerr brushed aside the "technical" defense to his technical theory; his statement boiled down to the argument that General Yamashita should have done something about the matter regardless of whether he had the right or the power to do it. This was the most bloody of crimes. The accused must answer for it, because—well, because he *is* the accused. There must be revenge.

XIX
AFFIDAVITS ALONE

THE Palawan incident was one of a number of items of the bills of particulars that was proved by document alone, that is, no witnesses appeared in court to face the accused and to be cross-examined by his counsel. At first, the commission refused to allow such procedure. To put it bluntly, it was too raw. If some items might be proved by affidavit alone, then they all might be. There would be no need for an open trial, and the generals might just as well sit in their offices and read the documents; there was nothing that the defendant or his lawyers could do about the matter anyway. And so on November 1, 1945, when the prosecution sought to prove a specification by unsupported affidavits, General Reynolds refused to accept the exhibits and added: "The commission feels that there must be witnesses introduced on each of the specifications or items. It has no objection to considering affidavits, but it is unwilling to form an opinion of a particular item based solely on an affidavit."

However, as in the case of the promised continuance, the commission changed its mind. A day or two later, General Reynolds read the following prepared statement: "The commission has an announcement to make. In the proceedings of 1 November, 1945, in the presentation concerning item No. 22 of the bill of particulars, the commission ruled against the receipt of affidavits or depositions proffered by the prosecution, on the grounds that they were not substantiated even in part by oral testimony.

"After further consideration, the commission reverses that ruling and affirms its prerogative of receiving and considering affidavits or depositions, if it choose to do so, for whatever probative value the commission believes they may have, without regard to the presentation of some partially corroborative oral testimony. Therefore, the commission *directs* the prosecution again to introduce the affidavits or depositions then in question, and other documents of a similar nature which the prosecution stated had been prepared for introduction."

Supreme Court Justice Rutledge later described this as "one of the commission's reversals of its earlier rulings in favor of the defense, a fact in itself conclusive demonstration of the necessity to the prosecution's case of the prohibited type of evidence and of its prejudicial effects upon the defense."

Of course, the defense lawyers continued to object to what we considered improper evidence. Most of the time General Reynolds answered our protestations by saying: "The objection is not sustained." After one particularly difficult day, General Muto asked Hamamoto: "Who is this Mr. Jackson that Captain Reel is always talking about? He always jumps up and says: 'Jackson.' " When it was ascertained that "Jackson" was Muto's understanding of the frequently voiced word "Objection," he was informed that Jackson's last name was: "Notsustained."

XX

THE ATTEMPT TO CONNECT

IT WOULD be inaccurate to leave the impression that no effort was made by the prosecution to show a direct connection between General Yamashita and some of the atrocities. There were a few witnesses produced for the purpose of showing that the accused knew of the crimes or had given general orders for their commission; but in each instance the attempt proved abortive, so clearly that the commission was unable to bolster its inevitable verdict of guilt with any finding of actual knowledge or direction on Yamashita's part.

One such witness was Colonel Hideu Nishiharu, who had been judge advocate of the Japanese Fourteenth Army Group. A trembling, wizened little fellow, he betrayed a confusion of mind that can most charitably be attributed to combat fatigue or shell shock. Defense counsel had interviewed Nishiharu numerous times, and, although we felt that he might be of some assistance to us, we had decided not to call him as our witness because of his painful inability to remember not only the history of events but also details of the Japanese court-martial system with which he should have been familiar. It is no exaggeration to say that in our interviews we never twice consecutively received the same answer to any important question.

Nishiharu was, however, called to the stand by the prosecution, apparently for the purpose of proving that General Yamashita knew of and countenanced a "streamlined" form of procedure in the trial of suspected guerrillas in Manila. He testified that a day or two before the general moved his headquarters from Fort McKinley to Baguio, he, Nishiharu, had informed his superior that the military police in Manila were holding approximately two thousand suspected guerrillas for trial, that "there would not be time" to have them tried by two or three judges, as had been the custom, and that therefore one judge would be assigned to each case. He said that, when he suggested such abbreviated technique to General Yamashita, the latter said nothing, merely nodding his head.

Even if the story were true, it did not indicate that Yamashita had countenanced any violation of law. As previously explained, although persons suspected of guerrilla activity must be given a trial, no particular form of trial is prescribed. International law merely indicates that it need not be so formal a procedure as is required for legitimate prisoners of war, who are entitled to the same safeguards that the captor gives his own troops. Actually, these guerrilla suspects in Manila were given the same type of trial that the Japanese accorded their own accused soldiers, with the exception that the hearing was conducted by and the court records were indorsed by one judge instead of by either two or three.

But I do not believe that Nishiharu told the truth. Not only did General Yamashita steadfastly deny that any such meeting had occurred, but there are too many discrepancies in the narrative to make it convincing. As in any properly organized military headquarters, access to the commanding general was normally channeled through his chief-of-staff. In this case General Muto as well as General Yamashita denied that he had ever been consulted about the matter, and it was not even alleged that Muto was present during the meeting. Nor did the story of General Yamashita's "nod" ring true—he was definitely not the nodding type but was ordinarily voluble on any subject having to do with the functions of his command. Furthermore, the recital that "there would not be time" to retain all trial formalities does not make sense under the circumstances. Manila was not under siege; indeed, the Americans had not yet landed on Luzon. It is true that General Yamashita had directed evacuation of the city, but that could not be an overnight operation, and control of the Manila area either had been or was about to be transferred to the newly formed "Shimbu army." Had General Yamashita desired to indicate that he would wash his hands of the problem supposedly posed by Nishiharu, he would have reminded him of the fact that the judge advocate should have known—namely, that under Japanese military law the new Shimbu army, immediately upon its activation, would assume all disciplinary functions, and responsibility for trial and disposition of the pending cases would be lifted from General Yamashita's shoulders. General Yokoyama, commander of the Shimbu group, would now have the final word on all judicial matters, including even the approval of death sentences.

But, most important, Nishiharu discredited his own reliability as a witness. His lapses of memory and factual inconsistencies were supplemented by an unbelievable ignorance of the Japanese court-martial system. It was after a particularly patent misstatement of one of the most elementary principles of Japanese military procedure that even the commission lost its patience. General Reynolds, after consulting with the other members of the commission, interrupted my cross-examination to ask the witness: "Are you an officer of the Japanese regular army?"

"Yes," replied Nishiharu.

"How many years have you served in the Japanese regular army?" was the next question.

"About twenty-three years."

"Have you been in the judge advocate's department all these years?"

"Yes."

"Are you thoroughly familar with the judicial processes of the Japanese army?"

"I generally know the procedure."

General Reynolds then turned to me and remarked significantly: "The commission doubts that further exploration of this point would serve any useful purpose. . . . We have great doubt that lengthy cross-examination will be worth consideration of this court."

And that, I believe, disposed of Nishiharu.

XXI

SOME PHILIPPINE HISTORY AND POLITICS

UNDOUBTEDLY the most exciting incident of the trial resulted from the testimony of two Filipinos who were brought to the witness stand by the prosecution from New Bilibid Prison, where they were confined pending charges of treason because of collaboration with the Japanese. An understanding of their testimony requires a brief excursion into the colorful history and unsavory politics of the Philippine Commonwealth.

In 1521, Ferdinand Magellan raised the Spanish flag over a group of East Asian islands that he called "Philippine" in honor of His Majesty, King Philip of Spain. For over three hundred and fifty years the archipelago remained a Spanish possession; and, although the Iberian rulers prospered more from the arrangement than did the native Filipinos, the latter managed to develop both a toughness of character and a restive spirit that eventually ripened into a desire for political independence. Fanned by the revolutionary winds that blew in fitful gusts around the world in the latter part of the nineteenth century, the smoldering unrest in the Philippines burst into armed revolt in 1896. Led by a group of intensely nationalistic libertarians, including Emilio Aguinaldo, Apolinario Mabini, and one "General" Artemio Ricarte, Filipinos took up arms against the king of Spain, and for sixteen months the blood of Spanish soldiers and native patriots flowed freely in the archipelago. The struggle might have been unduly protracted had not Admiral George Dewey sailed an American fleet into Manila Bay on May 1, 1898, and, with a few well-aimed volleys, settled the issue. Spain was through, but what was to follow? Such leaders as Aguinaldo and Ricarte had led a fight for Philippine independence, and they would not supinely countenance the exchange of Spanish rule for American rule.

In the United States the question "What shall be done with the Philippines?" became a nation-wide debate. The traditional American wish to set men free was met by a new feeling of national strength, a grasping for empire, a desire to share in assuming "the white man's burden," and a willingness to exploit whatever material resources might be found in lush tropical islands. Democrat William Jennings Bryan ran for president on an "anti-imperialism" platform. Republican George F. Hoar warned the United States Senate that our national honor would be irrevocably sullied if we "baffled the aspirations of a people for liberty." But the imperialists won, McKinley was re-elected, the Philippines would remain under the Stars and Stripes.

Aguinaldo, Ricarte, and their followers refilled their ammunition pouches, and once again the battle for independence raged. This was the "Philippine insurrection"—bloody pages that have been glossed into innocuous paragraphs in American history books. By 1902, superior American power had effectively suppressed the rebellion. Amnesty was offered to all revolutionary leaders who would pledge allegiance to the United States and admit its sovereignty over the islands, and only General Ricarte refused the proffer. Ricarte was exiled to Hong Kong in 1903, but he immediately returned to the Philippines as a stowaway, intending to foment and lead a second revolt against the Americans. Before he could muster any rebellious forces, Ricarte was apprehended, tried, and convicted of conspiring to create an armed revolution and sentenced to six years in prison. After he had served his term, Ricarte was again asked to swear allegiance to the

United States, but the unreconstructed patriot again refused, and he was once more exiled to Hong Kong. This was in 1910.

When World War I broke out, England ordered all foreigners to leave Hong Kong, so Ricarte and his wife moved to Japan. There they stayed for twenty-eight years, Ricarte teaching in a university and writing articles on behalf of Philippine independence. Naturally his compositions had a strong anti-American tone. In 1929 a grandson was born of Filipino parentage. Ricarte, now in his seventies, had the boy sent to Tokyo when he was two years of age, there to be educated and to furnish companionship for his grandparents. The little boy learned to speak Japanese, a language which neither his grandfather nor his grandmother had been able to master, and, combining this ability with a fluency in Tagalog, the lad became the old man's interpreter.

When, in 1942, the Japanese conquered the Philippines, they brought General Ricarte, his wife, and grandson to Manila. It was the plan of the Nipponese military leaders to "restore" Ricarte to the Filipinos as a patriot who had never given up the fight for freedom from the white man's domination, and they hoped that the natives would accept the aged general as president of a puppet "independent" state. But Ricarte was now in his eighties, there was no longer any fire in his speeches, the present generation of Filipinos neither knew nor honored him. The Japanese looked elsewhere for men to staff the new government, and Ricarte spent his time traveling about Luzon, making innocuous addresses to the natives, urging greater co-operation with the Japanese.

Some months after his arrival in the Philippines, Ricarte hired as his secretary a man who claimed to have fought under him as a boy in the Spanish insurrection of 1896. This was fifty-nine-year-old Narcisso Lapus, political opportunist and man of many trades, who was extricated from New Bilibid Prison on November 3, 1945, to become a "surprise" witness against General Yamashita.

As might be expected of a man facing charges of the capital crime of treason, Lapus' testimony was calculated to explain his own activities as a collaborator with the Japanese, as well as to please the authorities who were prosecuting General Yamashita. His somewhat fantastic story was designed to show that he was secretly helping the guerrillas, and he testified that he was arrested by the Japanese military police in June, 1942, on a charge of espionage, was sentenced to death, and was released only after he had pledged that he would "co-operate to the end" with General Ricarte. It later appeared that Lapus' arrest was for an entirely different reason.

The witness was unable to explain why he had to be asked to work with General Ricarte when he had already been employed as secretary for the aged patriot (with whom he had maintained a friendship for over two decades) for some months. However, it was established that Ricarte and Lapus had maintained some association, and this laid the groundwork for Lapus' contention that Ricarte had taken him into his confidence and had revealed to him the substance of four conversations that Ricarte had had with General Yamashita. Ricarte was now dead, but Lapus was permitted, over our continual objection, to testify as to what he claimed Ricarte had told him of what Yamashita allegedly had told Ricarte.

The testimony fell like a blockbuster in the courtroom. Lapus recited that the deceased had said that General Yamashita had called Ricarte to his headquarters for the purpose of informing him that he, Yamashita, had issued an order directing the "wiping-out" of all the Filipinos! Seventeen million people were to be slaughtered by the two hundred and fifty thousand Japanese, who were supposedly busy stemming the American advance. "There will not be a single Filipino living in the city of Manila," quoted Lapus; and he added that Ricarte reported that, although he had begged Yamashita to rescind the "order," the latter was adamant. The conversation, said Lapus, occurred in November, 1944.

Of course, there were many loopholes in that shocking narrative that were emphasized in cross-examination. Realizing that he was asking the commission to believe not only his own statements but those which he maintained were uttered by a dead man, Lapus had said: "I believe Ricarte all that he was, because I never experience any lie from that man for the long years that we have been related." However, when faced with the necessity of supporting the fanciful tale of his extracted pledge to work with Ricarte, Lapus contradicted himself. "General Ricarte," he explained, "has a sort of Japanese trait in his way of thinking. This Japanese have—you know, they are tricky. They never tell you the truth. Even if they treat you like a friend, they always have something in your back. That is the way General Ricarte thought, also."

But Lapus agreed that Ricarte was first and foremost a patriotic Filipino, and so he was unable to offer any satisfactory explanation of the fact that, after the old general had supposedly learned that the Japanese intended to massacre all his beloved countrymen, he had continued to work for the Japanese. Not only did Ricarte continue with his speechmaking but, together with two other men, Ramos and Pio Duran, he organized the so-called Filipino "Peace Army," the "Makipili," the avowed purpose of which was to recruit native laborers and fighters to help the Japanese defeat the impending American reinvasion of Luzon. This task was undertaken in December, 1944, only a few weeks after the alleged "revelation" that Lapus had so dramatically described.

Nor could Lapus convincingly explain why neither he nor Ricarte had published this startling information or why Ricarte had gone to Baguio with the Japanese military leaders late in December, leaving his wife and grandson behind in Manila to be massacred, assuming that that was truly General Yamashita's plan.

The coup de grâce was delivered to Lapus' testimony when the defense produced the American intelligence records that disclosed his true status. Lapus, it appeared, had actively aided the Japanese Kempeitai, by furnishing information about persons who were claiming to be pro-Japanese. He had set himself up as a sort of super-Japanese informer and had undertaken the task of ferreting out past incidents that might be grounds for a charge of pro-Americanism on the part of men who now sought Japanese favor. He apparently had earned considerable money by playing the dual role of informer on guerrilla suspects and then selling those same persons "passes" signed by General Ricarte that had the effect of procuring their release from the custody of the military police.

The records also revealed the true facts of Lapus' arrest in 1942. It appeared that Lapus was then living with a woman who left him because she preferred to cohabit with a Chinese acquaintance. This so infuriated Lapus that, in an attempt to obtain revenge, he charged both the Chinese and his lady friend with having stolen his jewelry. As a result, the two accused lovers were arrested and imprisoned by the Kempeitai. A week later they were released, and Lapus was, in turn, arrested for having filed false charges.

Lapus had sworn that he had never told his remarkable story to anyone until the day he took the witness stand and that he told it now solely "to serve the justice and to help my country." He insisted that he had no thought of aiding himself or the other members of his family who were in jail, and he denied that he had ever written a letter to the American Counter Intelligence Corps. But the defense produced four letters, signed by Lapus and dated in June and July, 1945, that were addressed to and received by the Counter Intelligence Corps, offering to "convey . . . certain facts of importance" in return for a promise of "favorable reconsideration of my case, that of my son and of my houseboy, all of us are now interned here under your custody since the month of February." More particularly, Lapus had demanded, as payment for his "facts," that "myself, my son and houseboy . . . must be given clearance, immediate release, immunity to any responsibility . . . and be freed from any further arrest, prosecution and punishment under the military laws. All properties . . . of my son . . . must be returned to him. . . . I must be furnished with an office . . . a residence . . . adequate amount to cover my personal expense, for the subsistence and maintenance of my family, such sum commensurate to the present high cost of living . . . free transportation facilities and the means to get away from the clutches of the black market in the securance of foodstuffs . . . the necessary papers of clearance, safe conduct, passport . . . and be sent immediately upon the end of my work, either to New York City or to any other Latin American country, preferably to Argentina or Cuba. . . ."

Of course, the Counter Intelligence Corps never made any such deal with Lapus. And I am sure that the prosecution made him no offer of any sort for his testimony. I believe that his concoction was the desperate attempt of a doomed man to escape the wrath of his liberated countrymen.

Lapus was followed on the stand by another denizen of New Bilibid Prison who was also enmeshed with the Philippine authorities as a treason suspect. His name was Joaquin Galang. Unlike Lapus, who affected the appearance of a scholar, this man was an unkempt, shifty-eyed individual of uncertain years. His narrative was even more fantastic than Lapus', and, like the latter's, would, if true, establish the fact that General Yamashita was the most blackhearted murderer of recorded history. He testified that one afternoon in mid-December he was visiting at General Ricarte's house in Manila, when, entirely unannounced and unaccompanied, General Yamashita walked in. Galang was sure that the accused had come alone, no aides, no officers, no interpreters—he just knocked on the door and entered. The only persons present, aside from Galang and Yamashita, were General Ricarte, his wife, and his twelve-year-old grandson. Ricarte and his wife were both dead, and Galang believed that the grandson was, too. General Yamashita, according to Galang, sat down and, in Galang's presence, conversed with Ricarte. Because Yamashita could not speak Tagalog and because Ricarte could not speak Japanese, the little grandson acted as interpreter. Galang testified that, as translated by the grandson, Yamashita had said: "All Filipinos are guerrillas and even the people who are supposed to be under Ricarte." Then, said Galang: "General Ricarte through the interpretation of the grandson said: 'I would like to take this occasion to ask you again for you to revoke your order to kill all the Filipinos and to destroy all the city.' " To which Yamashita replied: "An order is an order, is my order. And because of that it should not be broken or disobeyed."

Again there were glaring discrepancies. Not only was there the inexplicable fact that Ricarte later increased his efforts to aid the Japanese but we had the ridiculous story of a Japanese commanding general walking into a Filipino home unaccompanied by even an interpreter, apparently for no other reason than to reaffirm that he intended to kill seventeen million Filipinos. On cross-examination, Sandberg brought out the fact that, although Galang had been in jail for eight months, he had never told this story to anyone. For some mysterious reason he had regarded it as a secret that must be kept at all costs. He was friendly with Lapus—as a matter of fact, they were brothers-in-law—but, although they discussed the fact that they knew something about General Yamashita, neither divulged his particular secret to the other. There had been no collusion.

"You just told each other that you knew something, but you didn't tell each other what you knew?" asked Sandberg.

"Yes," was the astounding answer.

The witness, having thoroughly tangled himself in his lie, proceeded to make it worse. "You didn't even tell the prosecution the story?" asked Sandberg.

Galang seized the bait. "I did not tell them the case," he said, "they did not have any interest."

Captain Pace, who had examined Galang for the prosecution, attempted to extricate the witness from this obvious falsehood. When Sandberg had concluded his cross-examination, Pace took the witness on redirect. "Didn't I come and talk to you last night about the testimony that you have given in this case?" he asked.

"No," said Galang. Even General Reynolds smiled.

Once again the Counter Intelligence Corps records were helpful. It appeared that Galang, like Lapus, had been a spy for the Japanese and had also made considerable money selling "passes" signed by General Ricarte to guerrilla suspects who were in the custody of the Japanese and who may well have been the same persons on whom Galang had informed.

When Galang and Lapus had left the witness stand, however, Yamashita's counsel did not yet know of the Counter Intelligence Corps records or what they might contain. Although we felt that the credibility of the collaborators had been weakened by the results of the cross-examination, we nevertheless feared that, in view of the temper of the commission and the atmosphere of the trial, we were in a rather dangerous spot. Of course, General Yamashita unequivocally denied the incidents and would do so later in the witness chair. He emphatically stated that he had seen Ricarte on only two or three occasions that were essentially social in nature and that he had never made the idiotic statements attributed to him here. But Ricarte was dead, and the unsupported, self-serving statements of an accused Japanese general that were contradictory to those of even an unsavory Filipino could be expected to carry little weight in this courtroom.

Something more was needed. We set out to get it. The trail proved to be long and devious, and it led to an amazing conclusion.

XXII

BISLUMINO

IN THE evening after Galang had testified, the defense lawyers interviewed a Japanese prisoner who, Muto said, had been assigned to assist the collaborators in some of their activities. We asked many questions. What Filipino might be available who could throw light on this story? What Filipino might be alive who had worked with Ricarte in forming the "Peace Army"? The prisoner scratched his head—Ramos was dead, but there was Pio Duran. He was alive; in fact, he was also in New Bilibid Prison under charges of treason.

The following night Colonel Clarke, Sandberg, and I drove to New Bilibid. The inmates had gone to bed, but we had Pio Duran awakened and brought to a little room where we told him who we were and what we wanted. Duran was a collaborator but of an entirely different type from Lapus and Galang. There was no claim of reformation, no pretense that he had secretly been pro-American. "I just bet on the wrong horse," he said.

Duran substantiated what Yamashita and Muto had told us of their two or three meetings with General Ricarte. He had worked with Ricarte in organizing the "Peace Army" in December, 1944, and knew him intimately. Never had the old gentleman indicated in any way that he thought that General Yamashita intended to harm the Filipinos. On the contrary, Duran was certain that if Ricarte had harbored any such notion he would not have organized the Makapili or continued to work for the Japanese. But the really valuable information that Duran produced was his simple statement: "I think Ricarte's grandson is still alive."

Ricarte's grandson alive! Where was he? If we could locate him and bring him to the witness stand and if he would testify that the conversation described by Galang had never occurred, that he had never interpreted any such statement for General Yamashita—indeed, a bombshell.

"I don't know where he is," said Duran, "he may be around Manila. I don't even know his name, except that his first name has something to do with the names of the Philippine Islands—Luzon, Mindanao—something like that. It was his grandfather's idea." Duran thought for a moment and then continued: "I might be able to locate Ricarte's stepdaughter. She would know where the grandson is, and she's somewhere about Manila. If you could arrange to get me out of here for a few hours, I think I could get her address for you."

The arrangement was made. The following day, during the noon recess, Sandberg and I met Duran by appointment at our office. He gave us the address of a house in the outskirts of the city.

Fortunately, the next day was Sunday. Early in the morning we took off in a jeep and, after considerable difficulty, managed to locate the stepdaughter's residence. She was not at home, but her son, a pleasant Filipino youth, knew the boy we were seeking. He agreed to accompany us while we tried to find the lad, and it was fortunate that he did so, for our first stop was at a nipa hut a considerable distance from any traveled way, requiring a devious journey afoot through rice paddies and carabao wallows. The boy was not at home; he was visiting an uncle who lived in another part of the city. This time the trail led to a small shack hidden behind the wreckage of some blasted school buildings. We had to bend down to get through the only door.

Inside was a bright-eyed little Filipino boy who appeared to be seven or eight years of age. "Here's your man," said our guide. I was thunderstruck. This infant the interpreter for generals? I had forgotten, for the moment, that Filipino children generally look younger than their years when judged by American standards. When the lad spoke in Japanese and Tagalog and had had his sparkling words translated and when we had the opportunity to notice his poise and apparent maturity, we realized that this was a most unusual boy. Even his name corroborated the remarkable tale: it was Bislumino Romero. The Christian name is a contraction of the first syllables of the three major island groups of the Philippine archipelago—"Bis" for the Bisayan (or "Visayan," in English) group comprising Cebu, Leyte, Samar, Palawan, Negros, and many others of the middle area; "lu" for the largest island, Luzon; and "mino" for Mindanao, the second island in size located on the extreme south. The child's grandfather had always wanted the archipelago to be called the "Bislumino Islands," for "Philippine" was reminiscent of the hated Spanish overlords. And the old man had insisted that the boy be given this name.

Bislumino loved his grandfather very dearly. He refused to believe the newspaper reports of his death. "I know I'll see him again," he said. He remembered Lapus and Galang as men whom his grandmother had described as "making money out of General Ricarte, using his name for their own benefit." Galang, he said, had lied. Bislumino had never translated any statement for General Yamashita, he had never seen General Yamashita except once when the boy visited Fort McKinley and the general was pointed out to him from a considerable distance. Certainly, he would testify, he would tell the truth. He did not want to help the Japanese general because his Filipino friends would neither like nor understand that, but it was not right for men like Lapus and Galang to lie about his grandfather and leave the impression that the old patriarch would co-operate with the Japanese if he had had any idea that they meant to harm his countrymen. Later, on the witness stand, Bislumino put the matter succinctly. In reply to the question: "Did your grandfather ever tell you that General Yamashita had ordered the massacre of the Filipino people?" the boy answered: "Nothing like that was said. And if anybody had said that, my grandfather has been working for the freedom of the Philippines ever since the Spanish regime, and if right here on Philippine soil my grandfather was told that all the Filipinos, with the same colored skin as his own were to be killed, he could not have agreed to it. And I believe that if my grandfather knew that all the Filipinos were going to be killed it would not be reasonable for him to leave me living in the city."

Bislumino was a splendid witness. Not only did his clear and complete refutation of Galang's fabrication explode before the commission with dramatic force, but his unaffected, childlike spontaneity presented so brilliant a contrast to the appearance and manner of the two collaborators that not a soul in the courtroom could doubt his honesty. Captain Pace of the prosecution staff, who arose to cross-examine the boy, tried to make the best of a difficult task. His questions were aimed to show that, although he was a Filipino, Bislumino had been brought up in Japan and that therefore he had been pro-Japanese and anti-American. The lad answered all Pace's questions with the same disarming frankness he had displayed during the direct examination. "Did your grandfather devote his life to fighting the United States?" asked Pace.

"I have heard that he talked against the United States," said Bislumino.

"And did you believe and agree with his teachings?"

"I felt a little that way," the boy admitted. "But my playmates taught me that when the American Army came there would be plenty of bread, lots of sweet things to eat, and things would become cheaper."

Galang and Lapus had been held in the prison compound that had been erected on land adjacent to the high commissioner's residence, where Yamashita was on trial. Galang had told the prosecution lawyers that Ricarte's grandson, like the two grandparents, was dead; Galang had felt that he was on safe ground, that, aside from the accused, there was no living witness who could contradict his story. Now the two collaborators were brought to the courtroom where Bislumino was testifying. They stood in the wings, out of sight of the commission and the spectators. One of the prosecution lawyers pointed to the boy. "Well?" he asked.

Galang and Lapus looked at the witness and then at each other. There was a moment of silence. Confession was the obvious choice. "Yes," whispered Galang, "it's him."

XXIII
JEHOVAH'S WITNESS

THE day that Sandberg and I first located Bislumino, he had told us that he was planning to go to the southerly island of Cebu with his uncle, a Filipino seaman. Citing this reason, we obtained the commission's permission to bring the lad to the witness stand "out of order"—that is, we did not wait until the time when we would offer the major part of our defense case (which was still two weeks off) but were allowed to interrupt the prosecution's presentation. This suited our desires in another respect. The testimony of Lapus and Galang had, of course, been widely publicized in the local newspapers, and we feared that other collaborators, reading of the "success" of these two, would conceive the idea that they might win favor at the hands of the authorities and possible reduction of their own sentences by telling similar or even more fantastic tales. We knew that they would assume that Lapus and Galang would obtain some consideration for their services, regardless of the facts, and we feared that, unless something were done to stop it at its source, we should now see a veritable parade of prison denizens, the scum of the Philippines, each trying to outdo the other in inventive narrative on the witness stand. We decided that the publicizing of Bislumino's testimony might provide the antidote; the remaining collaborators would see that lies did not go unquestioned, that we meant business, and we hoped that the fear of perjury prosecution would operate to keep them in their lairs. Apparently we were right. In any event, no more collaborators were brought to the courtroom.

Nevertheless, Sandberg and I continued our independent

investigations whenever we could find the time. One day, before Bislumino testified, we were directed to the Manila headquarters of Jehovah's Witnesses. The local leader of that sect had been imprisoned as a collaborator, but he was out on bail, and we interviewed him in his office over the meeting hall. Although we told this self-professed "man of God" who we were, he obviously did not believe us and assumed that we were Army officers assigned to investigate his own activities. To show his loyalty, he insisted on giving us a document that he said he had just prepared to mail to the authorities who were prosecuting General Yamashita. He had read Lapus' testimony in the newspapers. Lapus, he maintained, had lied. General Ricarte had not said that Yamashita proposed to massacre *all* the Filipinos—he had planned to exterminate only *two-thirds* of the Filipinos. The document that our informant had prepared recited that this information had come from Ricarte via a guerrilla major—who now was also conveniently dead—and had been transmitted to the writer in September, 1944. We quizzed him about the time. Yes, he was sure it was September and no later, and he had a number of unassailable methods of remembering the date.

Of course, General Yamashita was thousands of miles away in Manchuria in September, 1944. It was just some more fabrication. Later we learned that this fine cleric had been a Japanese agent in Manila since long before Pearl Harbor; that he had used his pulpit to expound Japanese propaganda; that in December, 1941, he had guided the Japanese troops into the city; and that during the occupation his chief function had been to act as informer on guerrilla suspects for the Kempeitai.

This was one of the occasions when defense counsel felt it their duty to present evidence that they could not use in court, to the commission in chambers. In the presence of Major Kerr, Sandberg and I told General Reynolds of our interview and showed him the document that we had been given. Kerr asked to borrow it, so that he might "look into" the matter. We never heard any more about it. I think that by that time both the prosecution and the commission had had their fill of collaborators.

The other attempts to show a direct connection between General Yamashita and Japanese crimes were documentary. There was the affidavit of the American officer, who at the time of the trial was in the United States, who stated under oath that he knew that "the Japanese were confiscating Red Cross parcels for their own use" because "on one occasion, while at Bilibid [where he had been interned as a prisoner of war] I was sent on a work detail to clear the quarters of General Yamashita in his headquarters at Manila. . . . His headquarters were in a large building in Manila in which there were several rooms. In the course of cleaning the room, I noticed one room in which were piled to the ceiling American Red Cross parcels. Many had been opened, their contents rifled for the more desirable items, and the balance strewn about the room." The affiant went on to explain that by "the more desirable items" he referred to the fact that "the Japanese particularly liked American-made cigarettes."

This implication that a Japanese commanding general would steal cigarettes annoyed Yamashita by its very pettiness. "Do they really think I would do *that?*" he asked. Of course, as in the case of all affidavits, we were helpless. There could be no cross-examination. How did the witness know he was in General Yamashita's headquarters? What made him think these were the general's rooms? Was it hearsay? If so, who told him? And how did his informant know? Actually, General Yamashita had never had a headquarters in the city of Manila. His nearest office and residence was Fort McKinley, some distance out of town. The "evidence" was false evidence, but there it was unassailed, and, if believed, it would furnish grounds for finding, at the least, that the accused knew that Red Cross packages had been rifled and withheld from American prisoners.

There was also the affidavit of a man named Memmler, who had been an American prisoner of war at the Cabanatuan Camp. The document described the crowded conditions under which the prisoners were compelled to live and also their cruel treatment at the hands of prison guards, who apparently thought they were not working hard enough. Then the affiant added: "General Yamashita, Philippine Japanese commander, visited the Camp twice, saw the conditions there, and did nothing to improve the situation."

We knew that Yamashita had never been to Cabanatuan. But once again the unfairness of evidence by ex parte affidavit became obvious. Were the witness present in the courtroom, it would immediately appear that he could not identify the general as the man whom he had seen at the camp. The witness, however, was ten thousand miles away. If we had only been accorded the privilege of filing cross-interrogatories, we would have asked the affiant what made him think that the officer he saw was General Yamashita?—Who told him?—and we would have requested a full personal description.

But, worst of all, we knew that even the prosecuting authorities were extremely doubtful about this identification. Unknown to Major Kerr was the fact that Sandberg and I had seen a copy of a radiogram from the Manila War Crimes office to their Washington headquarters requesting additional information on Memmler. "Did the witness see Yamashita? How did he know it was Yamashita?" More than that, we knew that an answer to this radiogram had been received, addressed to the Pacific Theater judge advocate, which stated: "Steps undertaken to obtain additional statement from Memmler. No other information in this office that Yamashita visited Cabanatuan. Believe possibility of error in Memmler's statement."

At the time that Major Kerr introduced the Memmler affidavit, he denied any knowledge of the radiogram from Washington. We were forced to obtain it ourselves and introduce it as part of our case. It appeared, then, that for some weeks it had been in the very headquarters which Major Kerr occupied, although he insisted that it had never been brought to his personal attention. The chief prosecutor showed no more embarrassment over the incident than he had previously displayed over the unmasking of his two collaborators.

Perhaps the shoddiest bit of this type of "evidence" which the prosecution presented was a moving-picture film called *Orders from Tokyo*. The picture was made long before the war ended, and it was artfully designed to inflame the already ample American hatred of the Japanese enemy. In brief, it was a typical propaganda film. The scenes depicted the destruction of Manila and consequent death and maiming of Filipinos who were trapped in the ancient "Walled City" area. The commentary attributed all the death and damage to the Japanese, a bit of hyperbole that hardly squares with the facts. But, worse than that, the mysterious, omniscient sound-track voice, that, of course, was not under oath, had referred to the photographs as "evidence which will convict" and specifically mentioned General Yamashita by name. With bitter irony, Sandberg stated the defense objection to this inflammatory and prejudicial film: "It is not at all conducive to the calm, dispassionate sifting of the facts which has always been the cornerstone of American justice."

At one point in the film, the screen showed the picture of an American infantryman bending over the body of a dead Japanese soldier. The American reached into a pocket of the deceased's uniform, and slowly withdrew a piece of paper. As he read the paper, the movie voice intoned: "Orders from Tokyo. We have discovered the secret orders to destroy Manila." No explanation of how the infantryman could read Japanese was offered.

In vain we begged the prosecution to produce such an order if they had one. They never did. On the contrary, Captain Norman J. Sparnom, of the Australian army, chief of the translation division of the Allied Translator and Interpreter Section, testified that his organization had in its files all the Japanese documents that had been discovered or captured in the Philippine Islands and the Southwest Pacific area. These ran into the hundreds of thousands. All documents that possessed any intelligence value had passed through his hands, and he affirmed that invariably the captured orders of elements of the Japanese armed forces were regarded as having intelligence value. He also described the Japanese custom of mimeographing and distributing orders, including in all cases those which were originally issued orally. In response to our questions, Sparnom categorically stated that to his knowledge there were no orders by General Yamashita to destroy Manila or to kill civilians or prisoners of war. Then Sparnom was asked: "A film was shown before this commission in which a statement was made that the United States Army had captured an order from Tokyo for the destruction of Manila. Have you ever seen such an order among the captured documents?"

"No, I have not," answered Sparnom, and then he added: "I would like to say that if such an order was captured, the information would be of such high intelligence value that it would undoubtedly be translated and published."

There were no orders by General Yamashita to commit any of the long list of crimes with which he was charged. There was no evidence that he knew about the crimes, either before or after their commission. Every one of the attempts made by the prosecution to show any such connection ended in failure. But it was worse than failure; for no American who loves his country can read the record of the prosecution's efforts in this respect without an abiding and painful sense of shame.

XXIV

THE LONG ANSWER

AS IT became apparent that the prosecution's evidence was about to conclude and Yamashita's defense counsel were hastily preparing to introduce their affirmative case, Hamamoto remarked: "The prosecution has made this an ordinary police-court trial. It's up to us to raise it to the level of an international drama."

For the most part, we did. The first witness for the defense was General Muto. His statement of our case was flashed by radio and teletype to all parts of the globe, and, for the first time, the man in the streets of New York, London, Paris, and Chicago learned the story of the war from the Japanese side. The insurmountable problems faced by the Japanese in the Philippines, the confusion of divided command, poor communications, lack of food and oil, the overwhelming power of the American Army and Navy—all were sketched in accurate detail for the information of the military commission and a listening world. As the narrative unfolded, discerning observers saw a basic, inescapable fact that was never articulately recited, namely, that in so far as the all-important items of supply and organization were concerned, Japan had been ill equipped to fight a modern war against a first-rate military power. Just as Americans had underrated Japan before the attack on Pearl Harbor, so had we overrated her afterward.

Factually, General Muto presented our entire case. But corroboration was needed, and so there followed other witnesses who were Japanese prisoners of war, and seven leading citizens of Japan who had flown to Manila from Tokyo to appear as "character witnesses." These men described the high regard in which General Yamashita was held by the common people of Japan and also testified as to his reputation as a "moderate" who had been opposed to Japan's aggressive warfare and who represented a point of view that was contrary to that of the powerful Tojo clique. Muto's testimony was further bolstered by the submission of numerous American Army intelligence and operational reports.

The final witness for the defense was General Yamashita. Before the trial had opened, we had told the general that under American law he did not have to testify in his own behalf, that we wanted him to take the stand because we knew he would be an excellent witness, but that the decision was his alone. Yamashita was surprised. Up to that time he had assumed that he would be the first witness called by the prosecution.

"What will the American people think?" he asked. "In America is it considered proper for a man to testify in his own defense? In Japan it is not done, it is not considered dignified for an accused person to say anything in justification of himself. The Japanese leave that to heaven—the Omniscient knows the truth and will make the final judgment."

I told the general that we Americans did not trust heaven to that extent. Still he wanted further assurances—he was not worried about Japanese opinion, but he repeated: "What will the American people think? Your General Short and Admiral Kimmel are being accused of misbehavior at Pearl Harbor—would they take the stand in their own defense?"

"Not only would they," I answered, "but they have been begging for the chance to do so." That satisfied Yamashita. He would testify.

In connection with his appearance on the witness stand, Yamashita was worried only about the manner of interpretation of his Japanese into English and the interpretation of the lawyers' questions from English into Japanese. The official court interpreters were divided into two groups—American Nisei soldiers, whose Japanese was fairly good when restricted to elementary or "kindergarten" expressions but whose English left much to be desired, causing them frequently to take liberties in altering counsel's questions to fit their knowledge of the languages, and a number of American naval and marine officers, whose English was excellent but whose Japanese was spotty and required constant use of translation dictionaries. The court interpretation was therefore necessarily slow and required frequent correction. Because he was a prisoner of war, the commission refused to allow Hamamoto to act as an official interpreter, but he was permitted to sit beside Yamashita throughout the trial, to keep up a running translation of everything that was said in the English language. This was a tour de force of stupendous proportions that had the effect of shortening the proceedings by many weeks, for, without Hamamoto, the court interpreters would have had to translate the entire trial for the accused.

Before he took the stand, we instructed Yamashita to confine himself to the most elementary Japanese expressions. When his name was called, the general rose and strode toward the witness chair. As he passed the interpreters' table, he stopped and said to the surprised Nisei sergeant who was preparing to translate his history-making testimony: "Yamashita wants no mistakes. On long sentences I will repeat them twice. Listen carefully—with the brain as well as with the ear."

After General Yamashita had completed his direct testimony, Major Kerr cross-examined him for eleven hours. In all that time, employing all the craft and skill of the experienced trial lawyer, the chief prosecutor was unable to break down any part of the general's story, to find any inconsistencies, discrepancies, or falsehoods in it. Yamashita was in full command of the courtroom during the entire period.

Behind the witness chair on a large bulletin board, the

prosecution had posted an outline map of the Philippine Islands. As their case had gone on and the various atrocities had been described, prosecution lawyers had pinned small red disks on the map to show the locus of the crimes. The board was now covered by almost one hundred of the markers. As the fruitless cross-examination was drawing to a close, Major Kerr suddenly ordered the witness to turn around and face the map. Yamashita did so. "Each red pin or disk represents a major violation of the laws of war, which, according to the testimony in this case, was committed by your troops," said Kerr. "According to the evidence, approximately sixty thousand unarmed men, women, and children were killed in the Philippine Islands by men under your command. Do you deny to this commission that you knew of, or ever heard of, any of those killings?"

General Yamashita had answered that question many times during the past two-and-a-half days. Nevertheless, he turned around, faced the prosecutor, and repeated emphatically: "I never heard of nor did I know of these events."

Major Kerr paused, and then dramatically pointing his finger at the general, he shouted: "This is your opportunity to explain to this commission, if you care to do so, how you could have failed to know about those killings!"

The question truly set forth the basis of the prosecution's whole case—"There were so many that he *must* have known." The answer that it called for, likewise, would comprise the basic theory of the defense. The ground had been gone over and over again in the preceding fourteen hours that Yamashita had been on the stand. It may be for that reason that Major Kerr expected the witness to give only a desultory reply, simply referring to the previous testimony that he had given. Or perhaps the chief prosecutor was not surprised when the witness took full advantage of the "opportunity" that had been so ungraciously extended to him. At any rate, General Yamashita took a firm grip on the arms of his chair and began to speak. Talking slowly and with frequent pauses to allow the painstaking interpreters to translate his statement, Yamashita proceeded to answer the question for forty-two minutes. The "star witness" summarized his own defense thus:

"The facts are that I was constantly under attack by large American forces, and I have been under pressure day and night. Under these circumstances I had to plan, study, and carry out plans of how to combat superior American forces, and it took all of my time and effort.

"At the time of my arrival I was unfamiliar with the Philippine situation, and nine days after my arrival I was confronted with a superior American force. Another thing was that I was not able to make a personal inspection and to co-ordinate the units under my command. As a result of the inefficiency of the Japanese system—Japanese army system—it was impossible to unify my command, and my duties were extremely complicated.

"Another matter was that the troops were scattered about a great deal, and the communications would, of necessity, have to be good; but the Japanese communications were very poor and, therefore, the communications were not all they should have been.

"Reorganization of the military force takes quite a while, and these various troops, which were not under my command, such as the air force and the Third Maritime Command, were—and the navy—were gradually entering the command one at a time, and it created a very complicated situation. The source of command and co-ordination within a command is or lies in trusting in your subordinate commanders. Under the circumstances I was forced to confront the superior United States forces with subordinates whom I did not know and with whose character and ability I was unfamiliar.

"Besides this, I put all my efforts to get the maximum

efficiency and the best methods in the training of troops and the maintaining of discipline, and even during combat I demanded training and maintenance of discipline. However, they were inferior troops, and there simply was not enough time to bring them up to my expectations. These were insufficiently trained troops, and for a long time they had been under the influence of a tropical climate, and, due to the lowering of morale, my plan became even more difficult.

"I wished to augment my inefficient communications system by the use of airplanes, but even when they came under my command they proved to be all useless. I tried to dispatch staff officers and various people to the outlying units, but the situation was such that they would be attacked by guerrillas en route and would be cut off. Consequently, it became very difficult to know the situation in these separated groups. When the Americans landed on Leyte, Mindoro, and Luzon, the situation came to a point where our communications were completely disrupted.

"And under conditions like this and with both the communication equipment and personnel of low efficiency and old type, we managed to maintain some liaison, but it was gradually cut off, and I found myself completely out of touch with the situation.

"I believe that under the foregoing conditions I did the best possible job I could have done. However, due to the above circumstances, my plans and my strength were not sufficient to the situation, and if these things happened, they were absolutely unavoidable. They were beyond anything that I could have expected. If I could have foreseen these things, I would have concentrated all my efforts toward preventing it.

"If the present situation permits it, I will punish these people to the fullest extent of military law.

"Certain testimony has been given that I ordered the massacre of all the Filipinos, and I wish to say that I absolutely did not order this, nor did I receive the order to do this from any superior authority, nor did I ever permit such a thing, or if I had known of it would I have condoned such a thing, and I will swear to heaven and earth concerning these points.

"That is all I have to say."

XXV
ARGUMENTS

THE commission allowed one day for final argument, or "summation," as it is often called. The defense divided its presentation into four parts. Lieutenant Colonel Feldhaus led off with a discussion of the background of the events about which the case had revolved. He reviewed the history of General Yamashita's espousal of Japanese disarmament and his opposition to the Tojo program of aggressive warfare and then discussed the chaotic conditions and the divided command that the general faced when he arrived in the Philippine Islands. Colonel Clarke closed the argument by analyzing the abortive attempts of the prosecution to support a contention that the accused had ordered, or had had any knowledge of, the atrocities detailed in the bills of particulars and by pointing out that there was no precedent for the prosecution's theory that "command responsibility" imposed criminal liability on a man who did not order, condone, or even know about the actual misdeeds of his subordinates.

That left the task of dealing with the greater part of the prosecution's affirmative evidence to Sandberg and me. Sandberg commenced with a statement of our answer to the charge that General Yamashita was responsible for Japanese atrocities that occurred in the city of Manila. "No one will ever know the complete story of what happened in Manila in those bloody days of February, 1945," he began. "The Japanese who participated cannot tell because undoubtedly they are all dead. But if there is one fact which emerges clear and unmistakable from the welter of conflicting reports, rumor, and gossip, it is that General Yamashita did not want fighting in the city of Manila and that what happened occurred not only against his judgment and his wishes but against his express orders."

After reviewing Yamashita's strategic reasons for not wanting to defend the city, Sandberg asked:

"If Yamashita did not want to fight in Manila, why did he not declare it an open city? His answer to this is likewise the answer of a military man with no attempt to put a humanitarian gilding on the harshness of war. General Yamashita did not declare Manila an open city because if he had done so it would have been a fraud. The declaration of a city as an open city has the effect in international law of making the city immune from enemy bombardment. No city is properly an open city unless it has been cleared of all military fortifications and supplies.

"So long as Manila was full of war supplies, which he did not have the time, fuel, or transportation to remove, and so long as the navy was basing its main operations—activities which he never had authority to curtail—he had no right to label Manila 'open' and so invoke immunity from bombardment by the American forces. If he had declared Manila an open city, then, truly, he would have violated the laws of war, just as the Germans did in 1944 when they declared Rome an open city, knowing that, as a center of war supplies, Rome had no right to immunity from bombardment. Instead, General Yamashita took the conservative course of moving to put Manila outside the area of battle without demanding any special status from the American forces for so doing."

Sandberg then described the various attempts that General Yamashita had made to achieve complete evacuation of the city and the apparent reason why the naval forces remained behind. "For these basic facts the commission does not have to rely on the testimony of General Yamashita and his subordinates," he said. "Our own official intelligence and operational reports, in evidence, refer both to large-scale troop withdrawals from Manila and to the presence of only small residual army elements in the city at the time of the Battle of Manila."

There was little question but that the Manila atrocities had been committed by the naval troops, and under any definition of the term it was difficult to contend that these men had been under General Yamashita's "command." "It is true that they passed to his command on paper," continued Sandberg; "but it is also true that the only important order he ever gave them—the order to evacuate—they failed to carry out. In addition, even so far as land operations were concerned, General Yamashita's authority was limited to the tactical, the order to advance or retreat. Over supply, personnel, billeting and, most important—discipline—he had no control.

"But most important of all is the practical problem. How can the man possibly be held accountable for the action of troops which passed into his command only one month before, at a time when he was 150 miles away—troops which he had never seen, trained or inspected, whose commanding officers he cannot change or designate, and over whose actions he has only the most nominal control?

"The prosecution contends that there is a problem in the Manila atrocities. We do not see any. We see only wild, unaccountable looting, murder, and rape. If there be an explanation of the Manila story, we believe it lies in this: trapped in the doomed city, knowing that they had only a few days at best to live, the Japanese went berserk, unloosed their pent-up fears and passions in one last orgy of abandon. There are some phases of the Manila situation that point to antiguerrilla activity, it is true, but there are many others which do not. Can the rapes committed in the Bayview Hotel be explained on this basis?

"Does the prosecution contend that General Yamashita ordered these rapes? And if General Yamashita is not charged with ordering the Manila atrocities, what is the charge? Is he charged with having failed to punish the twenty thousand dead Japanese left in the city after the battle?"

Shortly before the close of the testimony, the prosecution had put into evidence a report of a liaison committee of the Japanese army then sitting in Tokyo. The document had recited that, because the Japanese War Ministry had burned all papers at the cessation of hostilities, the data it contained were based on the "recollections of staff officers" and that, "consequently, the information cannot be construed as absolutely correct." The "information" included a statement that the Southern Command had ordered Yamashita to defend Manila "to the utmost." General Yamashita and General Muto had, of course, denied that they ever received any such instruction. Sandberg now pointed out that the Japanese had been in the habit of using the word "Manila" to connote not only the city but the near-by hills and airfields that had been planned and utilized as defensive strongholds by Yamashita's army. "Read in the light of this meaning, the report of the liaison committee makes sense," he said. "If, however, the liaison report is using the term 'Manila' in the narrow sense of the city of Manila, it does not make sense, for the fact is that Manila was not defended to the utmost. Our own intelligence reports confirm the fact of constant withdrawal of troops from the city before the American advance. General Yamashita testified on the stand that he had received no orders to defend Manila to the utmost. And one fact is clear and certain: If he did receive such an order, he very definitely ignored and disobeyed it."

Captain Sparnom, of the Allied Translator and Interpreter Section, had testified that no Japanese order to destroy Manila had been found. The only order in the record was one issued by the Japanese *navy* to destroy factories, warehouses, and material. "It can hardly be pure coincidence that the only large-scale destruction in Manila was at the points of heaviest fighting," Sandberg pointed out. "Our own Fourteenth Corps report describes in great detail how we brought the point-blank fire of 155-mm. howitzers, tank destroyers, and tanks to bear on the large public buildings of Manila until the buildings collapsed or were demolished."

Captain Sandberg now turned his attention to the charge that General Yamashita was responsible for the brutalities of the Japanese military police in Manila. First he pointed to some significant dates:

"Until November 17, General Yamashita was not even the highest commander in the city of Manila. His immediate superior, Count Terauchi, was here. He was on the spot, and he was in charge. And, most important of all, it was Count Terauchi and not General Yamashita who was handling affairs concerning the civilian population—the relations with the civil government and the discouragement and suppression of anti-Japanese activities. The basic period, therefore, is from November 17 to December 26, a matter of merely five weeks, during which General Yamashita was in Manila and in charge of civilian affairs.

"Can it be seriously contended that a commander, beset and harassed by the enemy, staggering under a successful enemy invasion to the south, and expecting at any moment another invasion in the north—that such a commander could in the period of a handful of weeks gather in all the strings of administration? Could he in this period of time get a true picture of what the military police, with its three years of background in Manila and its long tradition of close contact with Tokyo, was up to, what it was doing right and what wrong, what legally and what illegally? Wasn't he forced by the very nature of the time and place and circumstances to rely on the course of conduct of the established, functioning, subordinate commands?"

But Yamashita had taken action as soon as he became charged with responsibility for civil matters. Shortly after the departure of Count Terauchi in November, he had met with

Filipino President Laurel for the first time. Yamashita spoke to Laurel of the military necessity of promoting friendly relations between the Filipino people and his troops. "Because of the difference between the Filipinos and the Japanese in religion, customs, and speech," he had said, "undoubtedly there would arise incidents." He asked the president to report any difficulties to him, to the end that such incidents might be kept to a minimum. Some time later, Laurel had taken advantage of that offer and had told Yamashita and Muto of complaints of overzealousness on the part of the military police. General Yamashita immediately called in the chief of that division, one Colonel Nagahama, and cautioned him. Simultaneously, General Muto instituted an investigation of the military police. Sandberg explained that "the Japanese army does not have an inspector-general's department comparable to that maintained in the United States. The only investigative agency in the Japanese army is the military police itself—the very agency it was desired to investigate, as General Muto pointed out. It would have been a very difficult and very long process indeed to get the real truth about what was going on inside the Kempeitai. When President Laurel complained again, this time about the arrests of a friend and relative, General Yamashita took firm and immediate action. He recommended the immediate removal of Colonel Nagahama."

Why merely a recommendation for removal? Why did not General Yamashita remove Nagahama outright? "He had no power to do so," Sandberg explained. "It is one of the peculiarities of the Japanese army system that a commander cannot remove on the spot a subordinate whose performance is unsatisfactory. He can only recommend it to higher authority. As officers of the United States Army, we may fail to understand this. But not only is this the case in the Japanese army, but it is also true that removal of an officer from the command which he holds by direct order of the emperor is a far more serious and drastic step than it is in our own army."

The papers recommending Nagahama's removal "had to follow the long, tortuous route to the supreme southern command at Saigon, from Saigon to Tokyo, from Tokyo back to Saigon, and from Saigon back to the Philippines. It took eight weeks to remove Colonel Nagahama, although ordinarily such a removal could be completed in two weeks. It was during these eight weeks—during the months of December and January—during the time that Colonel Nagahama was on the way out, yet not out, that the affairs of the military police took the turn that is the subject of consideration of this commission."

After Sandberg had concluded his argument, it was my turn. I began by reviewing the evidence of mistreatment of prisoners of war, the Palawan incident, and the charges that American prisoners and internees had received insufficient food. The seriousness of the food problem, General Yamashita's concern over it, and the steps he took to see to it that the internment camps received the same ration as the Japanese troops have all been detailed earlier in this work. In addition, I pointed out that General Yamashita had issued orders for the freeing of all prisoners and internees at the earliest possible time. The general, I said, had received "instructions from Tokyo to the effect that the prisoners of war were to be released if the Americans approached. What were General Yamashita's further orders in carrying out that basic order? His instructions were that if the United States troops landed, long before any approach—if they landed at all on Luzon, a roster of all the prisoners was to be made up and turned over to the United States Army through the protecting power, and that one month's supply of rations was to be prepared and was to be left with the prisoners."

Because Yamashita had ordered preparations for the prisoners' release upon an American landing rather than upon our "approach," he was reprimanded by the supreme southern commander. Yamashita's order had gone to the officer in command of the prisons, General Kou, who had mistakenly assumed that "protecting power" meant the neutral nation charged with supervision of the United States interests, namely, Switzerland, and he had looked in vain for a Swiss representative in Manila. Actually, Yamashita had intended Kou to deliver the roster to the representative of the protecting power of Japan, which at that time was Spain. Because of that misunderstanding, no list of prisoners reached the American authorities, but in all cases, with one slight exception, the prisoners and internees were delivered to their American liberators without difficulty. The single exception was at Santo Tomás internment camp in Manila, where there were approximately four thousand civilian internees. As I reminded the commission, "thirty-seven hundred of them were immediately turned over to the American forces. But the commander at Santo Tomás disobeyed the order in one particular: He refused to let three hundred, who were living in the Education Building, go until he got a safe conduct for himself and his troops. This was a violation of General Yamashita's order, which made no such provision. It was not, so far as we are aware, a violation of any international law, because these prisoners were not taken from a place of safety and put into a place of danger at all, but it was a violation of General Yamashita's orders. General Yamashita's orders, had they been carried out to the letter in Santo Tomás, would have had four thousand, not thirty-seven hundred, prisoners immediately released. As a matter of fact, the other prisoners were released after the safe conduct was granted."

The last part of my summation was devoted to a discussion of the crimes against Filipino civilians in the provinces outside of Manila. This, of course, necessitated a review of the evidence of guerrilla activity, much of which was contained in intelligence reports of our own Army that we had put into evidence. I had to try to make the American generals see the problem from their enemy's point of view. "To us," I argued, "the guerrillas were heroes who risked their lives and the lives of their loved ones to help us liberate the Philippine Islands. I, for one, certainly hope that the American people will some day realize the tremendous debt that they owe to the Filipino people, and in particular to the active guerrillas, for the heroic work they did in helping us to win this war. Not only throughout this trial, sir, but throughout the entire preparation, throughout interviews with the accused and the members of his staff, the defense counsel have had an unparalleled opportunity to see the tremendous effect that the guerrilla resistance movement had on the morale, on the communications, on the fighting ability of the Japanese soldiers.

"But in considering this case, this trial of General Yamashita, who is charged with being a war criminal—considering this case, we must put ourselves in the position of the Japanese forces. To us the guerrillas were patriots and heroes, and rightly so, but to the Japanese forces they were war criminals, and rightly so. They were the most dangerous form of war criminal: treacherous, ruthless, and effective.

"Perhaps we can understand this better if we remember that after V-E Day, when our armed forces began the occupation of Germany, there were rumors that a Nazi organization called the 'werewolves' was in existence with the avowed purpose of striking at night and from hidden places, to ambush isolated groups of American occupation soldiers. Now were we ready to regard those 'werewolves' as German patriots, as heroes willing to risk all for what they considered their homeland? Or were we ready to regard them as vermin that would have to be stamped out? Would we consider them honorable combatants entitled to the privileges of prisoners of war, or would we take the position that they would be subject to execution and that we would have the right to use stern methods to exterminate them?"

The defense was not, I explained, justifying punitive expeditions that resulted in the execution of small children and others who were not proved outlaws, but it was important to point out that General Yamashita had never "ordered or permitted or condoned or justified or excused in any way these atrocities." Just what had his attitude on this matter been? "Coming to these islands just before an imminent American landing, he finds confusion, deterioration, and the danger of active guerrilla preparations for actual combat. He is faced with a dilemma. As a military commander he must take all steps to put down armed forces who threaten him, whether from the front or from the rear. If he does not do this, he is guilty of a dereliction of duty. On the other hand, he must do his best to gain the friendship and the aid of other civilians, other than guerrillas, because they are equally important in the defense of these islands."

General Yamashita, I maintained, did precisely what he should have done under these circumstances. "He issued an order in which he directed action against *armed* guerrillas, and at the same time he informed his chiefs-of-staff 'to handle the Filipinos carefully, to co-operate with them and to get as much co-operation as possible from the Filipino people.'" He was forced to trust his subordinate officers to carry out those two orders.

How about the prosecution argument that the crimes were so widespread that he must have known about them? There were two answers to that:

"First of all, practically all the atrocities took place at times and in areas that made communication of such matters practically impossible. Land communication was cut off early in the game, and Japanese wireless communication at its best was apparently somewhat worse than ours at its worst. It was reserved only for matters of operational importance. General Yamashita testified that he tried and failed to augment his inefficient communication system by the use of airplanes, that he tried to send sufficient staff officers and others to outlying units, but that the situation was such that they were cut off; that after the American landings on Leyte, Mindoro, and Luzon, land communications were completely disrupted.

"In the second place, not only was he physically unable to know of these things, but it is ridiculous to suppose that he would be told about them. When these atrocities occurred, they were committed in violation of General Yamashita's orders, and it is quite natural that those who violate a superior's orders are not going to inform him, either before or after the fact that they intend to do so or have done so.

"It is not unknown, sir, that in many armies there may be some subordinate officers who break the law. Let us take, for example, in perhaps some army, a subordinate officer who actually organizes groups of enlisted men and others to highjack supplies and sell them in the black market in war-torn areas. Do these officers inform their superiors in advance of what they are going to do? Do they tell them afterward that they have done it? There have been some diaries put into evidence in this case which support the prosecution's testimony to the effect that certain subordinate officers ordered punitive expeditions, which resulted in the slaughter of innocent civilians. Now is it reasonable to suppose that those subordinate officers informed their battalion commanders, that their battalion commanders informed their regimental commanders, that their regimental commanders informed their divisional commander, that the divisional commander—suppose he was in Batangas—informed General Yokoyama, that General Yokoyama informed General Yamashita, and that perhaps General Yamashita informed Count Terauchi, and that Count Terauchi informed Imperial General Headquarters, and that Imperial General Headquarters informed the emperor—either before or after the commission of any such crime?"

Before the start of the final argument, Colonel Clarke informed me that he had been cautioned by the members of the military commission in chambers that we were not to allow possible American misdeeds to enter the discussion. Nevertheless, I thought it proper to remind the commission that the atrocities had been committed in the course of a bloody war. I may have been indelicate. "There is not a nation in the world that has taken part in this war on either side," I said, "that cannot produce a tale of death and torture of innocent, noncombatant civilians, including helpless women and babies, who suffered because of what someone on the other side decided was military necessity.

"Our answer to the torture of noncombatants, whether they were victims of Sherman's destruction of Atlanta, the shelling of French cities and villages in this war, or even the bombing of Hiroshima and Nagasaki, is that there was destruction by reason of military necessity.

"Now, what answer can be given to the noncombatant victims in the province of Batangas? Perhaps some subordinate commander thought there was military necessity for such action. If so, not only do we feel that he was wrong, but General Yamashita feels that the subordinate commander was wrong."

At the end of his cross-examination, immediately following his "long answer," General Yamashita had answered two questions relating to the "control" that he exercised over his troops. The questions were improper—they called for legal conclusions, and they tended to put the witness in an impossible situation. If he denied control, the prosecution would argue that their charge was proved, that Yamashita had "failed to control his troops." If he admitted that he retained control, which he eventually did, there would be claimed an added support for the theory of "command responsibility." Major Kerr's actual question was: "You admit, do you, that you failed to control your troops in the Philippines?"

"I have put forth my maximum effort in order to control

the troops," General Yamashita had answered, "and if this was not sufficient, then somehow I should have done more. Other people might have been able to do more, but I feel that I have done my very best."

But the prosecutor was not satisfied with this answer. "Did you fail to control your troops? Please answer 'Yes' or 'No'!" he screamed.

"I believe that I did control my troops," was the reply.

I quoted this exchange back to the commission, and then I said: "The answer is, of course, a legal and factual conclusion which only this commission can decide, and also it must be taken in the context of his previous answers, particularly the long answer which preceded it.

"Now, actually, there is no question about this. General Yamashita did not have full control over all his troops at all times. While these atrocities were being committed, he did not actually control the actual perpetrators in a strictly factual sense. Yet on paper, as a commander, he can give no other answer. I suppose that there have been rapes and that there has been mistreatment of prisoners of war by all armies—isolated cases, at least. And I do not suppose that any commander would say that he controlled a man while he was in the act of committing rape or mishandling a prisoner of war, but, if you asked any of those commanders whether they controlled their troops, they would certainly say they did."

Then, without naming the unit, I made an oblique reference to current accusations that were being noised about Manila with reference to an American Army supply outfit. "Suppose that it were a stated fact," I suggested, "that approximately 20 per cent of all the supplies shipped into a certain area by service troops were pilfered or stolen, in many cases by the troops themselves. Certainly, the commanding officer of that particular service of supply would not say that he did not have control of his troops, and yet actually he would not have real control of the perpetrators at the time that they committed the theft. And, furthermore, he would not be held criminally responsible as a thief, and he would not even be held responsible financially for the loss."

General Reynolds had ordered us to be "objective and dispassionate" in the summation. I had tried my best to obey the command, but, as I brought my hour-and-a-half argument to a close, I know that it was impossible to keep all traces of the pent-up emotion of the preceding six weeks out of my voice:

"General Yamashita's problem was not easy. Harassed by American troops, by our Air Forces, by the guerrillas, even by conflicting and unreasonable demands of his superiors, he was on the run from the moment he got here. Of course, he did not have time to inspect prisoners; of course, all he could do about the guerrilla situation was to give orders to suppress armed combatant guerrillas and befriend and co-operate with other civilians, and trust his subordinates to carry out his orders.

"When we judge him, sir, we must put ourselves in his place, and I say that, unless we are ready to plead guilty before the world to a charge of hypocrisy, to a charge that we supinely succumbed to the mob's desire for revenge, then we must find General Yamashita not guilty of these charges!"

When I had finished, the commission recessed. General Yamashita walked over to me and grasped my hand.

"Thank you," he said simply. "Thank you—thank you."

It was the only English he knew. But I looked into his eyes, and I realized that it was the most eloquent English I had ever heard.

XXVI

THE BURNING CIRCUS

MAJOR KERR handled the summation for the prosecution alone. His argument was uninspired, and he showed his fatigue. The only new and surprising matter to be found in it was his comparison of this case to an ordinary manslaughter charge based on "criminal negligence." "Under laws generally," explained the prosecutor, "any man who, having the control of the operation of a dangerous instrumentality, fails to exercise that degree of care which under the circumstances should be exercised to protect third persons is responsible for the consequences of his dereliction of duty. We say, apply that in this case! Apply that in the field of military law!"

Of course that elementary principle of civil negligence cannot be applied to military law, because the military always do, and by their very nature must, deal with "dangerous instrumentalities." A gun, a plane, a bomb, an army itself, is a dangerous instrument, unless it is a dud. But Major Kerr continued on this devious tack. Yamashita's ignorance of these atrocities showed "negligence" on his part, he said, and "that may be manslaughter."

"I have in mind," Kerr continued, "the case of the burning of the circus tent, I believe in Connecticut, a few years ago. Officers and employees of the circus company were charged and, I am informed, convicted of criminal charges and sentenced to prison terms. Not because they ordered that the circus tent be burned, not because they ordered that the innocent, helpless women and children there be killed, but because they failed to take action which, if taken, would have prevented that catastrophe. They had failed to take the steps which, if taken, would have prevented the tragedy; it was foreseeable, and they are charged with having had knowledge that, if they failed to take those ultimate precautions, this thing might have happened. We say the same thing of Yamashita."

It was hard to believe that the man who had but recently called Yamashita the murderer of sixty thousand people was now likening this case to a trial that a few years before had sent some circus officials to jail for manslaughter. "I think the man has joined our side," whispered Clarke, while Sandberg added: "Manslaughter!—he'll probably ask for a five-year sentence."

But he did not ask for a jail sentence. Major Kerr concluded his summation by saying: "We recommend that the sentence be—death—carried out by hanging."

At the conclusion of Major Kerr's remarks, General Reynolds, on behalf of the commission, read a statement thanking all counsel, interpreters, stenographers, military police, and others concerned for having co-operated with the commission in seeing to it that the trial was conducted with dispatch and without unnecessary disturbance. "He omitted the most important person," Sandberg remarked. "He should have added: 'The Commission thanks General Yamashita, without whose presence this trial could not have taken place.' "

Before adjourning, General Reynolds stated: "The commission will announce its findings at two o'clock in the afternoon, Friday next."

That was less than forty-six hours away! Of course, the commission could not review the more than four thousand pages of record and the four hundred and twenty-three exhibits in that time. It could not even properly study and digest the closing arguments. And how could the commission know how long it would take to discuss and vote on the two questions of findings and sentence and then to write its decision, unless those details had already been taken care of? We certainly were not surprised at the commission's haste, but many observers at the trial expressed the belief that, in view of the length of the proceedings, it would "look better" if the commission took a little more time over its decision.

General Reynolds' announcement of the fact that the findings would be made public at two o'clock on the following Friday was probably premised not alone on the appointing authority's evident desire for speed. Friday would be an excellent date for the final touch of retribution for the Japanese sneak attack on Pearl Harbor; for Friday would be more than just another Friday—it would be December the seventh.

XXVII

"DEATH BY HANGING"

FRIDAY, December 7, 1945. Long before the hour scheduled for the commission to reconvene, the courtroom was crowded. The tropical sun poured through the massive windows on the faces of the curious—the Filipinos, the American soldiers and sailors, the newspapermen, the stern-faced military police guards.

All eyes turned to the left, as General Yamashita entered the door behind his counsel table. Flanked by Muto, Utsunomiya, and Hamamoto, he carefully laid the envelope in which he kept notes and papers on the table, greeted his lawyers with a slight smile, and sat down. He betrayed no sign of nervousness or apprehension. To all appearances, this was just another day of trial.

Now grizzled Major Jack Kenworthy, chief of the military police guards, strode to the center of the bar inclosure and faced the audience. Veteran of two world wars, Kenworthy's weatherbeaten face seemed out of place under his shiny white pith helmet. His brass whistle and chain glistened, reflecting the sun's steady burning glare. He addressed the crowd. "There will be no demonstrations," he ordered. "When the judgment is pronounced, you will not utter any sound or make any display, either of pleasure or of dissatisfaction. I know there is a natural impulse to react to so dramatic an event, but in the interests of decorum, you will restrain yourselves."

Kenworthy stepped back and took his place behind the defense table. He had brought General Yamashita down from the hills at the time of the surrender, and Kenworthy's detachment had guarded the prisoner during the last three months. Now the major leaned forward and whispered in Hamamoto's ear: "Tell General Yamashita that no matter what the court says, I'll always think of him as a great guy—and as a real gentleman."

Kenworthy stepped back, stamped his foot on the floor, and shouted: "Atten—tion!" Two o'clock. The military commission entered the courtroom. The five generals looked unusually grave as they took their seats. General Reynolds glanced at his watch, then at the radio technician sitting in the balcony. Then he began to read a prepared statement.

The statement began by reciting the charge. It described the items of the two bills of particulars. Then it summarized the evidence produced by the two contending sides:

"The prosecution presented evidence to show that the crimes were so extensive and widespread, both as to time and area, that they must either have been wilfully permitted by the accused, or secretly ordered by the accused. Captured orders issued by subordinate officers of the accused were presented as proof that they, at least, ordered certain acts leading directly to exterminations of civilians under the guise of eliminating the activities of guerrillas hostile to Japan. With respect to civilian internees and prisoners of war, the proof offered to the commission alleged criminal neglect, especially with respect to food and medical supplies, as well as complete failure by the higher echelons of command to detect and prevent cruel and inhuman treatment accorded by local commanders and guards. The commission considered evidence that the provisions of the Geneva Convention received scant compliance or attention, and that the International Red Cross was unable to render any sustained help. The cruelties and arrogance of the Japanese military police, prison-camp guards, and officials, with like action by local subordinate commanders were presented at length by the prosecution."

Apparently the commission felt that there had been no evidence of acts, orders, or knowledge by General Yamashita himself that was worthy of their attention. As they listened, the defense counsel asked themselves whether this might not be a good omen.

General Reynolds then summarized what the commission had considered of import in the defense presentation:

"The defense established the difficulties faced by the accused with respect not only to the swift and overpowering advance of American forces, but also to the errors of his predecessors, weaknesses in organization, equipment, supply, with especial reference to food and gasoline, training, communication, discipline, and morale of his troops. It was alleged that the sudden assignment of naval and air forces to his tactical command presented almost insurmountable difficulties. This situation was followed, the defense contended, by failure to obey his orders to withdraw troops from Manila and the subsequent massacre of unarmed civilians, particularly by naval forces. Prior to the Luzon campaign, naval forces had reported to a separate ministry in the Japanese government, and naval commanders may not have been receptive or experienced in this instance with respect to a joint land operation under a single commander who was designated from the army service."

In Washington at this time, a bitter debate was in progress over the proposition that the War and Navy departments should be merged into a single Department of National Defense. Naval officers opposed the plan, and Army officials were equally vehement in its behalf. Might this not be an excellent argument for General Reynolds' superiors to cite in support of their position?

The commission president read on:

"As to the crimes themselves, complete ignorance that they had occurred was stoutly maintained by accused, his principal staff officers, and subordinate commanders; further, that all such acts, if committed, were directly contrary to the announced policies, wishes, and orders of the accused. The Japanese commanders testified that they did not make personal inspections or independent checks during the Philippine campaign to determine for themselves the established procedures by which their subordinates accomplished their missions. Taken at full face value, the testimony indicates that Japanese senior commanders operate in a vacuum, almost in another world, with respect to their troops, compared with standards American generals take for granted."

That last statement betrayed two unpleasant concepts: first, it showed the self-satisfaction of "desk" generals, whose experience in this war had borne no relation to that of a combat officer under constant military attack, forced to retreat for his very life; and, second, it presaged a judgment based not on objective standards dictated by the circumstances but on so-called "American" standards that these five men as American generals "took for granted." If national standards are relevant in passing judgment on an alleged war criminal, it would appear only fair to consider the patterns, customs, and values of the accused's nation rather than the apparently superior practices of his captors. When the defense counsel heard the commission refer to "standards American generals take for granted," they were prepared for the verdict.

General Reynolds continued:

"This accused is an officer of long years of experience, broad in its scope, who has had extensive command and staff duty in the Imperial Japanese Army in peace as well as war in Asia, Malaya, Europe, and the Japanese home islands. Clearly, assignment to command military troops is accompanied by broad authority and heavy responsibility. This has been true in all armies throughout recorded history. It is absurd, however, to consider a commander a murderer or rapist because one of his soldiers commits a murder or a rape. Nonetheless, where murder and rape and vicious, revengeful actions are widespread offenses and there is no effective attempt by a commander to discover and control the criminal acts, such a commander may be held responsible, even criminally liable, for the lawless acts of his troops, depending upon their nature and the circumstances surrounding them. *Should a commander issue orders* which lead directly to lawless acts, the criminal responsibility is definite and has always been so understood. It is for the purpose of maintaining discipline and control, among other reasons, that military commanders are given broad powers of administering military justice. The tactical situation, the character, training, and capacity of staff officers and subordinate commanders, as well as the traits of character and training of his troops, are other important factors in such cases. These matters have been the principal considerations of the commission during its deliberations."

Here General Reynolds paused. The preliminaries were over. The decision was at hand.

"The accused, his senior counsel, and personal interpreter, will take position before the commission."

Earlier in the day, General Yamashita had asked if he might make a statement to the court, that would then be interpreted by Hamamoto. The request was transmitted to General Reynolds, who answered that, if the statement were written out in advance, he would take it up with his fellow-members of the commission, and, if they found it unobjectionable, they would permit its introduction. Yamashita accordingly wrote his statement, Hamamoto transcribed it into English, and Colonel Clarke presented it to the commission in chambers. The generals agreed to allow Hamamoto to read the English version, explaining that the proceedings were to be broadcast on a world-wide radio hookup, that fifteen minutes had been allotted for the entire performance, and that there would not be time for General Yamashita to speak in Japanese.

Thus it was that when General Yamashita, Colonel Clarke, and Hamamoto stepped before the bench, Hamamoto read the following lines on behalf of the accused:

"In my capacity as commander-in-chief of the Japanese Fourteenth Area Army I met and fought, here in the Philippines, numerically and qualitatively superior armed forces of the United States. Throughout this engagement I have endeavored to fulfil to the best of my ability the requirements of my position and have done my best to conduct myself at all times in accordance with the principles of fairness and justice.

"I have been arraigned and tried before this honorable commission as a war criminal. I wish to state that I stand here today with the same clear conscience as on the first day of my arraignment and I swear before my Creator and everything sacred to me that I am innocent of the charges made against me.

"With reference to the trial itself I wish to take this opportunity to express my gratitude to the United States of America for having accorded to an enemy general the unstinted services of a staff of brilliant, conscientious, and upright American officers and gentlemen as defense counsel."

After Hamamoto concluded his reading, General Reynolds cleared his throat. The final judgment was at hand. It consisted of two factual conclusions—the finding and the sentence. General Reynolds spoke, and, as he did so, Hamamoto translated the fateful words for his chief:

"General Yamashita: The commission concludes: (1) That a series of atrocities and other high crimes have been committed by members of the Japanese armed forces under your command against the people of the United States, their allies, and dependencies throughout the Philippine Islands; that they were not sporadic in nature but in many cases were methodically supervised by Japanese officers and noncommissioned officers; (2) that during the period in question you failed to provide effective control of your troops as was required by the circumstances.

"Accordingly, upon secret written ballot, two-thirds or more of the members concurring, the commission finds you guilty as charged and sentences you to death by hanging."

There was no finding of any order, any knowledge, any condonation on General Yamashita's part. Crimes had been committed by his troops, and he had "failed" to provide effective control. That was all. He was to hang.

Yamashita nodded, turned, and calmly left the court. He was escorted to his cell upstairs.

More than fifty newspaper reporters had attended the Yamashita trial at some time or other during its devious course, but there were only twelve men, representing American, British, and Australian journals and news services, who had not missed a moment of the proceedings. After the conclusion of the final arguments on December 5, 1945, Pat Robinson, correspondent for the International News Service, had polled these twelve journalists in a secret ballot. The question was: "Having heard all the evidence, if you were on the commission would you vote to hang Yamashita?" The vote was 12 to 0, "No."

Yamashita's lawyers, however, were keenly aware of the fact that the newspapermen were not on the commission. Of the six of us, only Colonel Clarke had expressed a lingering hope for an acquittal, and even he had acknowledged that if the commission found Yamashita guilty, the sentence would be death by hanging. Nevertheless, after the sentence was pronounced, the fact that we had expected it failed to cushion its stunning effect. As Robert Shaplen, correspondent for *Newsweek* cabled his magazine: "Yamashita maintained to the end, and said so in his final statement, that his conscience was clear and that he was innocent of the charges. I believe he really thought so. What's more I think his legal counsel thought so too, because after the decision was announced they maintained this conviction privately. I never saw a defense staff take a decision any harder. Standing around the empty room when it was over, Colonel Clarke grimly planned appeal steps with Captain Reel and other members of his staff. Finally the colonel turned sadly to Reel. 'C'mon,' he said, 'I hate like hell to do this but we better go up and see him.' "

We did go up to see Yamashita. When we entered the cell, Muto spoke up bitterly: "Why can't they shoot us like soldiers?"

Yamashita looked at his chief-of-staff disapprovingly. Then he smiled and shook hands with each of us, trying to express his thanks for our efforts. He had some remembrances to distribute—his ribbons, his watch, Chinese good-luck coins, a tea set. He gave his spurs to Major Guy because the latter was a cavalry officer. And his huge leather belt was presented to Hendrix. "You're the only man fat enough to wear this," Yamashita said.

As lawyers will, we told Yamashita that there was still a chance. The sentence had to be approved by General MacArthur. And there was our habeas corpus proceeding, our attempt to get before the United States Supreme Court. It was not all over yet. It was apparent that the Japanese did not have much hope. And, truth to tell, we had little more.

Nevertheless, no sooner had Yamashita and his cohorts been taken on their way to the new Luzon prisoner-of-war camp than the defense counsel went back to work. We prepared two documents: the first a futile appeal to General MacArthur for clemency, and the second a cable to the clerk of the Supreme Court in Washington, asking that tribunal to stay Yamashita's execution until there had been an opportunity to consider our legal petition that was at that very moment winging its way over the Pacific.

That cable bore strange fruit. Two days later we learned that the secretary of war had ordered Yamashita's execution stayed. There was a chance—slim but alive.

XXVIII
THE GERMAN SABOTEURS

IN THE darkness of the night of June 13, 1942, a German submarine rose to the surface of the sea not more than a few hundred feet from Amagansett Beach, Long Island. Stealthily a small boat put in to the shore and landed four young men, who were dressed in the uniform of the German marine infantry. The men carried with them a supply of explosives, fuses, and incendiary and timing devices, as well as suits of civilian clothes. Immediately upon their landing, the four men buried their uniforms and demolition materials, donned the civilian clothing, and proceeded to New York City. The men were graduates of a German sabotage school near Berlin, where they had received instructions in the art of destroying war industries and facilities in the United States.

Four nights later, June 17, 1942, four classmates of those men, similarly garbed and carrying similar materials, were landed from another U-boat at Ponte Verde Beach, Florida. They made corresponding disposition of the articles and proceeded in citizen's dress to Jacksonville, Florida, and thence to various other points in this country.

Before the month was over, the eight Germans had been taken into custody in New York and Chicago by agents of the Federal Bureau of Investigation. President Roosevelt immediately appointed a military commission and directed it to try the captives for the offense of having violated the laws of war. The trial aroused tremendous public interest, since it was held during the bleakest days of the war. The commission eventually found the defendants guilty of being enemy belligerents who, acting under the directions of the

German army, had entered our territory behind the lines for the purpose of sabotaging and destroying vital industry. The accused men had gone about their mission, not in uniform, but in civilian disguise, a fact which made them violators of the laws of war—"unlawful belligerents"—and hence proper recipients of the death penalty to which seven of them were duly sentenced.

The Army officers who had been appointed to defend the accused Germans managed, by a series of legal maneuvers, to bring the case before the United States Supreme Court. The defense counsel argued that the Germans should never have been tried by a military commission at all, that they were entitled under the American Constitution to a trial by an ordinary civil jury. They pointed to the famous case of Milligan, a citizen of Indiana, who had been found guilty by a military commission of conspiring to aid the Confederacy during the Civil War and whose conviction had been later set aside by the Supreme Court on the grounds that there had been no active hostilities in Indiana, that the civil courts were open and functioning, and that therefore the accused should have had a jury trial. After all, the Fifth Amendment to our Constitution—one of the fundamental "Bill of Rights" upon which our forefathers had insisted before they would agree to ratify the Constitution—said: "No person shall be deprived of life, liberty, or property without due process of law," and due process of law meant trial by jury in a criminal case.

But the Supreme Court made short shrift of the German saboteurs. Milligan's case, said the judges, was quite different. Milligan was not a "belligerent"; he was an Indiana citizen who had not crossed the fighting lines as these Germans had. And, although the Civil War was not fought in Indiana, who could say that in these days of total war and the submarine and air-raid menace, the shores of Long Island and the beaches of Florida were not within the "theater of operations"? But, most important, the offenses with which the

Germans were charged—violation of the laws of war, spying, and sabotage—had never been held to require a jury trial in wartime. Warfare, said the Supreme Court, could not be conducted unless a military commander had the right to seize and punish *by military methods* enemies "who in their attempt to thwart or impede our military effort have violated the law of war." The Constitution was never intended to *enlarge* any ordinary rights to a jury trial; its object was merely to *preserve* rights that *had existed* at the time of its adoption, and, from time immemorial, alien spies and saboteurs during wartime could be subjected to trial by military tribunal. In fact, the court pointed out, the United States Congress had acknowledged this truth when it passed a law (called the "fifteenth Article of War") that recognized that "military commissions" might try "violations of the laws of war." The Supreme Court decision was unanimous—it was announced within forty-eight hours after the case was argued—and a few days later the saboteurs were executed.

The story of the saboteurs' case has a place here because it furnished the procedural pattern for the turbulent legal moves that General Yamashita's defense counsel pursued to bring their case to Washington. While the Yamashita trial was being fought in the Manila courtroom, another parallel battle was going on in our office by night, in research libraries, among lawyer's digests and tomes, finally in the chamber of the Philippine Supreme Court. After Yamashita's sentence, the two battle lines merged, and the final culmination of the offensive was to bring our case before the highest court in America.

The saboteurs' case was the starting point for our legal thinking. Among other things, we found in it three fundamental guiding lights:

1. It was a precedent for our belief that Army officers appointed to defend an accused enemy before a military commission could properly, within the terms of their appointment, carry his case into the civil courts.

2. It established the fact that the American courts, including the Supreme Court, would hear the plea of an enemy belligerent.

3. It showed that there was a basic question in the Yamashita case that the Supreme Court would decide, if we could only get it before the court.

What was that question?

On the very first day that the defense counsel met, the problem presented itself. We, of course, began by examining the "charge" that was designed to state the prosecution's case against General Yamashita. The reader is already familiar with the ambiguous and confusing language in which that memorable document was phrased; after some discussion we agreed that it apparently meant (what later developed to be the fact) that the general was charged with having failed to control certain persons other than himself, who had, in turn, committed crimes. After the bills of particulars were filed, implementing and explaining the charge, it became clear: General Yamashita was not accused of committing the crimes, aiding in their commission, ordering them, authorizing them before their perpetration, or condoning them afterward. He was accused of having failed to control his troops, and it was implied that this was a crime, regardless of whether or not he was *able* to control them. Why? Because he was in command. That was apparently the theory of "command responsibility."

But, we reasoned, that is the same as saying that General Yamashita is a criminal not because he had done something he should not have done or failed to do something he could have done but simply because he *was* somebody. That thought would be abhorrent to any American lawyer or to any American layman who had a feeling for the Anglo-Saxon tradition of justice. We just do not hang people because of crimes that others commit.

Nor did the annals of international law furnish a precedent for any such prosecution. Never before had any soldier been convicted in any court on a similar charge. And so, we reasoned, if this is all there is to it, General Yamashita has committed no crime; the charge fails to state any offense by him against the laws of war. He should not even be tried.

He should not be tried! There was a sorry jest! He was *going* to be tried, and by a military commission that we assumed was prepared to find him guilty and to order him hanged. It was reminiscent of the ancient story of the lawyer who told his client through the bars of the cell in which the latter was confined: "They can't do this to you."

Laymen often assume that a defendant who is aggrieved in any trial can "appeal" to "higher courts." This is not necessarily true in all civilian cases, and it is practically never true in military trials. Military tribunals constitute a sort of judicial system all their own, and the civilian courts will not interfere with them. They exist not so much to assure criminal justice in the armed forces as to aid the commanding officers in exercising discipline over their troops or in punishing captured enemy spies and other miscreants—all to achieve the end of a more efficient carrying-on of hostilities. Thus it is that civilian courts refuse to "review" or to intervene in military courts' proceedings. The only exception that is made to this rule is when an accused can show that the army court had no business in trying him at all, or, as the lawyers put it, that it had no "jurisdiction" over him. For example, Corporal John Smith, a member of the United States Army, is tried by court-martial for having disobeyed the order of his commanding officer. The court-martial commits various legal sins, and Smith does not get a fair trial. The civilian courts will refuse to interfere—he has no "appeal." But Sam Jones, who never was in the Army, is mistaken for a missing soldier and he is court-martialed for desertion. A United States court, upon his application, will order him released from custody because as a civilian he never should have been tried by the Army. The military had no "jurisdiction" over him.

Where did that leave us with General Yamashita? He was

to be tried for violation of the laws of war, and the saboteurs' case had established the rule that military commissions were the proper tribunals to try such offenses. But our reasoning had led us to the conclusion that the charge against Yamashita did not describe a violation of the laws of war, and, if our reasoning was correct, the military commission would be without jurisdiction in the case. Who could finally decide whether we were right—whether this *was* a violation of the laws of war? In the saboteurs' case, the Supreme Court had announced that it reserved that decision for itself, saying: "We must . . . inquire whether any of the acts charged is an offense against the law of war cognizable before a military tribunal."

The Supreme Court of the United States! At first it seemed fantastic. Less than one month before, this Japanese commander had been exerting his every effort in an attempt to destroy the United States. Now we were considering having him go before the highest court in our nation, to claim "rights" under our Constitution. And yet, was it preposterous? Again the saboteurs' case pointed the way, for there the Supreme Court had listened to the pleas of enemy war criminals while hostilities were still in progress. Yamashita's defense counsel had made their decision: if we could possibly get this case to the Supreme Court, it would be done.

That explains why we filed a motion to dismiss the entire case before the trial began. Along with the motion, we gave the commission a memorandum setting forth our views. Knowing that we were dealing with laymen, we phrased the brief in simple language and advanced the logic that we hoped would appeal to American generals. Analyzing the accusation, we pointed out that "the accused is not charged with having done something or having failed to do something, but solely with having *been* something. For the gravamen of the charge is that the accused was commander of

Japanese forces and, by virtue of that fact alone, is guilty.... American jurisprudence recognizes no such principle so far as its own military personnel is concerned.... No one would even suggest that the commanding general of an American occupational force becomes a criminal every time an American violates the law." Then, quoting the saboteurs' case, we informed the commission of our plan to try to take this matter to the United States Supreme Court and explained that we were filing the motion at this early stage to give the commission the opportunity of preventing what we considered would be an illegal trial.

Although none of the defense counsel entertained any substantial hope that the motion would be allowed, it was not until General Reynolds informed Colonel Clarke that action on the motion would be deferred until the opening day of trial that we were sure that it would be denied. It was obvious that, with the advance publicity buildup that this trial had received, once the show formally opened, it would run on to its bitter and inevitable end. It was this information that finally decided us to make the proceedings of the first day of trial the "record" on which to base our forthcoming legal moves.

Ordinarily, before initiating any legal "appeal," a lawyer waits until the original trial is over and then completes his papers. He takes advantage of the entire record of a completed case. But, in order to do that in our type of proceeding, we would require the co-operation of the prosecuting authorities. Assuming that Yamashita would be sentenced to death, if we followed a normal course we would then, after the sentence, prepare the documents in which we would question the commission's jurisdiction, for presentation to the first court to which we were entitled to go—in this case, the Philippine Supreme Court. That would take some time. Then the Philippine Supreme Court would hear argument on the matter and retire to consider the question and to write an opinion setting forth its views. That would take more time. Then, assuming that the Philippine justices held against us (and, of course, we did assume that), we would have to prepare further papers asking the United States Supreme Court to review the action of the Philippine court. That would consume still more time, especially since Washington is eight or ten thousand miles away from Manila, and even air-mail transmission requires more than a week. Then the American court would have to make up its mind whether it would hear the case, and, if a favorable decision was reached, there would be further documents, oral arguments, and another decision to be written. It was already being made quite clear to us that the supreme military authorities who had brought about this trial were in a rush to get it over with, and we simply could not imagine General MacArthur's sitting idly by for at least six or eight weeks after a death sentence, while the convicted criminal's lawyers maneuvered a tortuous path through the courts in an attempt to rob the commander-in-chief of his prey. Since the Army was in hurry, we would have to hurry, too.

As Yamashita's defense counsel studied the record of the saboteurs' case, they saw that it probably would never have reached the Supreme Court had it not been for the fact that the military authorities and the Department of Justice co-operated closely with the accuseds' lawyers to get it there. The government agencies in that case had expressed the desire to have the untried questions settled by the court for their own future guidance. Might we not expect the same co-operation here? After all, Yamashita's case was to be the first of many war-crimes trials that had been docketed. It presented a number of questions, including the untried theory of "command responsibility," which we presumed the prosecuting authorities would wish to have decided by a responsible court before going ahead with the trials of the other Japanese defendants. On the twenty-eighth of October, we put the question to Colonel Meek: Would the War Crimes Division co-operate with us in taking steps to present this case to the United States Supreme Court?

The answer was a resounding "No." Not only did we fail to enlist the aid of the Army authorities, but every step we had to take to bring the case to civilian courts was opposed with extraordinary zeal.

XXIX

OBSTACLES AND ISSUES

"THE accused by his duly appointed counsel, respectfully requests the commission to furnish sixteen (16) additional copies of the record of the arraignment and sixteen (16) additional copies of the report of the proceedings for the first day in the above entitled case. The extra copies of the arraignment and of the first day's proceedings are required for use in contemplated proceedings before a civil court."

That request was presented as a formal written motion to the commission four days after Yamashita's trial started. Normally the channel to the Supreme Court of the United States is routed through lower federal or state courts, but in the Philippine Islands there were no such bodies, and their place for appellate matters that raised constitutional questions was taken by the Philippine Supreme Court. During the first day of trial we had carefully raised the questions on which we planned to rely, and the record of that day and also of the arraignment contained all the pertinent papers in the case, including the cumbersome bills of particulars, rules of the commission, and various orders of appointment. To copy all that material for the Philippine court posed a tremendous clerical task. Not only that, but the Philippine Supreme Court demanded fifteen copies of all legal papers that were to be presented—the court consists of eleven judges, each of whom must have a copy, and the remaining copies were for the clerk and for service on the opposing side.

The stenographic record of our trial was being mechanically reproduced by mimeograph. Each day we received three copies of the previous day's record. But the commission was extremely jealous of the disposition of these booklets, and, before we were allowed to see any of them, we had to sign an agreement to return all copies to the commission at the end of the proceedings.

Now, however, we had come to a point where it was essential for us to submit fifteen copies of large portions of this record to the Philippine Supreme Court and to keep an additional copy for our files. We had prepared our petition to the court with numerous references to the pertinent passages in the official stenographic record of the arraignment and first day of trial, and we had planned to attach copies of the record as exhibits. That procedure was calculated to save the stupendous amount of typewriting and copying that we were not equipped to handle. And so we made a formal request for the copies and frankly stated our reason for wanting them.

The commission took our request "under advisement." A few days later, General Reynolds read the following announcement:

"The commission has received a motion from the chief defense counsel for additional copies of the record. This motion is not allowed by the commission, but counsel is advised that if they wish to do so, they may apply to the appointing authority."

Nothing that happened during the trial made me quite so furious as that announcement. I knew that the military commission was not anxious to have a civil court scrutinize their procedure, but I never believed that they would go so far as to force us into the entirely unnecessary labor involved in copying the mimeographed record. We did renew our request with General Styer, but, of course, he also turned us down. Did these generals think for one moment that their action would discourage us from going to court?

Angry but determined, we went to work. Colonel Clarke donated two typewriters and four stenographers. Hendrix rounded up half-a-dozen more typewriters and recruited more stenographers and enlisted men to volunteer to work nights until the job was done. Hendrix supervised the dreary routine of copying, typing, and proofreading, and by the end of a week the papers were filed.

Pandemonium reigned on the prosecution side. Hurried conferences were held, opinions were written, radiograms winged back and forth between Manila and General MacArthur's headquarters in Tokyo. From members of the prosecution's headquarters we received reports that the commander-in-chief was perturbed, that he had radioed orders to his Manila subordinates to ignore the Philippine Supreme Court, that it was well settled that the courts could not review the actions of a United States military commission—in short, that judicial interference should be avoided.

In any event, General Styer's office decided that it would literally ignore the Philippine Supreme Court. Not only would they fail to appear in the courtroom, but they would even attempt to avoid service of process. And on that peg hangs one of the more disgraceful incidents of this entire story.

The legal proceedings that we had commenced were what lawyers call "a petition for a writ of habeas corpus." As the name connotes, a writ of habeas corpus is a direction by a court addressed to the man who holds an aggrieved person in his custody, ordering the jailer to "produce the body" of his prisoner. As we have indicated, we based our request for the writ on the grounds that in this case the custodian had no "jurisdiction" over General Yamashita in the sense that he had no right to keep Yamashita in confinement as an accused war criminal under this charge. Inasmuch as Lieutenant General Wilhelm D. Styer, commanding general of AFWESPAC, was technically the custodian of our petitioner, he was named as the opposing party, or "respondent," in our papers. After we had filed the petition, the clerk of the Philippine court gave a copy to a bailiff to deliver to the respondent, General Styer, together with a "summons" informing him that he had five days in which to answer our declarations. The delivery of this summons and the obtaining of a signature acknowledging its receipt are called "service" of the process. What happened to the bailiff, a gentleman named Julio Arzadon, when he tried to perform this simple function is best described in his own expressive words. The following is a copy of an affidavit that he executed and filed with the papers in the case upon the direction of the Chief Justice of the Philippine Supreme Court:

"The undersigned went personally to the Office of the Commanding General, at the Far Eastern University, at about 2:30 o'clock, P.M. November 13, 1945. After being shown to a certain Major Jackson who, I believe, is in-charge of the Office of the General, I told him I was there to serve the summons—I handed him the papers which he immediately took to the General. Meantime I was told to wait. After waiting for some ten to fifteen minutes, the said Major came out with the summons unacknowledged, and informing me that the General wanted a certain Colonel Young to sign it for him. Colonel Young was called in the Phone, and he appeared after some time, took the papers, read and re-read them.

"Believing that I was unnecessarily delayed, I asked Jackson if there was anything they wanted to do yet before signing the papers, and he told me that Colonel Young and General Styer would take it up together first. Young could not see the General, however, because he was in a conference with a bunch of Army Officers by then. As it was getting late, it was almost five o'clock, I told Jackson and Young that if nobody would sign it yet, I would just leave the papers together with the original which I was asking anyone of them to sign, so that I would be back the following morning to get said original already signed. They would not let me leave the papers, and so told me to go back in the morning again with the papers.

"Went back this morning, at about 8:30 o'clock, directly to Major Jackson who told me that General Styer was out the whole day on an airplane trip. I inquired if there were no instructions left by the General for anyone to receive the papers, and at the same time asked him to receive them, but he said that there are no instructions and that he can not receive them. He told me to go back tomorrow morning at about 9:o'clock (Nov. 15th).

"Done at Manila, this 14th day of November, 1945.

(*sgd*) JULIO S. ARZADON
Act'g. Asst. Bailiff on the Supreme Court."

There we have the edifying spectacle of the most powerful military force in the world, the United States Army, running away from a Filipino process server just as an ordinary deadbeat dodges the sheriff. Fortunately, the Philippine court held that the facts detailed in the bailiff's affidavit constituted "service." The case was set down to be heard on November 23, 1945, and General Styer was notified of that fact by mail.

Our petition for relief was premised not only on the contention that the charge failed to state a legal violation by the accused but also on a number of other grounds that had occurred to us as we prepared for trial. First, there was the argument that, for whatever crimes Yamashita might be presumed to have committed, he should not be tried by a military commission in a territory over which the United States exercised sovereignty, where the local courts were open and functioning, and where there were no longer any hostilities in progress. Although this was not one of our stronger points, it caught the fancy of the newspaper reporters, probably because it was the easiest to explain to their readers. Americans who had had a high-school course in the history of their country had read about Milligan's case and remembered that, in general, it stood for the proposition that, except in cases of dire necessity, an accused man is entitled to a fair trial by a civilian court rather than by the often arbitrary and high-handed methods common to military tribunals. Citing the Milligan case, we contended that military commissions could properly be appointed in only three contingencies:

1. Where there is military government of occupied territory and the occupying army's military courts take the place of local courts, as in the case of occupied Japan and Germany.

2. Where there is so serious a threat to the existence of the state that civil courts are forced to shut their doors and martial law is declared, as in the case of an armed rebellion such as might result from certain strike or lockout situations.

3. Where a military commander, during wartime, tries a captured enemy for violation of the laws of war as a necessary adjunct of his successful prosecution of hostilities, as in the case of the trial of a captured spy or as in the saboteurs' case.

Here, we pointed out, there was no military government, and the Philippines were not "occupied" territory. We were in "recovered" territory—territory then belonging to the United States of America—territory that was being governed by a commonwealth government that had pledged allegiance to the United States. (It is to be remembered that the Philippines did not gain their independence until July 4, 1946, some eight months later.) The Army exercised no governmental functions here; General MacArthur had publicly restored "the full powers and responsibilities" of rule to President Osmeña and the Philippine Congress many months past. It is true that there were American soldiers stationed in the archipelago, but that did not make the Philippines "occupied territory" any more than Massachusetts was "occupied" because troops were stationed at Fort Devens and

Camp Edwards and Camp Myles Standish. Nor had martial law been declared in the islands. The local courts were in full operation.

As for the saboteurs' case, that, we said, had taken place while hostilities were in progress. It was true that a military commander could try accused war criminals by military commission, but we pointed out that the Supreme Court had called that power "an incident to the conduct of war," based on the mission of a commanding officer "not only to repel and defeat the enemy, but to seize and subject to disciplinary measures those enemies who in their attempt to thwart or impede our military effort have violated the law of war." Here a military commission had been appointed by an American general in his capacity as a commander in the field after his mission as a field commander was over. The enemy had unconditionally surrendered. Hostilities were at an end—there was no emergency. Was there still justification for replacing the ordinary judicial processes by this abnormally summary sort of trial?

The obvious answer, and the one we later received from the United States Supreme Court, was that the "war" was not yet over; there was still no peace treaty. A "technical" answer, perhaps, but I suppose that our contention could be called "technical," too. That is why I say that this was not one of our stronger arguments. But I still believe that it has merit; there is no magic in a "peace treaty," especially when one remembers that, although we think of World War I as ending on November 11, 1918, there was no declaration of peace by the United States Congress until 1922.

Another issue that we raised had to do with the Geneva Convention of July 27, 1929, relative to the treatment of prisoners of war. One of the agreements among the countries (including the United States) which entered into that treaty required that, before a prisoner of war is tried by the captor nation, notice shall be given at least three weeks before the commencement of the trial to the "protecting power" of the accused. The "protecting power" is a neutral nation that agrees to represent a belligerent nation in dealings between the warring countries. During the greater part of the conflict Japan's "protecting power" had been Spain, but Franco's government had broken off diplomatic relations shortly before the surrender, and, by the time Yamashita came to trial, Spain's place had been taken by Switzerland. Yamashita was a prisoner of war, and yet, on the opening day of trial, we had established the fact that no notice of the impending proceedings had been sent to Switzerland. This omission, we maintained, had deprived Yamashita of a substantial right, the possible intervention and assistance of a neutral power. We did not set much store by this argument, although it assumed greater proportions two months later when, during oral argument before the United States Supreme Court, Mr. Justice Rutledge pointed out that Yamashita was being accused as a criminal because his troops had made the same omission when they brought American prisoners of war to trial.

Perhaps our greatest reliance was placed on the contention that the sort of evidence that the commission was admitting over our strenuous objections denied Yamashita a fair trial. Our unsuccessful battles to keep out affidavits, depositions, opinions of the prosecutors, gossip, hearsay, and sound films have already been described. In our petition not only did we claim that the admission of this evidence deprived the accused of safeguards that were recognized as basic guaranties, but we argued that it violated two specific congressional statutes. This was not, like the Nuremberg trials, an international proceeding. This was an American commission, set up by an American general, trying a man in American territory, and therefore clearly subject to laws passed by the American Congress. One such law (called the "twenty-fifth Article of War") said that depositions (which are formal affidavits taken after notice is given to the opposite party to give him an opportunity to be represented) might be read in evidence before a military commission "*in any case not capital.*" This was a capital case—that is, it was one in which the death penalty might be adjudged—and so we maintained that Congress had clearly forbidden the use of depositions (and, of course, the less formal affidavits) as evidence on which to convict Yamashita. The other statute (called the "thirty-eighth Article of War") provided that the president of the United States might prescribe rules of evidence in cases before military commissions but that the procedures he prescribed should, so far as practicable, "apply the rules of evidence generally recognized in the trial of criminal cases in the district courts of the United States." Here, unlike the saboteurs' case, the president of the United States had played no part. *He* had made no rules. The logical deduction was that therefore the rules of evidence as recognized in United States district courts should prevail, and those rules, of course, prohibited the hearsay, opinion, gossip, and rumor which the military commission had used so extensively. Apparently, Congress had been afraid of just such a performance as was now going on in Manila. General Reynolds and his brethren were, to be sure, following "rules" that permitted this doubtful "evidence," but their rules had been handed down by General MacArthur and not, as the law provided, by President Truman, and they certainly strayed far from the paths followed by "district courts of the United States."

It was this directive by General MacArthur that gave us our entering wedge to bring the conduct of the trial before the courts. As I have explained, civil courts cannot review the actions of military tribunals—the petition for a writ of habeas corpus raises only the question of the *jurisdiction* of the military commission. But here, we said, the same document which gave the commission its powers, the foundation of its very existence—this order of the commander-in-chief—prescribed the illegal and improper rules which the commission declared itself bound to follow, and hence it raised the fundamental question of the commission's jurisdiction. Unbelievable though it may sound to a lawyer's ears, General MacArthur had decreed that the commission was to admit such evidence "as *in the Commission's opinion* would have probative value in the mind of a reasonable man"—that is, the *commission itself* was to be the sole judge of what it might or might not accept; and, further, the directive specifically included as "evidence" that might be proper: "any document which appears . . . to have been signed or issued officially by any officer, department, agency, or member of the armed forces of any government, without proof of the signature or of the issuance of the document. . . . Any report which appears . . . to have been signed or issued by the International Red Cross . . . or by a medical doctor or any medical service personnel, or by an investigator. . . . Affidavits, depositions, or other statements. . . . Any diary, letter, or other document appearing . . . to contain information relating to the charge. . . ."

The argument, then, went to General MacArthur's directive, and only incidentally to the commission's action under the directive. This is what brought our colleague Hendrix to Armageddon. He appeared for the petitioner before the Philippine Supreme Court; his task was to argue against the MacArthur *decree*, but his passionate revulsion against its injustice led him to give his plea a personal twist, and he found himself inveighing against the author of the document, the commander-in-chief himself. Hendrix' remarks were more undiplomatic than incorrect. I was not in the Philippine Supreme Court chamber on that memorable occasion, and so I have to rely on what I heard and read about the Hendrix explosion. Clarke, Sandberg, and I had just finished a rather dull day of trial before the military commission, when one of the press-service correspondents rushed up to us.

"Jesus Christ!" he said, "You fellows sure gave us a terrific story today!"

"What do you mean?" I asked in bewilderment. "Nothing exciting happened here."

"Hell, no, I don't mean here. Read this!" The reporter thrust a piece of yellow paper in my hand, apparently the carbon copy of a typewritten page, adding as he did so: "Here's my story for today. I just sent it in."

Clarke and Sandberg looked over my shoulders. Together, we read the sensational phrases. "Arguing for a writ of habeas corpus for Yamashita in the Philippine Supreme Court, Assistant Defense Counsel Lieutenant Colonel Walter Hendrix of Atlanta, Ga., implied that the 'Tiger of Malaya' was being railroaded," it began. And then Hendrix was quoted: " 'We contend,' Colonel Hendrix told the supreme court justices, 'that General MacArthur has taken the law into his own hands, is disregarding the laws of the United States and the Constitution, and that he has no authority from Congress or the President. He is a great soldier and general but not a great lawyer. His orders regarding this case are illegal.' " Nor had Hendrix spared the military commission, if the journalist's report was accurate. "The commission has violated every law in the world," it quoted him as saying. "The members are not justices and lawyers, such as you and I are, yet they are trying one of the greatest cases. If you could hear their decisions, you would be shocked and amazed." The story concluded: "One of the justices asked Colonel Hendrix why he did not appeal to General MacArthur. 'Well, sir,' Colonel Hendrix said after coughing, 'I don't believe I would do that.' "

Hendrix later complained that the dispatch was unfair. The various phrases, he explained, had been taken out of context—his argument had been a long one, and these quoted remarks had not all been run together. It had not sounded at all like that—at least not to him.

But Colonel Clarke was understandably perturbed. "This looks like court-martial," he said, "and I'll sure catch hell tomorrow. They'll have me in chambers first thing." Strangely, the members of the military commission never mentioned the matter until after the trial was over. Only then did General Reynolds discuss it with Colonel Clarke. The commission, Reynolds said, had read the newspaper reports of Hendrix' statement but felt that whatever occurred outside the trial court was none of their concern. He had heard talk of court-martial, but the proposal had apparently been discarded.

This was the only time during the trial that General Yamashita appeared worried. He was bothered about what might happen to Hendrix. "They won't do anything," I said; "they wouldn't be so foolish as to court-martial him. It would only make a martyr out of Hendrix, and it would throw the Army in a pretty bad light. He's O.K." Then jokingly I asked Yamashita: "What would you do if you were in General MacArthur's shoes? Suppose, when you were at the height of your power, some young lieutenant colonel way down the line had said such things about you—What would you do?"

Yamashita laughed. "I wouldn't feel insulted," he said. "I don't consider myself a lawyer."

XXX

AN UNORTHODOX STEP

ALTHOUGH no representative of the prosecution appeared before the Philippine court to oppose our petition, none of the defense counsel entertained any idea that it would be allowed. Not only was it inconceivable that the Philippine judges would veto any judicial action on the part of General MacArthur, the man whom Filipinos regarded and not infrequently described as their "savior," but some of the judges had been accused by politically minded newspapers of having been "collaborators," and our petition had presented them with a fine opportunity to give the lie to their detractors. We made no secret of the fact that we regarded our action in the local court as only a necessary steppingstone to a more definitive tribunal.

The question that troubled us was not whether we would get an adverse decision, but *when* we would get it; for the prosecution's case had closed, and we foresaw the conclusion of the trial in approximately two weeks. Suppose the Philippine judges kept our petition "under advisement" until the day that Yamashita was sentenced to death, or perhaps a few days before or a few days after? Then we would have to send our papers asking the United States Supreme Court to review the decision of the Philippine court to Washington and give the American justices a chance to act on the matter—and meanwhile our client would be dead. The case would be moot. For, by November 23, 1945, not only had the commission reversed itself and denied us a continuance, but it had been made very clear that the Army was anxious to avoid having this case ever get to the Supreme Court. Although we had announced to the newspapers our intention of appealing an adverse decision to the American court, still General MacArthur would have been within his legal rights, strictly speaking, in having a death sentence executed, and all indications supported our fear that exactly that would be done.

It must be borne in mind that one does not "appeal" to the United States Supreme Court as of "right." Whether or not they will review a decision of a lower court is discretionary with the nine justices who sit in Washington. The appellant files what is called a "petition for certiorari"—a request that he be allowed to present his case before the court.

Actually, the Supreme Court grants only about one in every seven such petitions that it receives. So we were not sure that the American judges would even consent to hear this plea, and, in any event, we were fearful of the additional time that might be required for them to decide such preliminary issue, after which the formal argument would take place. The sands were running fast. Delay on the part of the Philippine judges would be disastrous, and yet there was nothing we could do to hurry them along.

A desperate situation calls for desperate measures. We decided on a most unorthodox step. We prepared a new application for habeas corpus and sent it *direct* to the Supreme Court in Washington. Most important, we informed the newspapermen of what we had done.

The Supreme Court normally pays no attention to cases that do not come up on some sort of appeal from lower courts. It is not what lawyers call "a court of original jurisdiction." Indeed, the Constitution of the United States specifies that only in "cases affecting Ambassadors, other public Ministers and Consuls, and those in which a State shall be a Party" will the court have original jurisdiction, and "in all other cases . . . the Supreme Court shall have appellate jurisdiction." But might it not be argued that, if the threat of a speedy hanging really dissipated any chance of effective channeling through the Philippine court, this was an "appellate" proceeding—our only possible "appeal" from the actions of a military commission? Moreover, we knew that the Supreme Court had power to issue almost any sort of writ that it thought would aid it in the conduct of its functions, that is, we envisioned the possibility of this action being used as a stopgap until our proper petition might be received.

I may have stated a "good" reason for our new application. Professor Thomas Reed Powell, of Harvard Law School, used to warn his students that there is a difference between "good" reasons and "real" reasons. Our "real" reason was based on the hunch that, if we got any kind of a petition before the Supreme Court now, we might be able to stave off an execution, at least until the plea was turned down. And we calculated that it would not be turned down until after our more orthodox appeal had arrived in Washington. That is why it was so important for us to give this story to the press and for the press, in turn, to inform the public. By filing papers in Washington, we would be *in court.* General MacArthur might well take the position that he would ignore the Philippine court, but it was quite another thing publicly to ignore the Supreme Court of the United States. He would not dare to hang a man who had a case that was actually pending before the justices in Washington! Would not dare? The commander-in-chief might dare do anything. But it would have been embarrassing.

The defense counsel indicated their "real" reasons to the Supreme Court as frankly as was possible under the circumstances. The stopgap document recited the background of this unusual procedure, described the other petition that had been presented to the Philippine court, and then continued:

"Petitioner . . . believes and fears . . . that the Supreme Court of the Philippine Islands will deny the petition within a matter of hours or days set for execution of a probable sentence against petitioner. Manila is approximately 9,000 miles from Washington, D.C.; the fastest air mail delivery consumes approximately 7 days, and commercial cable transmission requires approximately 48 hours. It is therefore imperative that a considerable period of time elapse between an adverse decision of the Supreme Court of the Philippine Islands and the execution of a sentence of the military commission, in order to allow for the filing of a petition for a writ of certiorari in the Supreme Court of the United States." The document then detailed reasons why we thought that the questions raised were of sufficient importance to merit the court's consideration. It concluded by saying that "the trial of a General of a vanquished nation by the victor nation on a charge that presupposes that he is the guarantor of all actions of all of his troops . . . is a novel concept, and . . . any such trial by a purported agency of the United States of America, should be carefully scrutinized by the Courts, and *any attempt to avoid such judicial consideration should be circumvented.*" Strange language for a pleading addressed to the United States Supreme Court. But it was justified, and it proved effective.

In order to commence an action in the Philippine Supreme Court, a filing fee of twenty-four pesos (twelve dollars) was required. Upon his surrender, Yamashita's money had been taken from him, and, as prisoners, neither he nor his Japanese companions had been allowed to receive any cash. The six defense counsel were anxious to donate the small sum of two dollars apiece that would add up to the required amount, but, because of the fact that we were already being criticized for "carrying things too far," we were anxious to avoid, if possible, the technical objections that might be raised to our "going outside the scope of our appointment" and "financing the enemy as well as defending him."

Philippine law permits any litigant to apply for the waiver

of the filing fee upon his subscription to a pauper's oath. This appeared to be the logical course to follow, but defense counsel wondered whether General Yamashita would be willing to sign such an oath or whether it might involve "loss of face" in Japan. We broached the subject to the general.

As he did when the question of testifying in his own behalf arose, General Yamashita showed more concern over American sensibilities and customs than over those of the Japanese.

"He says he is not worried about 'loss of face' at home," said Hamamoto, "the Japanese people will understand. But he wants to know what the American people will think. He asks whether they won't think it cowardly for a man who is being tried by a military commission to run to the courts while the trial is on?"

We told Yamashita, through his interpreter, that fighting on to the last ditch and carrying legal appeals as far as possible was an old American custom. Indeed, the American people might think it cowardly for an accused man not to appeal to the courts. But, we added, the final decision must be his. Yamashita smiled—and signed.

Waiver of a filing fee *in forma pauperis* is not possible in the United States Supreme Court unless the appellant is an American citizen. But by the time that problem crystallized, Yamashita's character witnesses had arrived from Japan, and they contributed the required monies.

XXXI
"THE COURT DESIRES TO HEAR ARGUMENT"

ONE evening early in December, 1945, a fashionable Washington living-room was the scene of a gathering of bright intellectual souls. One of them was brilliant, waspish Felix Frankfurter, associate justice of the Supreme Court of the United States. A young lady who was seated across the room from him posed a question that was related to the topic that had been the subject of lively discussion for the past ten minutes: "Judge Frankfurter, what do you think of these war-crimes trials?"

The justice answered with his usual preciseness: "Had you told me yesterday that judicial ethics would prevent my answering such a question today, I would have thought it very strange," he said. "But today a most amazing thing happened, something that makes it impossible for me to talk about the subject. For today there came to my desk a petition filed by one of those accused of war crimes, actually a petition from a Japanese general, asking us to intervene in his case."

That same day the Manila newspapers carried the announcement of the clerk of the Supreme Court that our petition for an original writ of habeas corpus had arrived in Washington. The defense counsel were elated, although we feared that there was probably a note of sober truth behind the Associated Press reports from Washington that "it is believed by persons versed in such matters that the court's answer would be: 'No.' Yamashita's trial is considered here to be a purely military matter, with which the supreme court is in no way called upon to concern itself."

A few days later the Philippine court handed down the expected adverse decision. Our request for relief would not be granted, said the court, for various reasons, chief among which was the somewhat astounding proposition that for Filipino courts to interfere with acts of the United States Army "would be a violation of . . . faith" by the Philippine Commonwealth. We hastily completed our "petition for certiorari" and sent it off to Washington by air mail.

Before the papers arrived in Washington, General Yamashita was sentenced to hang. This was the moment we had feared. Would the execution be delayed until the Supreme Court had taken some action? Or might the court dispose of our original petition summarily, as prophesied by the "persons versed in such matters," before it had even received our more orthodox appeal? Perhaps, in view of the unsettled state of affairs, the court might be persuaded to order the execution postponed and thus save our having to rely on the "leniency" of General MacArthur. With this thought in mind, we immediately dispatched a cablegram to the clerk of the Supreme Court:

> GENERAL TOMOYUKI YAMASHITA SENTENCED TO HANG. IT IS FEARED SENTENCE WILL BE EXECUTED BEFORE COURT CAN ACT ON PETITION FOR WRIT HABEAS CORPUS NOW BEFORE COURT AND ON PETITION FOR WRIT CERTIORARI NOW EN ROUTE TO YOU. WE URGENTLY REQUEST COURT TO ORDER SECRETARY OF WAR TO STAY EXECUTION UNTIL COURT CAN ACT ON BOTH PETITIONS.

The immediate result of the cablegram was that the late Harlan F. Stone, then chief justice, communicated with the solicitor-general of the United States, who had already filed a brief in opposition to our first plea. Why should it be necessary that the Supreme Court order this execution stayed? Could not the Army do that itself? The solicitor-general would take the matter up with the War Department. Action followed. The high office of the secretary of war radioed to General MacArthur *suggesting* that he postpone further action until the court had had the opportunity to decide what to do about this case. General MacArthur forthwith radioed back to his superior, a point-blank refusal to stay the execution. He did not believe, he said, that the Supreme Court had any jurisdiction, and he proposed to proceed in the normal military manner.

General MacArthur's action constituted at once a verification of our worst fears and a justification for the unorthodox legal path that we had pursued. But even a supreme theater commander does not shake off a "suggestion" of the secretary of war so easily. Receipt of General MacArthur's reply was followed immediately by another message from the War Department, this time ordering him to stay the execution.

Defense counsel were jubilant. The Supreme Court had still not decided to grant us a hearing, but at least Yamashita's life was spared while the problem was under consideration.

A few days later the justices of the court adjourned for their annual Christmas recess. Before leaving the Supreme Court building, they added their judicial "stay of all further proceedings" to the record. Now even the secretary of war could not change his mind!

The court's Yule recess was to last for two weeks. But we were not to wait that long for an answer. On December 20, 1945, the judges interrupted their Christmas holiday to meet in "special term," only the third such event in the recent history of the tribunal. Now all our papers were before them. There was some discussion, and then Chief Justice Stone penned the order: "The Court desires to hear argument upon the questions presented . . . set down for oral argument on Monday, January 7th, next." To top it off, the chief justice again relayed a request to the War Department: Would they please see to it that some of the defense counsel were flown back to the United States so that the court might have the benefit of their argument?

Once again General MacArthur received a direct order from the secretary of war: three members of Yamashita's defense staff were to be given air transportation to Washington—No. 1 priority. Clarke, Sandberg, and I packed our bags.

XXXII
A GOODBYE

SINCE the time when he was removed from his cell in the high commissioner's residence and taken to the Luzon prisoner-of-war camp immediately after the sentence, General Yamashita had been held incommunicado. Even his lawyers had not been permitted to see him. We were angered and shocked by that ruling, but we were helpless. We finally appealed to General Styer in writing, but his chief-of-staff returned an adamant answer: "I am unaware of any essential reason justifying approval of the request made . . . to authorize members of the Defense Staff in the trial of the case of the U.S. against General Tomoyuki Yamashita to visit and confer with the latter at any time pending final disposition of the case. . . ."

After the stay of execution but before the Supreme Court decided to grant us a hearing, Sandberg and I drove to the prison camp to see Hamamoto, Muto, and Utsunomiya. We hoped that they might be able to get word of the stay of execution to General Yamashita, but they, too, were denied any access to him. Hamamoto told us of how the general had been stripped of his uniform and dressed in an old suit of Army "fatigues," and how all metal pieces and appliances were carefully kept from him. "They even took his glasses," said Hamamoto; "but I finally persuaded his guard to let him have them for a half-hour or so every day so he can read his book of Chinese poetry. They watch him while he reads, and then they take the glasses away." Then he added wistfully: "That's foolish. The 'old man' won't commit suicide—I know."

Sandberg asked Hamamoto whether Yamashita had said anything about the trial before they parted. "Just one thing," answered the interpreter. "He asked me: 'Do American generals really know everything that goes on in their commands?' I could not answer that."

"Neither can I," I said.

Then General Muto told us of Yamashita's last words to him. "When we parted," said Muto, "I asked him whether there was anything we could do for him in Japan. His answer was just like him—he said nothing about his wife or relatives or anything personal to him. He said: 'Muto, I told you just before we surrendered that I didn't see how I could go back to Japan. I had lost so many men. Once there were 250,000, now more than half were gone. But you remember I said it was my responsibility to see to it that those remaining men got home all right. Now it must be your responsibility. Take care of them, Muto—see that they get home. That is my last wish.' And then he added: 'That is my last command.' That was all."

Clarke, Sandberg, and I learned of our pending orders to fly to Washington, early Sunday morning, December 23. Now we had to see Yamashita. This was certainly an "essential reason." Colonel Clarke telephoned General Styer at his home and received the permission. That afternoon the three of us drove to the prison camp and, accompanied by the prison commandant and the indispensable Hamamoto, we were ushered through the barbed-wire inclosure that surrounded the pyramidal tent that had been Yamashita's home since December 7. He came out to greet us. Although clad only in a worn-out Army fatigue uniform and somewhat thinner in appearance, Yamashita still was the commanding general. He laughed, smiled, and joked as though we had conferred only the day before, but it was apparent that he was extremely happy to see us. We explained why we had been unable to visit him and how it happened that we had obtained permission today. In full detail we described the events of the last sixteen days, the various stays of execution, and the decision of the Supreme Court to grant a hearing on January 7. We explained again what he already understood—that the court hearing would not be like the Manila trial, that it would be concerned with law and not with the facts, that our chances of victory were slim, and that, if we won, the best we might hope for would be a new trial. We told him that it might be a long time before any results would be known—the court might act in a matter of days or it might take weeks. We spoke of other happenings—of the newspaper report that a petition signed by eighty-six thousand Japanese had been filed with General MacArthur in Tokyo requesting that his sentence be commuted to life-imprisonment or that he be given an opportunity to take his own life. Yamashita smiled, saying that he did not recognize the name of the man who had circulated the petition.

Then Yamashita became serious. He thanked us for what we were doing. We were giving up a great deal for him, he said, and it touched him deeply. We were going "all the way to America." We were giving up our Christmas.

"We'll have Christmas in the air," I said, pointing into the sky.

"Yes," he laughed, "Christmas in the air." Then he said: "I realize that the matters you will discuss before the American court do not concern my guilt or innocence. I know that there are important legal questions, judicial questions that should be decided, and some of them should be decided for the peace of the world." He paused while Hamamoto interpreted his words, and then the old smile crossed his face. "That is not to say," he added, "that I don't understand that I have a personal interest in the outcome."

The prison commandant coughed. It was time to leave. Goodbyes were said. "We'll see you again when we come back to Manila for the next trial," said Colonel Clarke. We shook hands, Hamamoto bowed, and we walked down the little hill to where our jeep was parked.

"The old man was very deeply touched," said Hamamoto, "he was almost ready to cry. He doesn't show it, but I know—I know."

As we climbed into our car, I looked back. Yamashita was still standing in front of his tent, his faded blue fatigues flapping in the tropical breeze. He raised his hand and waved.

Clarke, Sandberg, and I looked at one another. No one spoke. The jeep rattled down the gravel road, passed through the prison-camp gates, and rolled north on the highway to Manila.

Tomoyuki Yamashita—the little boy who watched the flowers grow in a garden in Shikoku, the Tiger of Malaya who conquered unassailable Singapore, the old man in the faded blue fatigues who stood in front of a tent and waited.

We were on our way home.

And so, I suppose, was he.

XXXIII
THE SUPREME COURT

YAMASHITA'S defense counsel, now reduced to three, left Manila airport on Christmas Day. On December 29, 1945, they disembarked at National Airport, Washington, D.C. They had flown halfway around the world, and yet I am afraid that, while this fantastic sphere revolved beneath them, their most absorbing occupation was sleep. It is perhaps well that this was so, because immediately upon arrival in the Capitol, they plunged into another grueling period of work.

We had but little more than a week in which to prepare a brief and argument for the Supreme Court. Research materials had been almost entirely lacking in the Philippines, and we were confronted with a mammoth task. But, much to our delight, we found that the co-operation and help which we received in Washington were directly proportionate to the opposition and obstacles that we had encountered in Manila. The Department of Justice, that was to represent the government (that is, the prosecution) before the Supreme Court, gave us office space, library facilities, stenographers, and mimeographing service. The Judge Advocate General donated the services of one of his most able international lawyers, Captain Wayne D. Williams, of Denver, who had been one of my classmates at Officer Candidate School. And the Supreme Court itself generously waived the requirement of printing of our brief and gave us additional time for argument. Although normally each side of a case is allotted one hour before the court, our debate consumed six hours and covered the better part of two days.

We divided the task of preparation of the brief and presentation of oral argument into three parts, falling under three basic headings. I undertook to present our first point, that the military commission was not the proper tribunal to try Yamashita. Like the use of "martial law" in a domestic situation, "the power of a commander in the field to dispense summary 'justice,' goes to the necessities of the prosecution of his mission, and not beyond. The justification for the use of a military commission has been the extreme necessity of the emergency situation. The historical procedures traditionally followed by Americans in their zeal to protect innocent persons accused of crime consume time and occasionally result in allowing the guilty to escape punishment. Such luxuries may not be indulged while the existence of the state is threatened. During wartime or during some domestic crises, martial law, quick justice, and absence of delay are essential. But the moment the emergency ends, the necessity for streamlined convictions ceases."

Colonel Clarke handled the second major contention, that there was not charged or proved or found here any violation of what had ever been held to be the laws of war. The laws of war were based on known standards, and they had never encompassed "command responsibility." "These standards are not to be taken lightly, for the case at bar involves more than a precedent to brandish before a defeated enemy. It involves a precedent which we must also be ready to apply within our own forces and to acknowledge in all cases of friend and foe alike."

Finally, Sandberg had the burden of maintaining that General Yamashita had been denied the fundamental right of a fair trial. His was the task of detailing what we claimed were the commission's violations of congressional laws and of demonstrating how the violations had damaged our cause. This, we agreed, was our strongest point. "The Anglo-Saxon nations take pride in their institutions of justice and in their guaranties of civil rights. It may seem to some that these fundamental guaranties were never intended for the benefit of a vanquished enemy general. But does not a defeated enemy represent that very example of a besieged and helpless human being caught in the net of overwhelming state power whom it was the impulse of the Bill of Rights to protect? The petitioner was denied the right to confront the witnesses against him and to cross-examine them. There was transcribed on the judicial records of the United States and published before the world the testimony of unsupported conclusions, opinions, rumors, and gossip, and the petitioner was judged and convicted thereon. This was not a trial as Americans know the term, and it should not be allowed to stand."

The government brief met ours fairly solidly on all points. The military commission, it said, was properly appointed because the war was not yet over; the charge and proof should be held to constitute a violation of the law of war because the principle of command responsibility had not been unknown in civil suits for damages and in domestic manslaughter cases; and the admission of the objectionable evidence was not a "jurisdictional" question, and, in any event, the acts of Congress which we had cited did not apply to this type of military commission. In addition, the government asserted that the Supreme Court should not interfere in this case, because the hanging of a war criminal was a "political act" of the executive and as such was none of the court's business.

Eventually it was noon on January 7, 1946. In the majestic chamber of the Supreme Court building in Washington sat Yamashita's lawyers, impatiently awaiting the moment when the exalted justices were to take their places on the highest bench in the land. Across a narrow aisle to our right sat the two frock-coated lawyers who were to represent the government—the solicitor-general of the United States, Mr. J. Howard McGrath, and the assistant solicitor, Mr. Harold Judson.

I believe that Clarke and Sandberg were as nervous as I

was. None of us had ever argued orally before the Supreme Court before. All but a very small percentage of the lawyers in the United States live through their professional lives without having the opportunity to represent a client before this bench. Now a fateful accident of Army life had brought us here. It was not only that it was the Supreme Court—but it was this particular 1946 Court. We had assumed that there was little purpose in preparing formal argument because we realized that our allotted time, and more, would be spent in answering the probing and keenly analytical questions that these searching minds would concoct; for this was probably as brilliant a Supreme Court as any in American history.

I glanced about the room. Every seat was filled. There were lawyers, members of the Department of Justice, officers from our own Judge Advocate's Department, throngs of spectators—the curious who had been attracted by the newspaper headlines: "Yamashita before Highest Court Today."

Yamashita before the court? Only a few days before, a news reporter actually had telephoned to ask us where Yamashita was staying in Washington!

Ten thousand miles away, underneath the world, was the Island of Luzon—and midnight. There, in his prison tent, General Yamashita was waiting, as he had already waited for many days and nights, waiting for the guard who might come at any moment and who, he supposed, would simply look at him and say: "Now." But was Yamashita really there? "For the first time in recorded history, a defeated general stands before the highest court of the mighty nation that has conquered him." Perhaps the newspapers were right. Perhaps Yamashita was here.

On the huge clock above the bench the minute hand jumped—it now pointed straight up and completely obscured the hour hand. The velvet curtains behind the bench parted. The clerk solemnly arose and intoned: "The Honorable, the Chief Justice and the Associate Justices of the Supreme

Court of the United States! Oyez! Oyez! Oyez! All persons having business before the Honorable, the Supreme Court of the United States, are admonished to draw near and give their attention, for the Court is now sitting! God save the United States and this Honorable Court."

In the order of their seniority, the black-robed judges entered the chamber and took their seats. First there was the Chief Justice, Harlan Fiske Stone, and following him came Associate Justices Black, Frankfurter, Douglas, Murphy, Rutledge, and Burton. Justice Reed was absent, confined to his home with a cold, and Mr. Justice Jackson was in far-off Nuremberg, where he was occupied with war-crimes problems of his own.

Mr. Cropley, the clerk, was reading: "Next Case: In the Matter of the Application of General Tomoyuki Yamashita. . . ."

As first counsel to address the court, I arose. I faced the judges. It was the final culmination of the lawyer's struggle. I was before the Supreme Court of the United States.

"In the Matter of the Application of General Tomoyuki Yamashita. . . ." Perhaps he *was* here before this court. And not only Yamashita, but all the thousands of Japanese soldiers and American and German and Russian and English soldiers who were victims of the military system, victims of man's still rampant cruelty and greed, victims of humanity's failure to become civilized. Perhaps they all were here before the world's highest apotheosis of reason and logic, this most carefully wrought human machine designed to aid man's striving for intelligence and domestic peace.

Chief Justice Stone peered over the bench. His kindly eyes seemed to search into the crannies of my brain. He nodded.

"May it please the Court—"

XXXIV
OPINIONS

AS YAMASHITA'S three defenders had anticipated, the oral argument before the Supreme Court proved to be a question-and-answer exercise. Attempting to gauge a judge's "slant" by the type of question he put, we guessed that we would lose the case and that Justices Murphy, Rutledge, and Black would dissent. We were wrong only about Black. Justice Frankfurter led in posing questions that seemed to be designed to aid the government's cause. I had studied under Frankfurter at Harvard Law School and had become somewhat acquainted with his particular mode of logical thinking and his extremely practical judicial philosophy. His questions indicated to me that he believed that the court must uphold Yamashita's conviction and that he was concerned with finding logical bases for that decision which might provide common ground on which the greatest possible number of his colleagues would agree.

Four weeks elapsed between the argument and February 4, 1946, when the court handed down its decision. Considering the unique measures that the court had taken to insure an early hearing and considering, also, the fact that during the middle two weeks of that period the court had been recessed for the purpose of preparing opinions, we were somewhat surprised that so much time had elapsed. Perhaps the judges were having trouble with this case?

The young lawyers in the Department of Justice had a ready answer to the riddle. Because of the effect that the decision would have on the country, they said, the chief justice was anxious that it be unanimous. Of course, the conviction would be upheld, and it would "look bad" if there were to be any dissenting opinion. The delay, they thought, was the result of Chief Justice Stone's difficulty in bringing one or two of his brethren into line.

That conjecture may have been accurate; for, after Chief Justice Stone had read the opinion of the court on that fateful Monday morning, Mr. Justice Murphy and Mr. Justice Rutledge read their dissenting opinions in tones so bitter and in language so sharp that it was readily apparent to all listeners that even more acrimonious expression must have marked the debate behind the scenes. Justice Rutledge commenced his statement by saying: "Not with ease does one find his views at odds with the Court's in a matter of this character and gravity. Only the most deeply felt convictions could force one to differ. That reason alone leads me to do so now, *against strong considerations for withholding dissent*"—and, as he uttered the last clause, Rutledge carefully turned and nodded in the chief justice's direction.

The opinion of the court and the two dissenting opinions deserve careful analysis, but not in a book of this type. Those three historic documents are attached as an appendix to this volume. They are recommended reading. It suffices here simply to describe the varying views and, where helpful, to quote revealing phrases.

Chief Justice Stone, speaking for the majority, read an opinion that appeared to be a patchwork of ideas and statements, pieced together to satisfy the divergent views of men who were seeking to find "good" reasons for a politically expedient result. If Stone's language seems labored, routine, and pedestrian, when compared with the razor-edged analysis of Rutledge and the literary sweep of Murphy, it must be remembered that the dissenters spoke for themselves alone, whereas the chief justice was constrained to convey the rationalizations of five men besides himself.

The majority opinion began by emphasizing the rule that, on the application for a writ of habeas corpus, the court was "not concerned with the guilt or innocence" of General Yamashita. It could consider "only the lawful power of the Commission" to try him for the offense charged. Military tribunals, said the chief justice, "are not courts whose rulings and judgments are made subject to review by this Court," and there could be no relief here "merely because they have made a wrong decision on disputed facts." Then there followed the significant sentence on which Yamashita's defense counsel would have to rest whatever hope might remain for their client: "Correction of their [the military commission's] errors of decision is not for the courts but for the military authorities which are alone authorized to review their decisions."

Chief Justice Stone next proceeded to dispose of the solicitor-general's contention that the matter of dealing with an accused war criminal was a political act of the executive, with which the courts could not interfere. Citing the saboteurs' case, Stone reaffirmed the right of an accused "to make a defense" and added that "the Executive branch of the Government could not . . . withdraw from the courts the duty and power to make such inquiry into the authority of the commission as may be made by habeas corpus."

That was our only victory. The opinion then proceeded to demolish our contentions, one by one. Military commissions might be used to try war crimes even after the cessation of hostilities "so long as a state of war exists" and "at least until peace has been officially recognized by treaty or proclamation of the political branch of the Government." The charge sufficiently stated a violation of the laws of war, because it described a failure to control troops as "*permitting* them to commit" atrocities, and therefore the commission had the right to hear the case (that is, it had "jurisdiction") and to determine whether or not Yamashita had taken such measures as were within his power to control his men. In this connection, Chief Justice Stone took care to point out:

"We do not here appraise the evidence on which petitioner

was convicted. We do not consider what measures, if any, petitioner took to prevent the commission, by the troops under his command, of the plain violations of the law of war detailed in the bill of particulars, or whether such measures as he may have taken were appropriate and sufficient to discharge the duty imposed upon him. These are questions within the peculiar competence of the military officers composing the commission and were for it to decide."

The opinion disposed of the alleged violation of the Geneva Convention by holding that the protections afforded by that treaty run only to prisoners of war who are tried by the captor for offenses they committed *while* they were prisoners and not for war crimes and other violations that occurred *before* their surrender.

The majority apparently experienced its greatest difficulty in dealing with our contention that the admission of questionable evidence violated the acts of Congress and the Fifth Amendment to the United States Constitution. The court stated that neither the twenty-fifth nor the thirty-eighth Article of War applied to the trial of an enemy combatant as a war criminal. To be sure, there is only *one kind* of military commission, but it can try *two* classes of persons, and Congress, said Stone somewhat obscurely, never intended the protections it imposed in those laws to apply to one of those classes.

The Fifth Amendment dictates that "no *person*" is to be deprived of his life, his liberty, or his property "without due process of law"—a stumbling block that produced the most confusing paragraph in the entire opinion. The majority stepped around the question by reiterating that "the Commission's rulings on evidence and the mode of conducting these proceedings . . . are not reviewable by the Courts, but only by the reviewing military authorities." But apparently the justices were worried about the danger of allowing military tribunals to ride roughshod over fundamental legal rights in other cases—perhaps in trials of American citizens who might face similar charges and who might encounter the same unfair treatment. And so they carefully added: "It is unnecessary to consider what, in other situations, the Fifth Amendment might require, and as to that no intimation one way or the other is to be implied. Nothing we have said is to be taken as indicating any opinion on the question of the wisdom of considering such evidence."

The question of the guaranties of the Fifth Amendment furnished the catapult from which Mr. Justice Murphy launched his powerful dissenting opinion. As soon as the Chief Justice had completed his reading of the majority decision, Murphy spoke, his voice ringing with indignation. "The significance of the issue facing the Court today cannot be overemphasized," he began. "The grave issue raised by this case is whether a military commission . . . may disregard the procedural rights of an accused person as guaranteed by the Constitution, especially by the due process clause of the Fifth Amendment."

"The answer," continued Justice Murphy, "is plain. The Fifth Amendment guarantee of due process of law applies to 'any person' who is accused of a crime by the Federal Government or any of its agencies. No exception is made as to those who are accused of war crimes or as to those who possess the status of an enemy belligerent. Indeed, such an exception would be contrary to the whole philosophy of human rights which makes the Constitution the great living document that it is. The immutable rights of the individual, including those secured by the due process clause of the Fifth Amendment, belong not alone to the members of those nations that excel on the battlefield or that subscribe to the democratic ideology. They belong to every person in the world, victor or vanquished, whatever may be his race, color, or beliefs. They rise above any status of belligerency or outlawry. They survive any popular passion or frenzy of the moment. No court or legislature or executive, not even the mightiest army in the world, can ever destroy them. Such is the universal and indestructible nature of the rights which the due process clause of the Fifth Amendment recognizes and protects when life or liberty is threatened by virtue of the authority of the United States.

"The existence of these rights, unfortunately, is not always respected. They are often trampled under by those who are motivated by hatred, aggression, or fear. But in this nation individual rights are recognized and protected, at least in regard to governmental action. They cannot be ignored by any branch of the government, even the military, except under the most extreme and urgent circumstances.

"The failure of the military commission to obey the dictates of the due process requirements of the Fifth Amendment is apparent in this case. The petitioner was the commander of an army totally destroyed by the superior power of this nation. While under heavy and destructive attack by our forces, his troops committed many brutal atrocities and other high crimes. Hostilities ceased, and he voluntarily surrendered. At that point he was entitled, as an individual protected by the due process clause of the Fifth Amendment, to be treated fairly and justly according to the accepted rules of law and procedure. He was also entitled to a fair trial as to any alleged crimes and to be free from charges of legally unrecognized crimes that would serve only to permit his accusers to satisfy their desires for revenge."

Justice Murphy then described the appointment of the American military commission to sit on soil that was under United States sovereignty. "No military necessity or other emergency demanded the suspension of the safeguards of due process," he said scornfully. "Yet petitioner was rushed to trial under an improper charge, given insufficient time to prepare an adequate defense, deprived of the benefits of some of the most elementary rules of evidence, and summarily sentenced to be hanged. In all this needless and unseemly haste there was no serious attempt to charge or to prove that he committed a recognized violation of the laws of war. He was not charged with personally participating in the acts of atrocity or with ordering or condoning their commission. Not even knowledge of these crimes was attributed to him. It was simply alleged that he unlawfully disregarded and failed to discharge his duty as commander to control the operations of the members of his command, permitting them to commit the acts of atrocity. The recorded annals of warfare and the established principles of international law afford not the slightest precedent for such a charge. This indictment in effect permitted the military commission to make the crime whatever it willed, dependent upon its biased view as to petitioner's duties and his disregard thereof, a practice reminiscent of that pursued in certain less respected nations in recent years.

"In my opinion, such a procedure is unworthy of the traditions of our people or of the immense sacrifices that they have made to advance the common ideals of mankind. The high feelings of the moment doubtless will be satisfied. But in the sober afterglow will come the realization of the boundless and dangerous implications of the procedure sanctioned today. No one in a position of command in an army, from sergeant to general, can escape those implications. Indeed, the fate of some future president of the United States and his chiefs of staff and military advisers may well have been sealed by this decision. But even more significant will be the hatred and ill-will growing out of the application of this unprecedented procedure. That has been the inevitable effect of every method of punishment disregarding the element of personal culpability. The effect in this instance, unfortunately, will be magnified infinitely for here we are dealing with the rights of man on an international level. To subject an enemy belligerent to an unfair trial, to charge him with an unrecognized crime, or to vent on him our retributive emotions only antagonizes the enemy nation and hinders the reconciliation necessary to a peaceful world."

Prior to his appointment as a justice of the Supreme Court, Frank Murphy had been governor-general of the Philippine Islands. He understood and loved the Filipino people, and he was aware of their long struggle for independence. His next words bore the imprimatur of the man who knew Philippine history: "That there were brutal atrocities inflicted upon the helpless Filipino people, to whom tyranny is no stranger," he said, ". . . is undeniable. . . . That just punishment should be meted out to all those responsible . . . is also beyond dispute. But these factors . . . do not justify the abandonment of our devotion to justice in dealing with a fallen enemy commander. To conclude otherwise is to admit that the enemy has lost the battle but has destroyed our ideals."

Listeners in the crowded courtroom realized by this time that not only judicial history but English literature was in the making. The justice read on: "War breeds atrocities. From the earliest conflicts of recorded history to the global struggles of modern times, inhumanities, lust and pillage have been the inevitable by-products of man's resort to force and arms. Unfortunately, such despicable acts have a dangerous tendency to call forth primitive impulses of vengeance and retaliation among the victimized peoples. The satisfaction of such impulses in turn breeds resentment and fresh tension. Thus does the spiral of cruelty and hatred grow.

"If we are ever to develop an orderly international community based upon a recognition of human dignity it is of the utmost importance that the necessary punishment of those guilty of atrocities be as free as possible from the ugly stigma of revenge and vindictiveness. Justice must be tempered by compassion rather than by vengeance. In this, the first case involving this momentous problem ever to reach this

Court, our responsibility is both lofty and difficult. We must insist, within the confines of our proper jurisdiction, that the highest standards of justice be applied in this trial of an enemy commander conducted under the authority of the United States. Otherwise stark retribution will be free to masquerade in a cloak of false legalism. And the hatred and cynicism engendered by that retribution will supplant the great ideals to which this nation is dedicated."

Justice Murphy then launched into an analysis of the question of whether General Yamashita had been convicted of any crime. After stating that he found "it impossible to agree that the charge . . . stated a recognized violation of the laws of war," the dissenter quoted at length from official United States Army reports that described the Japanese disorganization after the American invasion of Luzon. He cited the report of the chief-of-staff to the secretary of war, which said: "Yamashita's inability to cope with General MacArthur's swift moves, the guerrillas, and General Kenney's aircraft combined to place the Japanese in an impossible situation," forcing a "piecemeal commitment" of enemy troops, and he pointed out that it was at this time and place that most of the atrocities occurred. He then referred to the fact that the charge and the bills of particulars failed to allege any orders or knowledge on the part of Yamashita and that "the findings of the military commission bear out this absence of any direct personal charge." Finally, in a masterful summary, Murphy paraphrased the prosecution's real case: "In other words, read against the background of military events in the Philippines subsequent to October 9, 1944, these charges amount to this: 'We, the victorious American forces, have done everything possible to destroy and disorganize your lines of communication, your effective control of your personnel, your ability to wage war. In those respects we have succeeded. We have defeated and crushed your forces. And now we charge and condemn you for having been inefficient in maintaining control of your troops during the period when we were so effectively besieging and eliminating your forces and blocking your ability to maintain effective control. Many terrible atrocities were committed by your disorganized troops. Because these atrocities were so widespread we will not bother to charge or prove that you committed, ordered or condoned any of them. We will assume that they must have resulted from your inefficiency and negligence as a commander. In short, we charge you with the crime of inefficiency in controlling your troops. We will judge the discharge of your duties by the disorganization which we ourselves created in large part. Our standards of judgment are whatever we wish to make them.'

"Nothing in all history or in international law, at least as far as I am aware, justifies such a charge against a fallen commander of a defeated force. To use the very inefficiency and disorganization created by the victorious forces as the primary basis for condemning officers of the defeated armies bears no resemblance to justice or to military reality."

Nor was it remarkable that international law had failed to define the duties of an army commander who was under constant assault and that it imposed no liability under such circumstances for failure to meet the ordinary command responsibilities. "The omission is understandable," said Murphy. "Duties as well as the ability to control troops vary according to the nature and intensity of the particular battle. To find an unlawful deviation from duty under battle conditions requires difficult and speculative calculations. Such calculations become highly untrustworthy when they are made by the victor in relation to the actions of a vanquished commander. Objective and realistic norms of conduct are then extremely unlikely to be used in forming a judgment as to deviations from duty. The probability that vengeance will form the major part of the victor's judgment is an unfortunate but inescapable fact. So great is that probability that international law refuses to recognize such a judgment as a basis for a war crime, however fair the judgment may be in a particular instance. It is this consideration that undermines the charge against the petitioner in this case. The indictment permits, indeed compels, the military commission of a victorious nation to sit in judgment upon the military strategy and actions of the defeated enemy and to use its conclusions to determine the criminal liability of an enemy commander. Life and liberty are made to depend upon the biased will of the victor rather than upon objective standards of conduct."

In closing, Justice Murphy reviewed the high lights of the Manila trial—it had "proceeded with great dispatch without allowing the defense time to prepare an adequate case," Yamashita's rights under the Fifth Amendment had been "grossly and openly violated without any justification." And all this had been done "without any thorough investigation and prosecution of those immediately responsible for the atrocities, out of which might have come some proof or indication of personal culpability on petitioner's part. Instead the loose charge was made that great numbers of atrocities had been committed and that petitioner was the commanding officer; hence he must have been guilty of disregard of duty. Under that charge the commission was free to establish whatever standard of duty on petitioner's part that it desired. By this flexible method a victorious nation may convict and execute any or all leaders of a vanquished foe, depending upon the prevailing degree of vengeance and the absence of any objective judicial review."

What might be the implications of all this? The man of vision could see them. Mr. Justice Murphy concluded: "At a time like this when emotions are understandably high it is difficult to adopt a dispassionate attitude toward a case of this nature. Yet now is precisely the time when that attitude is most essential. While peoples in other lands may not share our beliefs as to due process and the dignity of the individual, we are not free to give effect to our emotions in reckless disregard of the rights of others. We live under the Constitution, which is the embodiment of all the high hopes and aspirations of the new world and which is applicable in both war and peace. We must act accordingly. Indeed, an uncurbed spirit of revenge and retribution, masked in formal legal procedure for purposes of dealing with a fallen enemy commander, can do more lasting harm than all of the atrocities giving rise to that spirit. The people's faith in the fairness and objectiveness of the law can be seriously undercut by that spirit. The fires of nationalism can be further kindled. And the hearts of all mankind can be embittered and filled with hatred, leaving forlorn and impoverished the noble ideal of malice toward none and charity to all. These are the reasons that lead me to dissent in these terms."

Mr. Justice Rutledge's dissenting opinion carried on where Murphy's had left off. Adopting the latter's conclusions with respect to the insufficiency of the charge and lack of substance of the "crime," Rutledge devoted thirty-two pages to an analysis of our other contentions. But he began with some cogent general observations. "More is at stake than General Yamashita's fate," he said. "There could be no possible sympathy for him if he is guilty of the atrocities for which his death is sought. But there can be and should be justice administered according to law. In this stage of war's aftermath it is too early for Lincoln's great spirit, best lighted in the Second Inaugural, to have wide hold for the treatment of foes. It is not too early, it is never too early, for the nation steadfastly to follow its great constitutional traditions, none older or more universally protective against unbridled power than due process of law in the trial and punishment of men, that is, of all men, whether citizens, aliens, alien enemies or enemy belligerents. It can become too late.

"This long-held attachment marks the great divide between our enemies and ourselves. Theirs was a philosophy of universal force. Ours is one of universal law, albeit imperfectly made flesh of our system and so dwelling among us. Every departure weakens the tradition, whether it touches the high or the low, the powerful or the weak, the triumphant or the conquered. If we need not or cannot be magnanimous, we can keep our own law on the plane from which it has not descended hitherto and to which the defeated foes' never rose."

Rutledge's basic concern was with the fact that General Yamashita had been denied "the fair trial our Constitution and laws command." So flagrant were the commission's "departures," that, according to the justice, it was "without jurisdiction from the beginning," and if it acquired jurisdiction, then "its power to proceed was lost in the course of what was done before and during the trial."

Damning the commission by quoting its own language, Justice Rutledge described those departures from "our time-tested road signs." "It is not in our tradition," he said, "for anyone to be charged with crime which is defined after his conduct, alleged to be criminal, has taken place; or in language not sufficient to inform him of the nature of the offense or to enable him to make defense. Mass guilt we do not impute to individuals, perhaps in any case but certainly in none where the person is not charged or shown actively to have participated in or knowingly to have failed in taking action to prevent the wrongs done by others, having both the duty and the power to do so.

"It is outside our basic scheme to condemn men without giving reasonable opportunity for preparing defense; in capital or other serious crimes to convict on 'official documents. . . ; affidavits; . . . documents or translations thereof; diaries . . . , photographs, motion picture films, and . . . newspapers' or on hearsay, once, twice or thrice removed, more particularly when the documentary evidence or some of it is prepared *ex parte* by the prosecuting authority and includes not only opinion but conclusions of guilt. Nor in such cases do we deny the rights of confrontation of witnesses and cross-examination.

"Our tradition does not allow conviction by tribunals both authorized and bound by the instrument of their creation to receive and consider evidence which is expressly excluded by Act of Congress or by treaty obligation; nor is it in accord with our basic concepts to make the tribunal, specially constituted for the particular trial, regardless of those prohibitions the sole and exclusive judge of the credibility, probative value and admissibility of whatever may be tendered as evidence. . . .

"One basic protection of our system and one only, petitioner has had. He has been represented by able counsel, officers of the army he fought. Their difficult assignment has been done with extraordinary fidelity, not only to the accused, but to their high conception of military justice, always to be administered in subordination to the Constitution and consistent Acts of Congress and treaties. But, as will appear, even this conceded shield was taken away in much of its value, by denial of reasonable opportunity for them to perform their function."

What about the holding of the majority that there was significance in the fact that we were technically still at war because peace had not been finally negotiated or declared? Rutledge admitted the fact, "but," he added, "there is no longer the danger which always exists before surrender and armistice. Military necessity does not demand the same measures. The nation may be more secure now than at any time after peace is officially concluded." He agreed with us that these facts were the basis for distinguishing this from the saboteurs' case, and he said: "Enemy aliens, including belligerents, need the attenuated protections our system extends to them more now than before hostilities ceased or than they may after a treaty of peace is signed." There was no question here "of what the military might have done in a field of combat. There the maxim about the law becoming silent in the noise of arms applies. The purpose of battle is to kill. But it does not follow that this would justify killing by trial after capture or surrender, without compliance with laws or treaties made to apply in such cases, whether trial is before or after hostilities end."

Justice Rutledge now turned his attention to the MacArthur directive on the basis of which the commission received into evidence "every conceivable kind of statement, rumor, report, at first, second, third or further hand . . . and one 'propaganda' film." After analyzing the terms of the directive, the dissenter summarized it in the following scathing terms: "A more complete abrogation of customary safeguards relating to the proof, whether in the usual rules of evidence or any reasonable substitute and whether for use in the trial of crime in the civil courts or military tribunals, hardly could have been made. So far as the admissibility and probative value of evidence was concerned, the directive made the commission a law unto itself.

"It acted accordingly."

There then followed a careful dissection of the commission's findings and the exposure of the mental confusion that they revealed. "This vagueness, if not vacuity, in the findings runs throughout the proceedings, from the charge itself through the proof and the findings, to the conclusion," Rutledge declared.

The justice attacked at length the prejudicial use of affidavits in evidence, the proof of certain items by document alone, the denial of time for preparation of an adequate defense. "Insufficient as this recital is to give a fair impression of what was done," he said, "it is enough to show that this was no trial in the traditions of the common law and the Constitution."

The reasoning of his brethren on the court in arriving at

what he termed their "strained construction" of the Articles of War was the object of Rutledge's next attack. After thoroughly reviewing the congressional history of those statutes, the justice scoffed at the "suggestion that there are two types of military commission, one bound by the procedural provisions of the Articles, the other wholly free from their restraints or, as the Court strangely puts the matter, that there is only one kind of commission, but that it is bound or not bound by the Articles applicable in terms, depending upon who is being tried and for what offense; for that very difference makes the difference between one and two."

Likewise, Rutledge was unable to find any historical or other basis for the majority's cavalier dismissal of the contention that the Geneva Convention covered Yamashita's trial. Not only did the language of the whole treaty support this view, but reasons of policy also dictated its acceptance. The construction that the defense had urged, said Rutledge, "is required for the security of our own soldiers, taken prisoner, as much as for that of prisoners we take. And the opposite one leaves prisoners of war open to any form of trial and punishment for offenses against the law of war their captors may wish to use, while safeguarding them, to the extent of the treaty limitations, in cases of disciplinary offense. This, in many instances, would be to make the treaty strain at a gnat and swallow the camel. . . .

"Furthermore the premise overlooks all the realities of the situation. Japan is a defeated power, having surrendered, if not unconditionally, then under the most severe conditions. Her territory is occupied by American military forces. She is scarcely in a position to bargain with us or to assert her rights. Nor can her nationals. She no longer holds American prisoners of war. Certainly, if there was the need of an independent neutral to protect her nationals during the war, there is more now."

Finally, Justice Rutledge, like Justice Murphy, had a few

words to say about the Fifth Amendment. He expressed himself as being "completely unable to accept or to understand the Court's ruling concerning the applicability of the due process clause of the Fifth Amendment to this case. Not heretofore has it been held that any human being is beyond its universally protecting spread in the guaranty of a fair trial in the most fundamental sense. That door is dangerous to open. I will have no part in opening it. For once it is ajar, even for enemy belligerents, it can be pushed back wider for others, perhaps ultimately for all. . . .

"I cannot accept the view that anywhere in our system resides or lurks a power so unrestrained to deal with any human being through any process of trial. What military agencies or authorities may do with our enemies in battle or invasion, apart from proceedings in the nature of trial and some semblance of judicial action, is beside the point. Nor has any human being heretofore been held to be wholly beyond elementary procedural protection by the Fifth Amendment. I cannot consent to even implied departure from the great absolute.

"It was a great patriot who said: 'He that would make his own liberty secure must guard even his enemy from oppression; for if he violates this duty he establishes a precedent that will reach himself.' "

XXXV

A GENERAL AND A PRESIDENT AND A HANGING

ALTHOUGH General Yamashita's defense counsel may have believed that the two dissenting opinions had more merit than the majority opinion, the latter was *the decision* of the Supreme Court in the case. It finally and effectively closed the door on any possibility of legal intervention. The defenders were compelled now to base their remaining hope on two pronouncements of the majority—first, the statement that "on application for habeas corpus we are not concerned with the guilt or innocence of the petitioners . . . we consider here only the lawful power of the commission to try the petitioner . . ." and, second, the suggestion that, since "the military tribunals have lawful authority to hear, decide and condemn, their action is not subject to judicial review merely because they have made a wrong decision on disputed facts . . . correction of their errors of decision is not for the courts but for the military authorities which are alone authorized to review their decisions." That second statement had received further amplification by Chief Justice Stone. In discussing the question of whether or not the charge stated a violation of the laws of war, he had been careful to say: "We do not here appraise the evidence on which petitioner was convicted," and, while considering the conduct of the trial, he had repeated: "We hold that the Commission's rulings on evidence and on the mode of conducting these proceedings against petitioner are not reviewable by the courts, but only by the reviewing military authorities."

Who were the "reviewing military authorities"? Before General Yamashita's sentence could be carried into effect, the record had to be reviewed and the sentence approved by General MacArthur. The stay of execution had operated to postpone that action. Although defense counsel did not anticipate any leniency from the Pacific commander-in-chief (we were convinced by his actions throughout the trial that his mind was set on execution), we had, immediately after Yamashita's sentence, composed a "recommendation for clemency" and attached it to the record for review. In it we had referred to the weakness of the commission's findings and to the unreliability of the "evidence" on which they were based. We had concluded: "This is the first time in the history of the modern world that a commanding officer has been held criminally liable for acts committed by his troops. It is the first time in modern history that any man has been held criminally liable for acts which according to the conclusion of the commission do not involve criminal intent or even gross negligence. The commission therefore by its findings created a new crime. The accused could not have known, nor could a sage have predicted, that at some time in the future a military commission would decree acts which involved no criminal intent or gross negligence to be a crime, and it is unjust, therefore, that the punishment for that crime should be the supreme penalty."

Now, we felt, there was additional reason for commutation of the sentence. In the first place, the Supreme Court was divided, and the very fact that there were dissenting opinions is often, in itself, held to constitute reason for the substitution of life-imprisonment for the death penalty. But more important was the nature of the opinions, both majority and minority. Eight justices of the United States Supreme Court had studied this matter. None of them had held that the trial had been properly conducted. Six of them had said that they had no power to inquire into that matter or into the question of Yamashita's guilt. The other two had maintained that they *could* examine the entire record, and they had both vehemently condemned the trial and its result. Surely—said people who had never been in the Pacific Theater—surely, General MacArthur would take the hint. Surely, he would be moved by Justice Murphy's logic and by Justice Rutledge's devastating analysis of the bitter farce that had been enacted in Manila.

But General MacArthur was apparently not interested in what the justices of the United States Supreme Court might have said. He affirmed Yamashita's sentence before he had even had a chance to receive the opinions.

Justice Rutledge had finished his remarks at about half-past three on the afternoon of February 4. Representatives of the Judge Advocate General's Department then obtained copies of the opinions and rushed them to a photostat machine. General MacArthur was notified by radio that the Supreme Court had refused to issue a writ of habeas corpus, and he was informed that copies of the opinions would be sent to him by air, to be delivered within a few days. On the following day, the photostatic copies of the majority decision and the two dissenting opinions were ready and were dispatched to Tokyo. But before they had even left the United States, General MacArthur had issued a statement to the press in which he disclosed that he had ordered that General Yamashita be hanged "stripped of uniform, decorations, and other appurtenances signifying membership in the military profession."

The opening remarks of the MacArthur announcement reveal just how "impartial" his review must have been. "It is not easy for me to pass judgment upon a defeated adversary in a major campaign," he began. "I have reviewed the proceedings in vain search for some mitigating circumstances on his behalf. I can find none."

The statement was premised on a lofty conception of what

some professional soldiers like to regard as their honorable code. "This officer," said General MacArthur, "has failed his duty to his troops, to his country, to his enemy and to mankind. He has failed utterly his soldier's faith. The transgressions ... are a stain upon civilization and constitute a memory of shame and dishonor that can never be forgotten."

General Yamashita's record, said MacArthur, was a "blot on the military profession," and, he added, "revolting as this may be in itself, it pales before the sinister and far-reaching implication thereby attached to the profession of arms. The soldier, be he friend or foe, is charged with the protection of the weak and unarmed. . . . When he violates this sacred trust, he not only profanes his entire cult but threatens the very fabric of international society."

To say that a soldier in a war of blockade and bomb—atomic and otherwise—is "charged with protection of the weak and unarmed" is somewhat less than realistic. But there were more serious errors in General MacArthur's declaration. Had he waited until he received the opinions of the Supreme Court justices, he might have avoided two of the errors. The first was the bald announcement that "no new or retroactive principles of law, either national or international, are involved. The case is founded upon basic fundamentals and practice as immutable and as standardized as the most matured and irrefragable of social codes." And the second was: "The proceedings were guided by that primary rationale of all judicial purpose—to ascertain the full truth unshackled by any artificialities of narrow method or technical arbitrariness. The results are beyond challenge."

Beyond challenge! Two Supreme Court justices had just written forty-five pages of American history, challenging the proceedings and the results. And long after the deeds of General MacArthur or General Yamashita or any other military commander are forgotten, the words of Mr. Justice Murphy's and Mr. Justice Rutledge's "challenge" will be remembered, remembered and recited by men, women, and children the world over, who will know that there can be no real victory without justice and no justice without law.

General MacArthur had described our attempts to get a fair trial for General Yamashita as "artificialities of narrow method" and "technical arbitrariness." Five days later, the two dissenting justices had an opportunity to explain the implications of MacArthur's words. While we were in Washington, Japanese General Homma had been tried, convicted, and sentenced by another military commission in Manila for responsibility for the Bataan "death march" and other 1942 atrocities. Although the case against Homma seemed to be considerably stronger than that against Yamashita, it had apparently been conducted in the same highhanded and prejudicial manner, and Homma's defense counsel had followed our path to the Supreme Court. The court, without opinion, refused to hear Homma's plea. After all, the issues had been decided in our case. But once again Justices Murphy and Rutledge dissented. "It may well be," wrote Murphy, "that the evidence of his [Homma's] guilt under the law of war is more direct and clear than in the case of General Yamashita, though this could be determined only by an examination of the evidence such as we have had no opportunity to make. But neither clearer proof of guilt nor the acts of atrocity of the Japanese troops could excuse the undue haste with which the trial was conducted or the promulgation of a directive containing such obviously unconstitutional provisions. . . . To try the petitioner in a setting of reason and calm, to issue and use constitutional directives and to obey the dictates of a fair trial are not impossible tasks. Hasty, revengeful action is not the American way. All those who act by virtue of the authority of the United States are bound to respect the principles of justice codified in our Constitution. Those principles which were established after so many centuries of struggle, can scarcely be dismissed [and here Justice Murphy used the words of MacArthur] as narrow artificialities or arbitrary technicalities. They are the very life blood of our civilization."

"Today," Justice Murphy concluded, "the lives of Yamashita and Homma, leaders of enemy forces vanquished in the field of battle, are taken without regard to due process of law. There will be few to protest. But tomorrow the precedent here established can be turned against others. A procession of judicial lynchings without due process of law may now follow. No one can foresee the end of this failure of objective thinking and of adherence to our high hopes of a new world. The time for effective vigilance and protest, however, is when the abandonment of legal procedure is first attempted. A nation must not perish because, in the natural frenzy of the aftermath of war, it abandoned its central theme of the dignity of the human personality and due process of law.

"Mr. Justice Rutledge agrees with these views."

General MacArthur's action left but one final recourse open to us. We appealed to President Truman as commander-in-chief of the armed forces for commutation of the sentence to life-imprisonment. The petition took the form of a letter that was delivered to the White House at our request by the secretary of war. Our plea was premised on the contention that the death sentence was disproportionate to the offense actually found by the military commission; that the commission had essentially created a new international crime—one that did not involve criminal intent; that, although the Supreme Court had refused to intervene, making no decision as to Yamashita's guilt or innocence or as to the propriety of the conduct of his trial, there had been two vehement dissenting opinions that described the proceedings as lacking "any semblance of trial"; and that commutation of the sentence would, as suggested by Mr. Justice Murphy, contribute to understanding among nations. Our petition closed with the following suggestion: "No member of the military commission that heard this case is a lawyer. The only lawyers who have published their reaction to a study of the proceedings before the commission are Justices Murphy and Rutledge. If there is any question in your mind as to the justice of this request for commutation, we urge that you assign to legal advisers the duty of reviewing and reporting to you on the record in this case."

After the appeal was delivered to the White House, Yamashita's counsel met with President Truman's military aide, Major General Harry H. Vaughan. Our purpose, we explained, was to let the President know that we were available and willing to answer any questions he might wish to put to us. General Vaughan had a few questions. He found it difficult to understand our objections to the conviction of Yamashita on a theory of "command responsibility." While we were conversing with him, General Vaughan was interrupted by a telephone call that had to do with the question of disposal of surplus military property. After the telephone conversation was concluded, Vaughan remarked about the difficulties in handling surplus property. "It's spread around the world," he said, "and the natives won't buy it because they're waiting for us to abandon it. The GI's have shown them that they don't want to stay around foreign countries just to guard supplies." General Vaughan's last statement referred to the mass meetings of American Army enlisted men that had taken place in various foreign theaters during the previous two or three weeks for the purpose of publicizing their desires for immediate demobilization. "They're just a bunch of crybabies," said the President's aide heatedly. "If I were in charge, I'd put a stop to that sort of thing. You know what I'd do? I'd get after the sergeants and the corporals—it's up to them to exercise some discipline." He paused a moment, and then added: "Damn it, I'd go even farther. I'd go after the lieutenants and the captains."

I couldn't resist asking General Vaughan: "And would you go after the commanding general, too?"

Vaughan looked at me as though bewildered. "The commanding general?" he asked incredulously. "What's he got to do with it?"

I told General Vaughan that he had just stated our objection to the theory of command responsibility as the basis for criminal punishment of General Yamashita. "Oh," he said, "atrocities are different."

We then called the military aide's attention to our expressed desire that the President assign the task of reviewing and reporting on the record to some legal advisers. General Vaughan agreed that would be a good idea, and he suggested that it might be well for the President to refer the matter to the Judge Advocate General. We said that, from our point of view, he would be a most happy choice.

"After all, the Judge Advocate General knows about these things, and the President doesn't," said Vaughan. "If the President knew about these things, *he* would be Judge Advocate General—"

But the record was not sent to the Judge Advocate General or to anyone else. The White House wasted very little time with the matter. The following afternoon, February 8, we received a copy of a War Department press release. It said simply: "The War Department has been advised that the President will take no action on the petition for clemency filed by counsel for General Tomoyuki Yamashita. General MacArthur has been given this information. End."

The last word was most significant. It was indeed the end of our efforts and of our client's chance to live.

On February 23, 1946, at three o'clock in the morning, at Los Baños—a town about thirty-five miles south of Manila—General Yamashita was hanged. According to the official press dispatch of General Styer's public relations section, Yamashita "appeared calm and stoical. Asked if he had any last words, he said: 'I will pray for the Emperor's long life and his prosperity forever!' "

The official release also contained what it described as "an interpreter's version of a statement written by Yamashita after the order of execution had been read to him." The interpreter obviously was not Hamamoto. The "pidgin English" into which the words were translated leaves much of the apparently intended meaning obscure. But the story of General Yamashita would not be complete without his valedictory, and so it is reproduced here as it appeared in the release:

"I were carrying out my duty, as Japanese high commander of Japanese Army in the Philippines islands, to control my army with my best during wartime. Until now I am believing that I have tried to my best throughout my army.

"As I said in the Manila Court that I have done with my all capacity, so I don't ashame in front of God for what I have done when I have die. But if you say to me 'you do not have any ability to command the Japanese Army' I should say nothing for it, because it is my own nature.

"I know that all your American and American military affairs officers always has tolerant and rightful judgment. When I have been investigated in Manila court I have had a good treatment, kindful attitude from your good natured officers who all the time protect me. I never forget for what they have done for me even if I have died. I don't blame my executioner. I'll pray God bless them.

"Please send my thankful word to Col. Clark and Lt. Col. Ferdhouse, Lt. Col. Hendric, Maj. Goi, Capt. Surburn, Capt. Real at Manila court."

XXXVI

MORE LASTING HARM

THE United States is no longer a young nation; it has grown to maturity. An adult people can afford to admit its mistakes. If we have deviated from the standard of fairness laid down by our Founding Fathers, if we have wandered from the ideals of tolerance expressed by Abraham Lincoln, we can at least recognize and analyze the fact, so that we may find future guidance to the restoration of the faith of humanity and our own self-respect.

General Yamashita was condemned unjustly, first, because the evidence against him was obtained and accepted in violation of the laws that Anglo-Saxon jurisprudence has developed over many centuries in order to protect just such persons as he against the prejudices of judges and the demands of the mob for vengeance. He did not have a fair trial.

There are those who have said that in the handling of this case our Army missed a great opportunity. Having fought and won a war against totalitarianism, they point out that we could have shown the world just what we meant. Instead of that, we fell to the level of our enemies. We adopted their judicial techniques. We gave the world a practical demonstration of the fact that, certainly in one corner of the globe, "the enemy has lost the battle but has destroyed our ideals."

It was more than a lost opportunity. Damage was done—affirmative damage, to ourselves and to the faith of men the world over in the honesty and objectiveness of our legal structure. As Mr. Justice Murphy said: "An uncurbed spirit of revenge and retribution, masked in formal legal procedure for purposes of dealing with a fallen enemy commander, can do more lasting harm than all of the atrocities giving rise to that spirit."

But let us assume that General Yamashita had been given a fair trial, that the rules of evidence and the constitutional guaranty of due process of law had been adhered to. In my opinion, even then the condemnation was unjust because Yamashita was held accountable for crimes committed by persons other than himself, crimes committed without his knowledge and, in fact, against his orders. He was held so accountable on the basis of a "principle" of command responsibility, a principle that in this perverted form has no basis in either law or logic.

Here we find a fundamental difference between the German war-crimes trials in Nuremberg and the Yamashita case. In the Nuremberg trials three types of crime were alleged: first, offenses against the peace, conspiring and planning and undertaking to wage a war of aggression; second, offenses on racial and religious grounds, covering pre-war years as well as wartime; third, offenses against persons and property in the conduct of the war, in violation of the laws of war. Only those Nuremberg defendants who were charged within the third category can be compared to General Yamashita. And it is interesting to note that in the Nuremberg indictments great care was taken to allege that these particular prisoners "authorized, directed, or participated in" the actual crimes. Nowhere in the record of the Nuremberg trials can there be found the cavalier disregard of that touchstone of our criminal law—the element of personal culpability—that signalizes the Yamashita case.

There are, however, certain similarities to be found in all these war-crimes trials. They are, for example, all subject to the objection that they are not really trials in the sense that there is an honest possibility of acquittal. Although it seemed likely from the beginning that a few of the Nuremberg defendants would be acquitted, it was even more obvious that such important German prisoners as Hermann Goering had no more chance of being found not guilty than there was of our military commission letting Yamashita go. The fallacy is that we have been trying to cover what is essentially a political act with a cloak of legalism.

In Nuremberg as well as in Manila one might well inquire as to whether or not there was a violation of one of the first principles of Anglo-Saxon law, namely, that no man shall be a judge in his own cause. Although the Nuremberg cases were not heard by an American military commission composed of generals subject to American law, they were tried before an international tribunal of jurists recruited from Allied countries. In both instances representatives of the vanquished nation were being judged by representatives of the victor nations, whose wartime leaders had publicly promised the forthcoming retribution.

The significant defendants at Nuremberg were those charged with conspiring and undertaking to initiate a war of aggression, a far cry from the allegations against Yamashita. Yet here, too, there is an important similarity. Both convictions are subject to the accusation that they were for ex post facto offenses. Never before had it been a crime to plan an invasion, any more than it had been a crime to be in command of troops who committed crimes. Ever since the days of the Magna Carta, our judicial canons have had no place for the idea of punishing a man for having done something that was not illegal at the time that he did it.

The apologists for Nuremberg have given two answers to that charge. The first is that the Briand-Kellogg Treaty of 1928 outlawed war, so that the planning of war has been a crime since that date—in other words, the Nuremberg situation is not ex post facto at all. The second answer, and the only one that can have any reference to the Yamashita case, is that we have to start somewhere—in other words, ex post facto prosecutions are justifiable in this instance. Laws, so the argument runs, are made either by a legislative body or by a court declaring accepted customs. There is no international legislative body, and hence the only way that international law can be evolved is either through agreements (that is, treaties) or through original declaration by a war-crimes court.

In his opening statement to the Nuremberg tribunal, Mr. Justice Robert H. Jackson, chief American prosecutor, gave voice to this view: "Every custom has its origins in some single act, and every agreement has to be initiated by the action of some state. . . . Our own day has its right to institute customs," he said. And further: "The fact is that when the law evolves by the case method, as did the Common Law and as International Law must do if it is to advance at all, it advances at the expense of those who wrongly guessed the law and learned too late their error."

In the first place, no man who loves liberty can agree that the prohibition of ex post facto laws may be relaxed for an instant. It is one thing to say that civil law is evolved by judicial decision, but it is something else to say that a judge may order a man hanged for having done something that was permitted at the time that he did it, or for having occupied an office that was legal at the time that he held it.

The dangers inherent in any abandonment of that fundamental doctrine were well known to our Founding Fathers. James Madison, in the *Federalist*, explained why the proposed Constitution of the United States contained a prohibition of all ex post facto laws, by describing them as "contrary to the first principles of the social compact." He pointed out that a similar interdiction was to be found in then existing state constitutions, and he added: "Our own experience has taught us, nevertheless, that additional fences against these dangers ought not to be omitted."

And the terror caused by a system that permits retroactive punishment is even better known to the victims of dictatorships who live in constant fear of secret police dragging them from their homes not because of some act that they knew was forbidden but because of some "crime" of which they were hitherto unaware. Perhaps tomorrow it may be a felony to have been yesterday a Social Democrat—or a Catholic or a Jew.

But, even if we agree with this analogy to the evolution of civil law, it can have no counterpart in the creation of new rules of war. Judge-made common law is valid only because it binds the judge to apply his ruling to all similar cases, even against himself. That is not what has happened here.

Thus there are those who say that the execution of Yamashita because he was in command of troops who committed atrocities is a good thing. In the next war, they argue, commanding generals will take more care to see to it that their troops behave decently. But in the next war the results may be quite to the contrary, because the wary commander will have to concentrate on winning at all costs. For Yamashita was not hanged because he was in command of troops who committed atrocities. He was hanged because he was in command of troops who committed atrocities *on the losing side.*

At Lichfield prison camp in England, our own American soldier-prisoners were cruelly beaten by their American soldier-guards. One of the victims subsequently died from massive cerebral hemorrhage, apparently caused by having his head rammed against a wall. The evidence in the ensuing court-martial cases disclosed that the camp commander had ordered his subordinates to indulge in rough treatment, cautioning them not to "break too many bones." This same commander, while General Eisenhower was his superior, had been awarded the Legion of Merit, and his name was sent to Congress on the promotion list. Should General Eisenhower be tried?

According to an Army chaplain, an American general on Luzon announced just before the invasion: "I do not want to see our hospitals cluttered up with Jap wounded. Kill them or let them die." Such statements in the Pacific Theater during the war were apparently not unusual. General MacArthur is reported to have remarked when he saw a Japanese corpse on a beachhead: "A dead Jap is the only good Jap." Certainly, that was not an extreme pronouncement, considering the time it was supposedly made; but might it not be construed as condonation or even encouragement of his subordinate's cruel suggestion? Should General MacArthur be hanged?

Aerial bombardment killed many noncombatants throughout the war. Our military leaders took the position that this did not constitute a violation of the rules because the bombs were dropped on military objectives and the wiping-out of civilians was unintended and incidental. It was obvious, however, that the loosing of atomic bombs on Hiroshima and Nagasaki could not entirely be explained in this way and must be a violation of the letter of the laws of war. It was not until February, 1947, however, that a definitive statement of the rationale of the bombing was made public.

Writing in *Harper's* magazine on that date, Henry L. Stimson, who had been secretary of war throughout the conflict, described "The Decision To Use the Atomic Bomb," admittedly a "decision that brought death to over a hundred thousand Japanese," as "deliberate, premeditated," and for the purpose of producing "exactly the kind of shock" it did. Specifically, Mr. Stimson said: "The ultimate responsibility for the recommendation to the President rested upon me, and I have no desire to veil it. . . . I felt that to extract a genuine surrender from the Emperor and his military advisers, they must be administered a tremendous shock which would carry convincing proof of our power to destroy the Empire." Here is no talk of munitions factories as primary targets; here is the candid description of the bomb as a "psychological weapon," the recognition that its great value came from its terrorization of civilians: "the experience of what an atomic bomb will actually do to a community, *plus the dread of many more.*"

Yet we do not try Mr. Stimson. On the contrary, most Americans probably take the realistic view that this decision undoubtedly saved many lives. It tremendously shortened the war. It made unnecessary the costly invasion and probable piecemeal destruction of Japan. We honor Mr. Stimson's candor, and we respect his sincerity when he tells us that he could not have failed to use the bombs and "afterwards looked his countrymen in the face."

Why must we judge our enemies by a different standard? Mr. Stimson was the American secretary of war for five years. Looking back over that period, he concluded: "I see too many stern and heartrending decisions to be willing to pretend that war is anything else than what it is. The face of war is the face of death; death is an inevitable part of every order that a wartime leader gives."

So may it have been with General Yamashita.

We have been unjust, hypocritical, and vindictive. We have defeated our enemies on the battlefield, but we have let their spirit triumph in our hearts.

What is past is past, but in more sober days we may find resolution not to compound our sins. The United States will live to see other victories. We must learn that victory without justice is a dead thing, that humanity cannot live without charity, and that we cannot have freedom for the strong as long as we bring oppression to the weak. As we judge, so will we be judged; our own rights and privileges are those we grant to the lowliest and most despised of culprits.

From the tragedy of the Yamashita case there does emerge one great contribution to the cause of human freedom. I refer, of course, to the magnificent dissenting opinions of Mr. Justice Rutledge and Mr. Justice Murphy. Not only are they embodied forever in the annals of our legal literature, but they must eventually be recognized as beacons of our best tradition. In the years to come, the words of Rutledge and of Murphy will be read and read again by a grateful people, a people who will have risen above the hatred and revenge and injustice of our angry day, a people who, as they read, will hear the sound of truth and who will say: "This was the best in our nation. This was the voice of hope. This protest was the triumph of humanity and of reason and of right. Here was the thread of our heritage—here was America's soul."

APPENDIX

APPENDIX

327 U.S. 1

CASES ADJUDGED

IN THE

SUPREME COURT OF THE UNITED STATES

AT

OCTOBER TERM, 1945

IN RE YAMASHITA

NO. 61, MISC. APPLICATION FOR LEAVE TO FILE PETITION FOR WRIT OF HABEAS CORPUS AND WRIT OF PROHIBITION.*

Argued January 7, 8, 1946.—Decided February 4, 1946.

No. 61, Misc. Application for leave to file a petition for writs of habeas corpus and prohibition in this Court challenging the jurisdiction and legal authority of a military commission which convicted applicant of a violation of the law of war and sentenced him to be hanged. *Denied.*

No. 672. Petition for certiorari to review an order of the Supreme Court of the Commonwealth of the Philippines, 42 Off. Gaz. 664, denying an application for writs of habeas corpus and prohibition likewise challenging the jurisdiction and legal authority of the military commission which tried and convicted petitioner. *Denied.*

Colonel Harry E. Clarke, pro hac vice, Captain A. Frank Reel and *Captain Milton Sandberg* argued the cause for petitioner. With them on the brief were *Lt. Col. Walter C. Hendrix, Lt. Col. James G. Feldhaus* and *Major George F. Guy.*

* Together with No. 672, *Yamashita* v. *Styer, Commanding General,* on petition for writ of certiorari to the Supreme Court of the Commonwealth of the Philippines. For earlier orders in these cases see 326 U.S. 693, 694.

Solicitor General McGrath and *Assistant Solicitor General Judson* argued the cause for respondent. With them on the brief were *The Judge Advocate General of the Army, Frederick Bernays Wiener, George Thomas Washington, David Reich, Irving Hill, Colonel William J. Hughes, Jr.*, and *Captain D. C. Hill.*

Mr. Chief Justice Stone delivered the opinion of the Court.

No. 61 Miscellaneous is an application for leave to file a petition for writs of habeas corpus and prohibition in this Court. No. 672 is a petition for certiorari to review an order of the Supreme Court of the Commonwealth of the Philippines (28 U. S. C. § 349), denying petitioner's application to that court for writs of habeas corpus and prohibition. As both applications raise substantially like questions, and because of the importance and novelty of some of those presented, we set the two applications down for oral argument as one case.

From the petitions and supporting papers it appears that prior to September 3, 1945, petitioner was the Commanding General of the Fourteenth Army Group of the Imperial Japanese Army in the Philippine Islands. On that date he surrendered to and became a prisoner of war of the United States Army Forces in Baguio, Philippine Islands. On September 25th, by order of respondent, Lieutenant General Wilhelm D. Styer, Commanding General of the United States Army Forces, Western Pacific, which command embraces the Philippine Islands, petitioner was served with a charge prepared by the Judge Advocate General's Department of the Army, purporting to charge petitioner with a violation of the law of war. On October 8, 1945, petitioner, after pleading not guilty to the charge, was held for trial before a military commission of five Army officers appointed by order of General Styer. The order appointed six Army officers, all lawyers, as defense counsel. Throughout the proceedings which followed, including those before this Court, defense counsel have demonstrated their professional skill and resourcefulness and their proper zeal for the defense with which they were charged.

On the same date a bill of particulars was filed by the prosecution, and the commission heard a motion made in petitioner's behalf to dismiss the charge on the ground that it failed to state a violation of the law of war. On October 29th the commission was reconvened, a supplemental bill of particulars was filed, and the motion to dismiss was denied. The trial then proceeded until its conclusion on December 7, 1945, the commission hearing two hundred and eighty-six witnesses, who gave over three thousand pages of testimony. On that date petitioner was found guilty of the offense as charged and sentenced to death by hanging.

The petitions for habeas corpus set up that the detention of petitioner for the purpose of the trial was unlawful for reasons which are now urged as showing that the military commission was without lawful authority or jurisdiction to place petitioner on trial, as follows:

(a) That the military commission which tried and convicted petitioner was not lawfully created, and that no military commission to try petitioner for violations of the law of war could lawfully be convened after the cessation of hostilities between the armed forces of the United States and Japan;

(b) That the charge preferred against petitioner fails to charge him with a violation of the law of war;

(c) That the commission was without authority and jurisdiction to try and convict petitioner because the order governing the procedure of the commission permitted the admission in evidence of depositions, affidavits and hearsay and opinion evidence, and because the commission's rulings admitting such evidence were in violation of the 25th and 38th Articles of War (10 U. S. C. §§ 1496, 1509) and the Geneva Convention (47 Stat. 2021), and deprived petitioner of a fair trial in violation of the due process clause of the Fifth Amendment;

(d) That the commission was without authority and jurisdiction in the premises because of the failure to give advance notice of petitioner's trial to the neutral power representing the interests of Japan as a belligerent as required by Article 60 of the Geneva Convention, 47 Stat. 2021, 2051.

On the same grounds the petitions for writs of prohibition set up that the commission is without authority to proceed with the trial.

The Supreme Court of the Philippine Islands, after hearing argument, denied the petition for habeas corpus presented to it, on the ground, among others, that its jurisdiction was limited to an inquiry as to the jurisdiction of the commission to place petitioner on trial for the offense charged, and that the commission, being validly constituted by the order of General Styer, had jurisdiction over the person of petitioner and over the trial for the offense charged.

In *Ex parte Quirin*, 317 U. S. 1, we had occasion to consider at length the sources and nature of the authority to create military commissions for the trial of enemy combatants for offenses against the law of war. We there pointed out that Congress, in the exercise of the power conferred upon it by Article I, § 8, Cl. 10 of the Constitution to "define and punish . . . Offences against the Law of Nations . . . ," of which the law of war is a part, had by the Articles of War (10 U. S. C. §§ 1471–1593) recognized the "military commission" appointed by military command, as it had previously existed in United States Army practice, as an appropriate tribunal for the trial and punishment of offenses against the law of war. Article 15 declares that the "provisions of these articles conferring jurisdiction upon courts martial shall not be construed as depriving military commissions . . . or other military tribunals of concurrent jurisdiction in respect of offenders or offenses that by statute or by the law of war may be triable by such military commissions . . . or other military tribunals." See a similar provision of the Espionage Act of 1917, 50 U. S. C. § 38. Article 2 includes among those persons subject to the Articles of War the personnel of our own military establishment. But this, as Article 12 indicates, does not exclude from the class of persons subject to trial by military commissions "any other person who by the law of war is subject to trial by military tribunals," and who, under Article 12, may be tried by court-martial, or under Article 15 by military commission.

We further pointed out that Congress, by sanctioning trial of enemy combatants for violations of the law of war by military commission, had not attempted to codify the law of war or to mark its precise boundaries. Instead, by Article 15 it had incorporated, by reference, as within the preexisting jurisdiction of military commissions created by appropriate military command, all offenses which are defined as such by the law of war, and which may constitutionally be included within that jurisdiction. It thus adopted the system of military common law applied by military tribunals so far as it should be recognized and deemed applicable by the courts, and as further defined and supplemented by the Hague Convention, to which the United States and the Axis powers were parties.

We also emphasized in *Ex parte Quirin*, as we do here, that on application for habeas corpus we are not concerned with the guilt or innocence of the petitioners. We consider here only the lawful power of the commission to try the petitioner for the offense charged. In the present cases it must be recognized throughout that the military tribunals which Congress has sanctioned by the Articles of War are not courts whose rulings and judgments are made subject to review by this Court. See *Ex parte Vallandigham*, 1 Wall. 243; *In re Vidal*, 179 U. S. 126; cf. *Ex parte Quirin*, *supra*, 39. They are tribunals whose determinations are reviewable by the military authorities either as provided in the military orders constituting such tribunals or as provided by the Articles of War. Congress conferred on the courts no power to review their determinations save only as it has granted judicial power "to grant writs of habeas corpus for the purpose of an inquiry into the cause of restraint of liberty." 28 U. S. C. §§ 451, 452. The courts may inquire whether the detention complained of is within the authority of those detaining the petitioner. If the military tribunals have lawful authority to hear, decide and condemn, their action is not subject to judicial review merely because they have made a wrong decision on disputed facts. Correction of their errors of decision is not for the courts but for the military authorities which are alone authorized to review their decisions. See *Dynes* v. *Hoover*, 20 How. 65, 81; *Runkle* v. *United States*, 122 U. S. 543, 555–556; *Carter* v. *McClaughry*, 183 U. S. 365; *Collins* v. *McDonald*, 258 U. S. 416. Cf. *Matter of Moran*, 203 U. S. 96, 105.

Finally, we held in *Ex parte Quirin, supra*, 24, 25, as we hold now, that Congress by sanctioning trials of enemy aliens by military commission for offenses against the law of war had recognized the right of the accused to make a defense. Cf. *Ex parte Kawato*, 317 U. S. 69. It has not foreclosed their right to contend that the Constitution or laws of the United States withhold authority to proceed with the trial. It has not withdrawn, and the Executive branch of the Government could not, unless there was suspension of the writ, withdraw from the courts the duty and power to make such inquiry into the authority of the commission as may be made by habeas corpus.

With these governing principles in mind we turn to the consideration of the several contentions urged to establish want of authority in the commission. We are not here concerned with the power of military commissions to try civilians. See *Ex parte Milligan*, 4 Wall. 2, 132; *Sterling* v. *Constantin*, 287 U. S. 378; *Ex parte Quirin, supra*, 45. The Government's contention is that General Styer's order creating the commission conferred authority on it only to try the purported charge of violation of the law of war committed by petitioner, an enemy belligerent, while in command of a hostile army occupying United States territory during time of war. Our first inquiry must therefore be whether the present commission was created by lawful military command and, if so, whether authority could thus be conferred on the commission to place petitioner on trial after the cessation of hostilities between the armed forces of the United States and Japan.

The authority to create the commission. General Styer's order for the appointment of the commission was made by him as Commander of the United States Army Forces, Western Pacific. His command includes, as part of a vastly greater area, the Philippine Islands, where the alleged offenses were committed, where petitioner surrendered as a prisoner of war, and where, at the time of the order convening the commission, he was detained as a prisoner in custody of the United States Army. The congressional recognition of military commissions and its sanction of their use in trying offenses against the law of war to which we have referred, sanctioned their creation by military command in conformity to long-established American precedents. Such a commission may be appointed by any field commander, or by any commander competent to appoint a general court-martial, as was General Styer, who had been vested with that power by order of the President. 2 Winthrop, Military Law and Precedents, 2d ed., *1302; cf. Article of War 8.

Here the commission was not only created by a commander competent to appoint it, but his order conformed to the established policy of the Government and to higher military commands authorizing his action. In a proclamation of July 2, 1942 (56 Stat. 1964), the President proclaimed that enemy belligerents who, during time of war, enter the United

States, or any territory or possession thereof, and who violate the law of war, should be subject to the law of war and to the jurisdiction of military tribunals. Paragraph 10 of the Declaration of Potsdam of July 26, 1945, declared that "... stern justice shall be meted out to all war criminals, including those who have visited cruelties upon our prisoners." U. S. Dept. of State Bull., Vol. XIII, No. 318, pp. 137–138. This Declaration was accepted by the Japanese government by its note of August 10, 1945. U. S. Dept. of State Bull., Vol. XIII, No. 320, p. 205.

By direction of the President, the Joint Chiefs of Staff of the American Military Forces, on September 12, 1945, instructed General MacArthur, Commander in Chief, United States Army Forces, Pacific, to proceed with the trial, before appropriate military tribunals, of such Japanese war criminals "as have been or may be apprehended." By order of General MacArthur of September 24, 1945, General Styer was specifically directed to proceed with the trial of petitioner upon the charge here involved. This order was accompanied by detailed rules and regulations which General MacArthur prescribed for the trial of war criminals. These regulations directed, among other things, that review of the sentence imposed by the commission should be by the officer convening it, with "authority to approve, mitigate, remit, commute, suspend, reduce or otherwise alter the sentence imposed," and directed that no sentence of death should be carried into effect until confirmed by the Commander in Chief, United States Army Forces, Pacific.

It thus appears that the order creating the commission for the trial of petitioner was authorized by military command, and was in complete conformity to the Act of Congress sanctioning the creation of such tribunals for the trial of offenses against the law of war committed by enemy combatants. And we turn to the question whether the authority to create the commission and direct the trial by military order continued after the cessation of hostilities.

An important incident to the conduct of war is the adoption of measures by the military commander, not only to repel and defeat the enemy, but to seize and subject to disciplinary measures those enemies who, in their attempt to thwart or impede our military effort, have violated the law of war. *Ex parte Quirin, supra,* 28. The trial and punishment of enemy combatants who have committed violations of the law of war is thus not only a part of the conduct of war operating as a preventive measure against such violations, but is an exercise of the authority sanctioned by Congress to administer the system of military justice recognized by the law of war. That sanction is without qualification as to the exercise of this authority so long as a state of war exists—from its declaration until peace is proclaimed. See *United States* v. *Anderson,* 9 Wall. 56, 70; *The Protector,* 12 Wall. 700, 702; *McElrath* v. *United States,* 102 U. S. 426, 438; *Kahn* v. *Anderson,* 255 U. S. 1, 9–10. The war power, from which the commission derives its existence, is not limited to victories in the field, but carries with it the inherent power to guard against the immediate renewal of the conflict, and to remedy, at least in ways Congress has recognized, the evils which the military operations have produced. See *Stewart* v. *Kahn,* 11 Wall. 493, 507.

We cannot say that there is no authority to convene a commission after hostilities have ended to try violations of the law of war committed before their cessation, at least until peace has been officially recognized by treaty or proclamation of the political branch of the Government. In fact, in most instances the practical administration of the system of military justice under the law of war would fail if such authority were thought to end with the cessation of hostilities. For only after their cessation could the greater number of offenders and the principal ones be apprehended and subjected to trial.

No writer on international law appears to have regarded the power of military tribunals, otherwise competent to try violations of the law of war, as terminating before the formal state of war has ended.[1] In our own military history there have been numerous instances in which offenders were tried by military commission after the cessation of hostilities and before the proclamation of peace, for offenses against the law of war committed before the cessation of hostilities.[2]

The extent to which the power to prosecute violations of the law of war shall be exercised before peace is declared rests, not with the courts, but with the political branch of the Government, and may itself be governed by the terms of an armistice or the treaty of peace. Here, peace has not been agreed upon or proclaimed. Japan, by her acceptance of the Potsdam Declaration and her surrender, has acquiesced in the trials of those guilty of violations of the law of war. The conduct of the trial by the military commission has been authorized by the political branch of the Government, by military command, by international law and usage, and by the terms of the surrender of the Japanese government.

The charge. Neither congressional action nor the military orders constituting the commission authorized it to place petitioner on trial unless the charge preferred against him is of a violation of the law of war. The charge, so far as now

1 The Commission on the Responsibility of the Authors of the War and on the Enforcement of Penalties of the Versailles Peace Conference, which met after cessation of hostilities in the First World War, were of the view that violators of the law of war could be tried by military tribunals. See Report of the Commission, March 9, 1919, 14 Am. J. Int. L. 95, 121. See also memorandum of American commissioners concurring on this point, *id.*, at p. 141. The treaties of peace concluded after World War I recognized the right of the Allies and of the United States to try such offenders before military tribunals. See Art. 228 of Treaty of Versailles, June 28, 1919 Art. 173 of Treaty of St. Germain, Sept. 10, 1919; Art. 157 of Treaty of Trianon, June 4, 1920.

The terms of the agreement which ended hostilities in the Boer War reserved the right to try, before military tribunals, enemy combatants who had violated the law of war. 95 British and Foreign State Papers (1901–1902) 160. See also trials cited in Colby, War Crimes, 23 Michigan Law Rev. 482, 496–7.

2 See cases mentioned in *Ex parte Quirin*, *supra*, p. 32, note 10, and in 2 Winthrop, *supra*, *1310–1311, n. 5; 14 Op. A. G. 249 (Modoc Indian Prisoners).

relevant, is that petitioner, between October 9, 1944 and September 2, 1945, in the Philippine Islands, "while commander of armed forces of Japan at war with the United States of America and its allies, unlawfully disregarded and failed to discharge his duty as commander to control the operations of the members of his command, permitting them to commit brutal atrocities and other high crimes against people of the United States and of its allies and dependencies, particularly the Philippines; and he . . . thereby violated the laws of war."

Bills of particulars, filed by the prosecution by order of the commission, allege a series of acts, one hundred and twenty-three in number, committed by members of the forces under petitioner's command during the period mentioned. The first item specifies the execution of "a deliberate plan and purpose to massacre and exterminate a large part of the civilian population of Batangas Province, and to devastate and destroy public, private and religious property therein, as a result of which more than 25,000 men, women and children, all unarmed noncombatant civilians, were brutally mistreated and killed, without cause or trial, and entire settlements were devastated and destroyed wantonly and without military necessity." Other items specify acts of violence, cruelty and homicide inflicted upon the civilian population and prisoners of war, acts of wholesale pillage and the wanton destruction of religious monuments.

It is not denied that such acts directed against the civilian population of an occupied country and against prisoners of war are recognized in international law as violations of the law of war. Articles 4, 28, 46, and 47, Annex to the Fourth Hague Convention, 1907, 36 Stat. 2277, 2296, 2303, 2306–7. But it is urged that the charge does not allege that petitioner has either committed or directed the commission of such acts, and consequently that no violation is charged as against him. But this overlooks the fact that the gist of the charge is an unlawful breach of duty by petitioner as an army commander to control the operations of the members of his command by "permitting them to commit" the extensive and widespread atrocities specified. The question then is whether the law of war imposes on an army commander a duty to take such appropriate measures as are within his power to control the troops under his command for the prevention of the specified acts which are violations of the law of war and which are likely to attend the occupation of hostile territory by an uncontrolled soldiery, and whether he may be charged with personal responsibility for his failure to take such measures when violations result. That this was the precise issue to be tried was made clear by the statement of the prosecution at the opening of the trial.

It is evident that the conduct of military operations by troops whose excesses are unrestrained by the orders or efforts of their commander would almost certainly result in violations which it is the purpose of the law of war to prevent. Its purpose to protect civilian populations and prisoners of war from brutality would largely be defeated if the commander of an invading army could with impunity neglect to take reasonable measures for their protection. Hence the law of war presupposes that its violation is to be avoided through the control of the operations of war by commanders who are to some extent responsible for their subordinates.

This is recognized by the Annex to the Fourth Hague Convention of 1907, respecting the laws and customs of war on land. Article 1 lays down as a condition which an armed force must fulfill in order to be accorded the rights of lawful belligerents, that it must be "commanded by a person responsible for his subordinates." 36 Stat. 2295. Similarly Article 19 of the Tenth Hague Convention, relating to bombardment by naval vessels, provides that commanders in chief of the belligerent vessels "must see that the above Articles are properly carried out." 36 Stat. 2389. And Article 26 of the Geneva Red Cross Convention of 1929, 47 Stat. 2074, 2092, for the amelioration of the condition of the wounded and sick in armies in the field, makes it "the duty of the commanders-in-chief of the belligerent armies to provide for the details of execution of the foregoing articles, [of the convention] as well as for unforeseen cases . . ." And, finally, Article 43 of the Annex of the Fourth Hague Convention, 36 Stat. 2306, requires that the commander of a force occupying enemy territory, as was petitioner, "shall take all the measures in his power to restore, and ensure, as far as possible, public order and safety, while respecting, unless absolutely prevented, the laws in force in the country."

These provisions plainly imposed on petitioner, who at the time specified was military governor of the Philippines, as well as commander of the Japanese forces, an affirmative duty to take such measures as were within his power and appropriate in the circumstances to protect prisoners of war and the civilian population. This duty of a commanding officer has heretofore been recognized, and its breach penalized by our own military tribunals.[3] A like principle has been applied so as to impose liability on the United States in international arbitrations. *Case of Jeannaud*, 3 Moore, International Arbitrations, 3000; *Case of The Zafiro*, 5 Hackworth, Digest of International Law, 707.

We do not make the laws of war but we respect them so far as they do not conflict with the commands of Congress or the Constitution. There is no contention that the present charge, thus read, is without the support of evidence, or that the commission held petitioner responsible for failing to take measures which were beyond his control or inappropriate for

[3] Failure of an officer to take measures to prevent murder of an inhabitant of an occupied country committed in his presence. Gen. Orders No. 221, Hq. Div. of the Philippines, August 17, 1901. And in Gen. Orders No. 264, Hq. Div. of the Philippines, September 9, 1901, it was held that an officer could not be found guilty for failure to prevent a murder unless it appeared that the accused had "the power to prevent" it.

a commanding officer to take in the circumstances.[4] We do not here appraise the evidence on which petitioner was convicted. We do not consider what measures, if any, petitioner took to prevent the commission, by the troops under his command, of the plain violations of the law of war detailed in the bill of particulars, or whether such measures as he may have taken were appropriate and sufficient to discharge the duty imposed upon him. These are questions within the peculiar competence of the military officers composing the commission and were for it to decide. See *Smith* v. *Whitney*, 116 U. S. 167, 178. It is plain that the charge on which petitioner was tried charged him with a breach of his duty to control the operations of the members of his command, by permitting them to commit the specified atrocities. This was enough to require the commission to hear evidence tending to establish the culpable failure of petitioner to perform the duty imposed on him by the law of war and to pass upon its sufficiency to establish guilt.

Obviously charges of violations of the law of war triable before a military tribunal need not be stated with the precision of a common law indictment. Cf. *Collins* v. *McDonald, supra*, 420. But we conclude that the allegations of the charge, tested by any reasonable standard, adequately allege a violation of the law of war and that the commission had authority to try and decide the issue which it raised. Cf. *Dealy* v. *United States*, 152 U. S. 539; *Williamson* v. *United States*, 207 U. S. 425, 447; *Glasser* v. *United States*, 315 U. S. 60, 66, and cases cited.

[4] In its findings the commission took account of the difficulties "faced by the Accused with respect not only to the swift and overpowering advance of American forces, but also to the errors of his predecessors, weaknesses in organization, equipment, supply . . . , training, communication, discipline and morale of his troops," and the "tactical situation, the character, training and capacity of staff officers and subordinate commanders as well as the traits of character . . . of his troops." It nonetheless found that petitioner had not taken such measures to control his troops as were "required by the circumstances." We do not weigh the evidence. We merely hold that the charge sufficiently states a violation against the law of war, and that the commission, upon the facts found, could properly find petitioner guilty of such a violation.

The proceedings before the commission. The regulations prescribed by General MacArthur governing the procedure for the trial of petitioner by the commission directed that the commission should admit such evidence "as in its opinion would be of assistance in proving or disproving the charge, or such as in the commission's opinion would have probative value in the mind of a reasonable man," and that in particular it might admit affidavits, depositions or other statements taken by officers detailed for that purpose by military authority. The petitions in this case charged that in the course of the trial the commission received, over objection by petitioner's counsel, the deposition of a witness taken pursuant to military authority by a United States Army captain. It also, over like objection, admitted hearsay and opinion evidence tendered by the prosecution. Petitioner argues, as ground for the writ of habeas corpus, that Article 25[5] of the Articles of War prohibited the reception in evidence by the commission of depositions on behalf of the prosecution in a capital case, and that Article 38[6] prohibited the reception of hearsay and of opinion evidence.

We think that neither Article 25 nor Article 38 is applicable to the trial of an enemy combatant by a military commission for violations of the law of war. Article 2 of the Articles of War enumerates "the persons . . . subject to these articles," who are denominated, for purposes of the Articles, as "persons subject to military law." In general, the persons so enumerated are members of our own Army and of the per-

[5] Article 25 provides: "A duly authenticated deposition taken upon reasonable notice to the opposite party may be read in evidence before any military court or commission in any case not capital, or in any proceeding before a court of inquiry or a military board, . . . *Provided*, That testimony by deposition may be adduced for the defense in capital cases."

[6] Article 38 provides: "The President may, by regulations, which he may modify from time to time, prescribe the procedure, including modes of proof, in cases before courts-martial, courts of inquiry, military commissions, and other military tribunals, which regulations shall insofar as he shall deem practicable, apply the rules of evidence generally recognized in the trial of criminal cases in the district courts of the United States: *Provided*, That nothing contrary to or inconsistent with these articles shall be so prescribed: . . ."

sonnel accompanying the Army. Enemy combatants are not included among them. Articles 12, 13 and 14, before the adoption of Article 15 in 1916, made all "persons subject to military law" amenable to trial by courts-martial for any offense made punishable by the Articles of War. Article 12 makes triable by general court-martial "any other person who by the law of war is subject to trial by military tribunals." Since Article 2, in its 1916 form, includes some persons who, by the law of war, were, prior to 1916, triable by military commission, it was feared by the proponents of the 1916 legislation that in the absence of a saving provision, the authority given by Articles 12, 13 and 14 to try such persons before courts-martial might be construed to deprive the nonstatutory military commission of a portion of what was considered to be its traditional jurisdiction. To avoid this, and to preserve that jurisdiction intact, Article 15 was added to the Articles.[7] It declared that "The provisions of these articles conferring jurisdiction upon courts-martial shall not be construed as depriving military commissions . . . of concurrent jurisdiction in respect of offenders or offenses that . . . by the law of war may be triable by such military commissions."

By thus recognizing military commissions in order to preserve their traditional jurisdiction over enemy combatants unimpaired by the Articles, Congress gave sanction, as we held in *Ex parte Quirin*, to any use of the military commis-

[7] General Crowder, the Judge Advocate General, who appeared before Congress as sponsor for the adoption of Article 15 and the accompanying amendment of Article 25, in explaining the purpose of Article 15, said:

"Article 15 is new. We have included in article 2 as subject to military law a number of persons who are also subject to trial by military commission. A military commission is our common-law war court. It has no statutory existence, though it is recognized by statute law. As long as the articles embraced them in the designation 'persons subject to military law,' and provided that they might be tried by court-martial, I was afraid that, having made a special provision for their trial by court-martial, [Arts. 12, 13, and 14] it might be held that the provision operated to exclude trials by military commission and other war courts; so this new article was introduced: . . ." (Sen. R. 130, 64th Cong., 1st Sess., p. 40.)

sion contemplated by the common law of war. But it did not thereby make subject to the Articles of War persons other than those defined by Article 2 as being subject to the Articles, nor did it confer the benefits of the Articles upon such persons. The Articles recognized but one kind of military commission, not two. But they sanctioned the use of that one for the trial of two classes of persons, to one of which the Articles do, and to the other of which they do not, apply in such trials. Being of this latter class, petitioner cannot claim the benefits of the Articles, which are applicable only to the members of the other class. Petitioner, an enemy combatant, is therefore not a person made subject to the Articles of War by Article 2, and the military commission before which he was tried, though sanctioned, and its jurisdiction saved, by Article 15, was not convened by virtue of the Articles of War, but pursuant to the common law of war. It follows that the Articles of War, including Articles 25 and 38, were not applicable to petitioner's trial and imposed no restrictions upon the procedure to be followed. The Articles left the control over the procedure in such a case where it had previously been, with the military command.

Petitioner further urges that by virtue of Article 63 of the Geneva Convention of 1929, 47 Stat. 2052, he is entitled to the benefits afforded by the 25th and 38th Articles of War to members of our own forces. Article 63 provides: "Sentence may be pronounced against a prisoner of war only by the same courts and according to the same procedure as in the case of persons belonging to the armed forces of the detaining Power." Since petitioner is a prisoner of war, and as the 25th and 38th Articles of War apply to the trial of any person in our own armed forces, it is said that Article 63 requires them to be applied in the trial of petitioner. But we think examination of Article 63 in its setting in the Convention plainly shows that it refers to sentence "pronounced against a prisoner of war" for an offense committed while a prisoner of war, and not for a violation of the law of war committed while a combatant.

Article 63 of the Convention appears in part 3, entitled "Judicial Suits," of Chapter 3, "Penalties Applicable to Prisoners of War," of § V, "Prisoners' Relations with the Authorities," one of the sections of Title III, "Captivity." All taken together relate only to the conduct and control of prisoners of war while in captivity as such. Chapter 1 of § V, Article 42 deals with complaints of prisoners of war because of the conditions of captivity. Chapter 2, Articles 43 and 44, relates to those of their number chosen by prisoners of war to represent them.

Chapter 3 of § V, Articles 45 through 67, is entitled "Penalties Applicable to Prisoners of War." Part 1 of that chapter, Articles 45 through 53, indicate what acts of prisoners of war, committed while prisoners, shall be considered offenses, and defines to some extent the punishment which the detaining power may impose on account of such offenses.[8] Punish-

[8] Part 1 of Chapter 3, "General Provisions," provides in Articles 45 and 46 that prisoners of war are subject to the regulations in force in the armies of the detaining power, that punishments other than those provided "for the same acts for soldiers of the national armies" may not be imposed on prisoners of war, and that "Collective punishment for individual acts" is forbidden. Article 47 provides that "Acts constituting an offense against discipline, and particularly attempted escape, shall be verified immediately; for all prisoners of war, commissioned or not, preventive arrest shall be reduced to the absolute minimum. Judicial proceedings against prisoners of war shall be conducted as rapidly as the circumstances permit . . . In all cases, the duration of preventive imprisonment shall be deducted from the disciplinary or judicial punishment inflicted . . ."

Article 48 provides that prisoners of war, after having suffered "the judicial or disciplinary punishment which has been imposed on them," are not to be treated differently from other prisoners, but provides that "prisoners punished as a result of attempted escape may be subjected to special surveillance." Article 49 recites that prisoners "given disciplinary punishment may not be deprived of the prerogatives attached to their rank." Articles 50 and 51 deal with escaped prisoners who have been retaken or prisoners who have attempted to escape. Article 52 provides: "Belligerents shall see that the competent authorities exercise the greatest leniency in deciding the question of whether an infraction committed by a prisoner of war should be punished by disciplinary or judicial measures. This shall be the case especially when it is a

ment is of two kinds—"disciplinary" and "judicial," the latter being the more severe. Article 52 requires that leniency be exercised in deciding whether an offense requires disciplinary or judicial punishment. Part 2 of Chapter 3 is entitled "Disciplinary Punishments," and further defines the extent of such punishment, and the mode in which it may be imposed. Part 3, entitled "Judicial Suits," in which Article 63 is found, describes the procedure by which "judicial" punishment may be imposed. The three parts of Chapter 3, taken together, are thus a comprehensive description of the substantive offenses which prisoners of war may commit during their imprisonment, of the penalties which may be imposed on account of such offenses, and of the procedure by which guilt may be adjudged and sentence pronounced.

We think it clear, from the context of these recited provisions, that part 3, and Article 63, which it contains, apply only to judicial proceedings directed against a prisoner of war for offenses committed while a prisoner of war. Section V gives no indication that this part was designed to deal with offenses other than those referred to in parts 1 and 2 of Chapter 3.

We cannot say that the commission, in admitting evidence to which objection is now made, violated any act of Congress, treaty or military command defining the commission's authority. For reasons already stated we hold that the commission's rulings on evidence and on the mode of conducting these proceedings against petitioner are not reviewable by the courts, but only by the reviewing military authorities. From this viewpoint it is unnecessary to consider what, in other situations, the Fifth Amendment might require, and as to that no intimation one way or the other is to be implied. Nothing we have said is to be taken as indicating any opinion

---

question of deciding on acts in connection with escape or attempted escape. . . . A prisoner may not be punished more than once because of the same act or the same count."

on the question of the wisdom of considering such evidence, or whether the action of a military tribunal in admitting evidence, which Congress or controlling military command has directed to be excluded, may be drawn in question by petition for habeas corpus or prohibition.

Effect of failure to give notice of the trial to the protecting power. Article 60 of the Geneva Convention of July 27, 1929, 47 Stat. 2051, to which the United States and Japan were signatories, provides that "At the opening of a judicial proceeding directed against a prisoner of war, the detaining Power shall advise the representative of the protecting Power therof as soon as possible, and always before the date set for the opening of the trial." Petitioner relies on the failure to give the prescribed notice to the protecting power[9] to establish want of authority in the commission to proceed with the trial.

For reasons already stated we conclude that Article 60 of the Geneva Convention, which appears in part 3, Chapter 3, § V, Title III of the Geneva Convention, applies only to persons who are subjected to judicial proceedings for offenses committed while prisoners of war.[10]

[9] Switzerland, at the time of the trial, was the power designated by Japan for the protection of Japanese prisoners of war detained by the United States, except in Hawaii. U.S. Dept. of State Bull., Vol. XIII, No. 317, p. 125.

[10] One of the items of the bill of particulars, in support of the charge against petitioner, specifies that he permitted members of the armed forces under his command to try and execute three named and other prisoners of war, "subjecting to trial without prior notice to a representative of the protecting power, without opportunity to defend, and without counsel; denying opportunity to appeal from the sentence rendered; failing to notify the protecting power of the sentence pronounced; and executing a death sentence without communicating to the representative of the protecting power the nature and circumstances of the offense charged." It might be suggested that if Article 60 is inapplicable to petitioner it is inapplicable in the cases specified, and that hence he could not be lawfully held or convicted on a charge of failing to require the notice, provided for in Article 60, to be given.

As the Government insists, it does not appear from the charge and specifications that the prisoners in question were not charged with offenses committed by them as prisoners rather than with offenses against the law of war committed by them as enemy combatants. But apart from this consideration,

It thus appears that the order convening the commission was a lawful order, that the commission was lawfully constituted, that petitioner was charged with violation of the law of war, and that the commission had authority to proceed with the trial, and in doing so did not violate any military, statutory or constitutional command. We have considered, but find it unnecessary to discuss, other contentions which we find to be without merit. We therefore conclude

---

independently of the notice requirements of the Geneva Convention, it is a violation of the law of war, on which there could be a conviction if supported by evidence, to inflict capital punishment on prisoners of war without affording to them opportunity to make a defense. 2 Winthrop, *supra*, *434–435, 1241; Article 84, Oxford Manual, Laws and Customs of War on Land; U.S. War Dept., Basic Field Manual, Rules of Land Warfare (1940) par. 356; Lieber's Code, G. O. No. 100 (1863) Instructions for the Government of Armies of the United States in the Field, par. 12; Spaight, War Rights on Land, 462, n.

Further, the commission, in making its findings, summarized as follows the charges, on which it acted, in three classes, any one of which, independently of the others if supported by evidence, would be sufficient to support the conviction: (1) execution or massacre without trial and maladministration generally of civilian internees and prisoners of war; (2) brutalities committed upon the civilian population, and (3) burning and demolition, without adequate military necessity, of a large number of homes, places of business, places of religious worship, hospitals, public buildings and educational institutions.

The commission concluded: "(1) That a series of atrocities and other high crimes have been committed by members of the Japanese armed forces" under command of petitioner "against people of the United States, their allies and dependencies . . . ; that they were not sporadic in nature but in many cases were methodically supervised by Japanese officers and noncommissioned officers"; (2) that during the period in question petitioner "failed to provide effective control of . . . [his] troops, as was required by the circumstances." The commission said: ". . . where murder and rape and vicious, revengeful actions are widespread offenses, and there is no effective attempt by a commander to discover and control the criminal acts, such a commander may be held responsible, even criminally liable, for the lawless acts of his troops, depending upon their nature and the circumstances surrounding them."

The commission made no finding of non-compliance with the Geneva Convention. Nothing has been brought to our attention from which we could conclude that the alleged non-compliance with Article 60 of the Geneva Convention had any relation to the commission's finding of a series of atrocities committed by members of the forces under petitioner's command, and that he failed to provide effective control of his troops, as was required by the circumstances; or which could support the petitions for habeas corpus on the ground that petitioner had been charged with or convicted for failure to require the notice prescribed by Article 60 to be given.

that the detention of petitioner for trial and his detention upon his conviction, subject to the prescribed review by the military authorities, were lawful, and that the petition for certiorari, and leave to file in this Court petitions for writs of habeas corpus and prohibition should be, and they are

Denied.

Mr. Justice Jackson took no part in the consideration or decision of these cases.

Mr. Justice Murphy, dissenting.

The significance of the issue facing the Court today cannot be overemphasized. An American military commission has been established to try a fallen military commander of a conquered nation for an alleged war crime. The authority for such action grows out of the exercise of the power conferred upon Congress by Article I, § 8, Cl. 10 of the Constitution to "define and punish . . . Offences against the Law of Nations . . ." The grave issue raised by this case is whether a military commission so established and so authorized may disregard the procedural rights of an accused person as guaranteed by the Constitution, especially by the due process clause of the Fifth Amendment.

The answer is plain. The Fifth Amendment guarantee of due process of law applies to "any person" who is accused of a crime by the Federal Government or any of its agencies. No exception is made as to those who are accused of war crimes or as to those who possess the status of an enemy belligerent. Indeed, such an exception would be contrary to the whole philosophy of human rights which makes the Constitution the great living document that it is. The immutable rights of the individual, including those secured by the due process clause of the Fifth Amendment, belong not alone to the members of those nations that excel on the battlefield or that subscribe to the democratic ideology. They belong to every person in the world, victor or vanquished, whatever may be his race, color or beliefs. They rise above any status of belligerency or outlawry. They survive any popular passion or frenzy of the moment. No court or legislature or executive, not even the mightiest army in the world, can ever destroy them. Such is the universal and indestructible nature of the rights which the due process clause of the Fifth Amendment recognizes and protects when life or liberty is threatened by virtue of the authority of the United States.

The existence of these rights, unfortunately, is not always respected. They are often trampled under by those who are motivated by hatred, aggression or fear. But in this nation individual rights are recognized and protected, at least in regard to governmental action. They cannot be ignored by any branch of the Government, even the military, except under the most extreme and urgent circumstances.

The failure of the military commission to obey the dictates of the due process requirements of the Fifth Amendment is apparent in this case. The petitioner was the commander of an army totally destroyed by the superior power of this nation. While under heavy and destructive attack by our forces, his troops committed many brutal atrocities and other high crimes. Hostilities ceased and he voluntarily surrendered. At that point he was entitled, as an individual protected by the due process clause of the Fifth Amendment, to be treated fairly and justly according to the accepted rules of law and procedure. He was also entitled to a fair trial as to any alleged crimes and to be free from charges of legally unrecognized crimes that would serve only to permit his accusers to satisfy their desires for revenge.

A military commission was appointed to try the petitioner for an alleged war crime. The trial was ordered to be held in territory over which the United States has complete sovereignty. No military necessity or other emergency demanded the suspension of the safeguards of due process. Yet petitioner was rushed to trial under an improper charge, given insufficient time to prepare an adequate defense, deprived of the benefits of some of the most elementary rules of evidence and summarily sentenced to be hanged. In all this needless and unseemly haste there was no serious attempt to charge or to prove that he committed a recognized violation of the laws of war. He was not charged with personally participating in the acts of atrocity or with ordering or condoning their commission. Not even knowledge of these crimes was attributed to him. It was simply alleged that he unlawfully disregarded and failed to discharge his duty as commander to control the operations of the members of his command, permitting them to commit the acts of atrocity. The recorded annals of warfare and the established principles of international law afford not the slightest precedent for such a charge. This indictment in effect permitted the military commission to make the crime whatever it willed, dependent upon its biased view as to petitioner's duties and his disregard thereof, a practice reminiscent of that pursued in certain less respected nations in recent years.

In my opinion, such a procedure is unworthy of the traditions of our people or of the immense sacrifices that they have made to advance the common ideals of mankind. The high feelings of the moment doubtless will be satisfied. But in the sober afterglow will come the realization of the boundless and dangerous implications of the procedure sanctioned today. No one in a position of command in an army, from sergeant to general, can escape those implications. Indeed, the fate of some future President of the United States and his chiefs of staff and military advisers may well have been sealed by this decision. But even more significant will be the hatred and ill-will growing out of the application of this unprecedented procedure. That has been the inevitable effect of every method of punishment disregarding the element of personal culpability. The effect in this instance, unfortunately, will be magnified infinitely, for here we are dealing with the rights of man on an international level. To subject an enemy belligerent to an unfair trial, to charge him with an unrecognized crime, or to vent on him our retributive emotions only antagonizes the enemy nation and hinders the reconciliation necessary to a peaceful world.

That there were brutal atrocities inflicted upon the helpless Filipino people, to whom tyranny is no stranger, by Japanese armed forces under the petitioner's command is undeniable. Starvation, execution or massacre without trial, torture, rape, murder and wanton destruction of property were foremost among the outright violations of the laws of war and of the conscience of a civilized world. That just punishment should be meted out to all those responsible for criminal acts of this nature is also beyond dispute. But these factors do not answer the problem in this case. They do not justify the abandonment of our devotion to justice in dealing with a fallen enemy commander. To conclude otherwise is to admit that the enemy has lost the battle but has destroyed our ideals.

War breeds atrocities. From the earliest conflicts of recorded history to the global struggles of modern times inhumanities, lust and pillage have been the inevitable byproducts of man's resort to force and arms. Unfortunately, such despicable acts have a dangerous tendency to call forth primitive impulses of vengeance and retaliation among the victimized peoples. The satisfaction of such impulses in turn breeds resentment and fresh tension. Thus does the spiral of cruelty and hatred grow.

If we are ever to develop an orderly international community based upon a recognition of human dignity it is of the utmost importance that the necessary punishment of those guilty of atrocities be as free as possible from the ugly stigma of revenge and vindictiveness. Justice must be tempered by compassion rather than by vengeance. In this, the first case involving this momentous problem ever to reach this Court, our responsibility is both lofty and difficult. We must insist, within the confines of our proper jurisdiction, that the highest standards of justice be applied in this trial of an enemy commander conducted under the authority of the United States. Otherwise stark retribution will be free to masquerade in a cloak of false legalism. And the hatred and cynicism engendered by that retribution will supplant the great ideals to which this nation is dedicated.

This Court fortunately has taken the first and most important step toward insuring the supremacy of law and justice in the treatment of an enemy belligerent accused of violating the laws of war. Jurisdiction properly has been asserted to inquire "into the cause of restraint of liberty" of such a person. 28 U. S. C. § 452. Thus the obnoxious doctrine asserted by the Government in this case, to the effect that restraints of liberty resulting from military trials of war criminals are political matters completely outside the arena of judicial review, has been rejected fully and unquestionably. This does not mean, of course, that the foreign affairs and policies of the nation are proper subjects of judicial inquiry. But when the liberty of any person is restrained by reason of the authority of the United States the writ of habeas corpus is available to test the legality of that restraint, even though direct court review of the restraint is prohibited. The conclusive presumption must be made, in this country at least, that illegal restraints are unauthorized and unjustified by any foreign policy of the Government and that commonly accepted juridical standards are to be recognized and enforced. On that basis judicial inquiry into these matters may proceed within its proper sphere.

The determination of the extent of review of war trials calls for judicial statesmanship of the highest order. The ultimate nature and scope of the writ of habeas corpus are within the discretion of the judiciary unless validly circumscribed by Congress. Here we are confronted with a use of the writ under circumstances novel in the history of the Court. For my own part, I do not feel that we should be confined by the traditional lines of review drawn in connection with the use of the writ by ordinary criminals who have direct access to the judiciary in the first instance. Those held by the military lack any such access; consequently the judicial review available by habeas corpus must be wider than usual in order that proper standards of justice may be enforceable.

But for the purposes of this case I accept the scope of review recognized by the Court at this time. As I understand it, the following issues in connection with war criminal trials are reviewable through the use of the writ of habeas corpus: (1) whether the military commission was lawfully created and had authority to try and to convict the accused of a war crime; (2) whether the charge against the accused stated a violation of the laws of war; (3) whether the commission, in admitting certain evidence, violated any law or military command defining the commission's authority in that respect; and (4) whether the commission lacked jurisdiction because of a failure to give advance notice to the protecting power as required by treaty or convention.

The Court, in my judgment, demonstrates conclusively that the military commission was lawfully created in this instance and that petitioner could not object to its power to try him for a recognized war crime. Without pausing here to discuss the third and fourth issues, however, I find it impossible to agree that the charge against the petitioner stated a recognized violation of the laws of war.

It is important, in the first place, to appreciate the background of events preceding this trial. From October 9, 1944, to September 2, 1945, the petitioner was the Commanding General of the 14th Army Group of the Imperial Japanese Army, with headquarters in the Philippines. The reconquest of the Philippines by the armed forces of the United States began approximately at the time when the petitioner assumed this command. Combined with a great and decisive sea battle, an invasion was made on the island of Leyte on October 20, 1944. "In the six days of the great naval action the Japanese position in the Philippines had become extremely critical. Most of the serviceable elements of the Japanese Navy had been committed to the battle with disastrous results. The strike had miscarried, and General MacArthur's land wedge was firmly implanted in the vulnerable flank of the enemy . . . There were 260,000 Japanese troops scattered over the Philippines but most of them might as well have been on the other side of the world so far as the enemy's ability to shift them to meet the American thrusts was concerned. If General MacArthur succeeded in establishing himself in the Visayas where he could stage, exploit, and spread under cover of overwhelming naval and air superiority, nothing could prevent him from overrunning the Philippines." Biennial Report of the Chief of Staff of the United States Army, July 1, 1943, to June 30, 1945, to the Secretary of War, p. 74.

By the end of 1944 the island of Leyte was largely in American hands. And on January 9, 1945, the island of Luzon was invaded. "Yamashita's inability to cope with General MacArthur's swift moves, his desired reaction to the deception measures, the guerrillas, and General Kenney's aircraft combined to place the Japanese in an impossible situation. The enemy was forced into a piecemeal commitment of his troops." *Ibid.*, p. 78. It was at this time and place that most of the alleged atrocities took place. Organized resistance around Manila ceased on February 23. Repeated land and air assaults pulverized the enemy and within a few months there was little left of petitioner's command except a few remnants which had gathered for a last stand among the precipitous mountains.

As the military commission here noted, "The Defense established the difficulties faced by the Accused with respect not only to the swift and overpowering advance of American forces, but also to the errors of his predecessors, weaknesses in organization, equipment, supply with especial reference to food and gasoline, training, communication, discipline and morale of his troops. It was alleged that the sudden assignment of Naval and Air Forces to his tactical command presented almost insurmountable difficulties. This situation was followed, the Defense contended, by failure to obey his orders to withdraw troops from Manila, and the subsequent massacre of unarmed civilians, particularly by Naval forces. Prior to the Luzon Campaign, Naval forces had reported to a separate ministry in the Japanese Government and Naval Commanders may not have been receptive or experienced in this instance with respect to a joint land operation under a single commander who was designated from the Army Service."

The day of final reckoning for the enemy arrived in August, 1945. On September 3, the petitioner surrendered to the United States Army at Baguio, Luzon. He immediately became a prisoner of war and was interned in prison in conformity with the rules of international law. On September 25, approximately three weeks after surrendering, he was served with the charge in issue in this case. Upon service of the charge he was removed from the status of a prisoner of war and placed in confinement as an accused war criminal. Arraignment followed on October 8 before a military commission specially appointed for the case. Petitioner pleaded not guilty. He was also served on that day with a bill of particulars alleging 64 crimes by troops under his command. A supplemental bill alleging 59 more crimes by his troops was filed on October 29, the same day that the trial began. No continuance was allowed for preparation of a defense as to the supplemental bill. The trial continued uninterrupted until December 5, 1945. On December 7 petitioner was found guilty as charged and was sentenced to be hanged.

The petitioner was accused of having "unlawfully disregarded and failed to discharge his duty as commander to control the operations of the members of his command, permitting them to commit brutal atrocities and other high crimes." The bills of particulars further alleged that specific acts of atrocity were committed by "members of the armed forces of Japan under the command of the accused." Nowhere was it alleged that the petitioner personally committed any of the atrocities, or that he ordered their commission, or that he had any knowledge of the commission thereof by members of his command.

The findings of the military commission bear out this absence of any direct personal charge against the petitioner. The commission merely found that atrocities and other high crimes "have been committed by members of the Japanese armed forces under your command . . . that they were not sporadic in nature but in many cases were methodically supervised by Japanese officers and noncommissioned officers; . . . That during the period in question you failed to provide effective control of your troops as was required by the circumstances."

In other words, read against the background of military events in the Philippines subsequent to October 9, 1944, these charges amount to this: "We, the victorious American forces, have done everything possible to destroy and disorganize your lines of communication, your effective control of your personnel, your ability to wage war. In those respects we have succeeded. We have defeated and crushed your forces. And now we charge and condemn you for having been inefficient in maintaining control of your troops during the period when we were so effectively besieging and eliminating your forces and blocking your ability to maintain effective control. Many terrible atrocities were committed by your disorganized troops. Because these atrocities were so widespread we will not bother to charge or prove that you committed, ordered or condoned any of them. We will assume that they must have resulted from your inefficiency and negligence as a commander. In short, we charge you with the crime of inefficiency in controlling your troops. We will judge the discharge of your duties by the disorganization which we ourselves created in large part. Our standards of judgment are whatever we wish to make them."

Nothing in all history or in international law, at least as far as I am aware, justifies such a charge against a fallen commander of a defeated force. To use the very inefficiency and disorganization created by the victorious forces as the primary basis for condemning officers of the defeated armies bears no resemblance to justice or to military reality.

International law makes no attempt to define the duties of a commander of an army under constant and overwhelming assault; nor does it impose liability under such circumstances for failure to meet the ordinary responsibilities of command. The omission is understandable. Duties, as well as ability to control troops, vary according to the nature and intensity of the particular battle. To find an unlawful deviation from duty under battle conditions requires difficult and speculative calculations. Such calculations become highly untrustworthy when they are made by the victor in relation to the actions of a vanquished commander. Objective and realistic norms of conduct are then extremely unlikely to be used in forming a judgment as to deviations from duty. The probability that vengeance will form the major part of the victor's judgment is an unfortunate but inescapable fact. So great is that probability that international law refuses to recognize such a judgment as a basis for a war crime, however fair the judgment may be in a particular instance. It is this consideration that undermines the charge against the petitioner in this case. The indictment permits, indeed compels, the military commission of a victorious nation to sit in judgment upon the military strategy and actions of the defeated enemy and to use its conclusions to determine the criminal liability of an enemy commander. Life and liberty are made to depend upon the biased will of the victor rather than upon objective standards of conduct.

The Court's reliance upon vague and indefinite references in certain of the Hague Conventions and the Geneva Red Cross Convention is misplaced. Thus the statement in Article 1 of the Annex to Hague Convention No. IV of October 18, 1907, 36 Stat. 2277, 2295, to the effect that the laws, rights and duties of war apply to military and volunteer corps only if they are "commanded by a person responsible for his subordinates," has no bearing upon the problem in this case. Even if it has, the clause "responsible for his subordinates" fails to state to whom the responsibility is owed or to indicate the type of responsibility contemplated. The phrase has received differing interpretations by authorities on international law. In Oppenheim, International Law (6th ed., rev. by Lauterpacht, 1940, vol. 2, p. 204, fn. 3) it is stated that "The meaning of the word 'responsible' . . . is not clear. It probably means 'responsible to some higher authority,' whether the person is appointed from above or elected from below; . . ." Another authority has stated that the word "responsible" in this particular context means "presumably to a higher authority," or "Possibly it merely means one who controls his subordinates and who therefore can be called to account for their acts." Wheaton, International Law (7th ed., by Keith, London, 1944, p. 172, fn. 30). Still another authority, Westlake, International Law (1907, Part II, p. 61), states that "Probably the responsibility intended is nothing more than a capacity of exercising effective control." Finally, Edmonds and Oppenheim, Land Warfare (1912, p. 19, par. 22) state that it is enough "if the commander of the corps is regularly or temporarily commissioned as an officer or is a person of position and authority . . ." It seems apparent beyond dispute that the word "responsible" was not used in this particular Hague Convention to hold the commander of a defeated army to any high standard of efficiency when he is under destructive attack; nor was it used to impute to him any criminal responsibility for war crimes committed by troops under his command under such circumstances.

The provisions of the other conventions referred to by the Court are on their face equally devoid of relevance or significance to the situation here in issue. Neither Article 19 of Hague Convention No. X, 36 Stat. 2371, 2389, nor Article 26 of the Geneva Red Cross Covention of 1929, 47 Stat. 2074, 2092, refers to circumstances where the troops of a commander commit atrocities while under heavily adverse battle conditions. Reference is also made to the requirement of Article 43 of the Annex to Hague Convention No. IV, 36 Stat. 2295, 2306, that the commander of a force occupying enemy territory "shall take all the measures in his power to restore, and ensure, as far as possible, public order and safety, while respecting, unless absolutely prevented, the laws in force in the country." But the petitioner was more than a commander of a force occupying enemy territory. He was the leader of an army under constant and devastating attacks by a superior re-invading force. This provision is silent as to the responsibilities of a commander under such conditions as that.

Even the laws of war heretofore recognized by this nation fail to impute responsibility to a fallen commander for excesses committed by his disorganized troops while under attack. Paragraph 347 of the War Department publication, Basic Field Manual, Rules of Land Warfare, FM 27–10 (1940), states the principal offenses under the laws of war recognized by the United States. This includes all of the atrocities which the Japanese troops were alleged to have committed in this instance. Originally this paragraph concluded with the statement that "The commanders ordering the commission of such acts, or under whose authority they are committed by their troops, may be punished by the belligerent into whose hands they may fall." The meaning of the phrase "under whose authority they are committed" was not clear. On November 15, 1944, however, this sentence was deleted and a new paragraph was added relating to the personal liability of those who violate the laws of war. Change 1, FM 27–10. The new paragraph 345.1 states that "Individuals and organizations who violate the accepted laws and customs of war may be punished therefor. However, the fact that the acts complained of were done pursuant to order of a superior or government sanction may be taken into consideration in determining culpability, either by way of defense or in mitigation of punishment. The person giving such orders may also be punished." From this the conclusion seems inescapable that the United States recognizes individual criminal responsibility for violations of the laws of war only as to those who commit the offenses or who order or direct their commission. Such was not the allegation here. Cf. Article 67 of the Articles of War, 10 U.S.C. § 1539.

There are numerous instances, especially with reference to the Philippine Insurrection in 1900 and 1901, where commanding officers were found to have violated the laws of war by specifically ordering members of their command to commit atrocities and other war crimes. Francisco Frani, G. O. 143, Dec. 13, 1900, Hq. Div. Phil.; Eugenio Fernandez and Juan Soriano, G. O. 28, Feb. 6, 1901, Hq. Div. Phil.; Ciriaco Cabungal, G. O. 188, Jul. 22, 1901, Hq. Div. Phil.; Natalio Valencia, G. O. 221, Aug. 17, 1901, Hq. Div. Phil.; Aniceta Angeles, G. O. 246, Sept. 2, 1901, Hq. Div. Phil.; Francisco Braganza, G. O. 291, Sept. 26, 1901, Hq. Div. Phil.; Lorenzo Andaya, G. O. 328, Oct. 25, 1901, Hq. Div. Phil. And in other cases officers have been held liable where they knew that a crime was to be committed, had the power to prevent it and failed to exercise that power. Pedro Abad Santos, G. O. 130, June 19, 1901, Hq. Div. Phil. Cf. Pedro A. Cruz, G. O. 264, Sept. 9, 1901, Hq. Div. Phil. In no recorded instance, however, has the mere inability to control troops under fire or attack by superior forces been made the basis of a charge of violating the laws of war.

The Government claims that the principle that commanders in the field are bound to control their troops has been applied so as to impose liability on the United States in international arbitrations. *Case of Jeannaud* (1880), 3 Moore, International Arbitrations (1898) 3000; *Case of The Zafiro* (1910), 5 Hackworth, Digest of International Law (1943) 707. The difference between arbitrating property rights and charging an individual with a crime against the laws of war is too obvious to require elaboration. But even more significant is the fact that even these arbitration cases fail to establish any principle of liability where troops are under constant assault and demoralizing influences by attacking forces. The same observation applies to the common law and statutory doctrine, referred to by the Government, that one who is under a legal duty to take protective or preventive action is guilty of criminal homicide if he willfully or negligently omits to act and death is proximately caused. *State* v. *Harrison*, 107 N.J. L. 213, 152 A. 867; *State* v. *Irvine*, 126 La. 434, 52 So. 567; Holmes, The Common Law, p. 278. No one denies that inaction or negligence may give rise to liability, civil or criminal. But it is quite another thing to say that the inability to control troops under highly competitive and disastrous battle conditions renders one guilty of a war crime in the absence of personal culpability. Had there been some element of knowledge or direct connection with the atrocities the problem would be entirely different. Moreover, it must be remembered that we are not dealing here with an ordinary tort or criminal action; precedents in those fields are of little if any value. Rather we are concerned with a proceeding involving an international crime, the treatment of which may have untold effects upon the future peace of the world. That fact must be kept uppermost in our search for precedent.

The only conclusion I can draw is that the charge made against the petitioner is clearly without precedent in international law or in the annals of recorded military history. This is not to say that enemy commanders may escape punishment for clear and unlawful failures to prevent atrocities. But that punishment should be based upon charges fairly drawn in light of established rules of international law and recognized concepts of justice.

But the charge in this case, as previously noted, was speedily drawn and filed but three weeks after the petitioner surrendered. The trial proceeded with great dispatch without allowing the defense time to prepare an adequate case. Petitioner's rights under the due process clause of the Fifth Amendment were grossly and openly violated without any justification. All of this was done without any thorough investigation and prosecution of those immediately responsible for the atrocities, out of which might have come some proof or indication of personal culpability on petitioner's part. Instead the loose charge was made that great numbers of atrocities had been committed and that petitioner was the commanding officer; hence he must have been guilty of disregard of duty. Under that charge the commission was free to establish whatever standard of duty on petitioner's part that it desired. By this flexible method a victorious nation may convict and execute any or all leaders of a vanquished foe, depending upon the prevailing degree of vengeance and the absence of any objective judicial review.

At a time like this when emotions are understandably high it is difficult to adopt a dispassionate attitude toward a case of this nature. Yet now is precisely the time when that attitude is most essential. While peoples in other lands may not share our beliefs as to due process and the dignity of the individual, we are not free to give effect to our emotions in reckless disregard of the rights of others. We live under the Constitution, which is the embodiment of all the high hopes and aspirations of the new world. And it is applicable in both war and peace. We must act accordingly. Indeed, an uncurbed spirit of revenge and retribution, masked in formal legal procedure for purposes of dealing with a fallen enemy commander, can do more lasting harm than all of the atrocities giving rise to that spirit. The people's faith in the fairness and objectiveness of the law can be seriously undercut by that spirit. The fires of nationalism can be further kindled. And the hearts of all mankind can be embittered and filled with hatred, leaving forlorn and impoverished the noble ideal of malice toward none and charity to all. These are the reasons that lead me to dissent in these terms.

MR. JUSTICE RUTLEDGE, dissenting.

Not with ease does one find his views at odds with the Court's in a matter of this character and gravity. Only the most deeply felt convictions could force one to differ. That reason alone leads me to do so now, against strong considerations for withholding dissent.

More is at stake than General Yamashita's fate. There could be no possible sympathy for him if he is guilty of the atrocities for which his death is sought. But there can be and should be justice administered according to law. In this stage of war's aftermath it is too early for Lincoln's great spirit, best lighted in the Second Inaugural, to have wide hold for the treatment of foes. It is not too early, it is never too early, for the nation steadfastly to follow its great constitutional traditions, none older or more universally protective against unbridled power than due process of law in the trial and punishment of men, that is, of all men, whether citizens, aliens, alien enemies or enemy belligerents. It can become too late.

This long-held attachment marks the great divide between our enemies and ourselves. Theirs was a philosophy of universal force. Ours is one of universal law, albeit imperfectly made flesh of our system and so dwelling among us. Every departure weakens the tradition, whether it touches the high or the low, the powerful or the weak, the triumphant or the conquered. If we need not or cannot be magnanimous, we can keep our own law on the plane from which it has not descended hitherto and to which the defeated foes' never rose.

With all deference to the opposing views of my brethren, whose attachment to that tradition needless to say is no less than my own, I cannot believe in the face of this record that the petitioner has had the fair trial our Constitution and laws command. Because I cannot reconcile what has occurred with their measure, I am forced to speak. At bottom my concern is that we shall not forsake in any case, whether Yamashita's or another's, the basic standards of trial which, among other guaranties, the nation fought to keep; that our system of military justice shall not alone among all our forms of judging be above or beyond the fundamental law or the control of Congress within its orbit of authority; and that this Court shall not fail in its part under the Constitution to see that these things do not happen.

This trial is unprecedented in our history. Never before have we tried and convicted an enemy general for action taken during hostilities or otherwise in the course of military operations or duty. Much less have we condemned one for failing to take action. The novelty is not lessened by the trial's having taken place after hostilities ended and the enemy, including the accused, had surrendered. Moreover, so far as the time permitted for our consideration has given opportunity, I have not been able to find precedent for the proceeding in the system of any nation founded in the basic principles of our constitutional democracy, in the laws of war or in other internationally binding authority or usage.

The novelty is legal as well as historical. We are on strange ground. Precedent is not all-controlling in law. There must be room for growth, since every precedent has an origin. But it is the essence of our tradition for judges, when they stand at the end of the marked way, to go forward with caution keeping sight, so far as they are able, upon the great landmarks left behind and the direction they point ahead. If, as may be hoped, we are now to enter upon a new era of law in the world, it becomes more important than ever before for the nations creating that system to observe their greatest traditions of administering justice, including this one, both in their own judging and in their new creation. The proceedings in this case veer so far from some of our time-tested road signs that I cannot take the large strides validating them would demand.

I.

It is not in our tradition for anyone to be charged with crime which is defined after his conduct, alleged to be criminal, has taken place;[1] or in language not sufficient to inform him of the nature of the offense or to enable him to make defense.[2] Mass guilt we do not impute to individuals, perhaps in any case but certainly in none where the person is not charged or shown actively to have participated in or knowingly to have failed in taking action to prevent the wrongs done by others, having both the duty and the power to do so.

It is outside our basic scheme to condemn men without giving reasonable opportunity for preparing defense;[3] in capital or other serious crimes to convict on "official documents

[1] *Cummings* v. *Missouri*, 4 Wall. 277; *Kring* v. *Missouri*, 107 U.S. 221.

[2] *Armour Packing Co.* v. *United States*, 209 U.S. 56, 83–84; *United States* v. *Cohen Grocery Co.*, 255 U.S. 81; cf. *Screws* v. *United States*, 325 U.S. 91. See note 17 and text.

[3] *Hawk* v. *Olson*, 326 U.S. 271; *Snyder* v. *Massachusetts*, 291 U.S. 97, 105: "What may not be taken away is notice of the charge and an adequate opportunity to be heard in defense of it." See Part III.

. . .; affidavits; . . . documents or translations thereof; diaries . . ., photographs, motion picture films, and . . . newspapers"[4] or on hearsay, once, twice or thrice removed,[5] more particularly when the documentary evidence or some of it is prepared *ex parte* by the prosecuting authority and includes not only opinion but conclusions of guilt. Nor in such cases do we deny the rights of confrontation of witnesses and cross-examination.[6]

Our tradition does not allow conviction by tribunals both authorized and bound[7] by the instrument of their creation to receive and consider evidence which is expressly excluded by Act of Congress or by treaty obligation; nor is it in accord with our basic concepts to make the tribunal, specially constituted for the particular trial, regardless of those prohibitions the sole and exclusive judge of the credibility, probative value and admissibility of whatever may be tendered as evidence.

The matter is not one merely of the character and admissibility of evidence. It goes to the very competency of the tribunal to try and punish consistently with the Constitution, the laws of the United States made in pursuance thereof, and treaties made under the nation's authority.

All these deviations from the fundamental law, and others, occurred in the course of constituting the commission, the

[4] The commission's findings state: "We have received for analysis and evaluation 423 exhibits consisting of official documents of the United States Army, The United States State Department, and the Commonwealth of the Philippines; affidavits; captured enemy documents or translations thereof; diaries taken from Japanese personnel, photographs, motion picture films, and Manila newspapers." See notes 19 and 20.

Concerning the specific nature of these elements in the proof, the issues to which they were directed, and their prejudicial effects, see text *infra* and notes in Part II.

[5] *Queen* v. *Hepburn*, 7 Cranch 290; *Donnelly* v. *United States*, 228 U.S. 243, 273. See Part II; note 21.

[6] *Motes* v. *United States*, 178 U.S. 458; *Paoni* v. *United States*, 281 F. 801. See Parts II and III.

[7] See Part II at notes 10, 19; Part III.

preparation for trial and defense, the trial itself, and therefore, in effect, in the sentence imposed. Whether taken singly in some instances as departures from specific constitutional mandates or in totality as in violation of the Fifth Amendment's command that *no* person shall be deprived of life, liberty or property without due process of law, a trial so vitiated cannot withstand constitutional scrutiny.

One basic protection of our system and one only, petitioner has had. He has been represented by able counsel, officers of the army he fought. Their difficult assignment has been done with extraordinary fidelity, not only to the accused, but to their high conception of military justice, always to be administered in subordination to the Constitution and consistent Acts of Congress and treaties. But, as will appear, even this conceded shield was taken away in much of its value, by denial of reasonable opportunity for them to perform their function.

On this denial and the commission's invalid constitution specifically, but also more generally upon the totality of departures from constitutional norms inherent in the idea of a fair trial, I rest my judgment that the commission was without jurisdiction from the beginning to try or punish the petitioner and that, if it had acquired jurisdiction then, its power to proceed was lost in the course of what was done before and during trial.

Only on one view, in my opinon, could either of these conclusions be avoided. This would be that an enemy belligerent in petitioner's position is altogether beyond the pale of constitutional protection, regardless of the fact that hostilities had ended and he had surrendered with his country. The Government has so argued, urging that we are still at war with Japan and all the power of the military effective during active hostilities in theatres of combat continues in full force unaffected by the events of August 14, 1945, and after.

In this view the action taken here is one of military necessity, exclusively within the authority of the President as Commander-in-Chief and his military subordinates to take in warding off military danger and subject to no judicial restraint on any account, although somewhat inconsistently it is said this Court may "examine" the proceedings generally.

As I understand the Court, this is in substance the effect of what has been done. For I cannot conceive any instance of departure from our basic concepts of fair trial, if the failures here are not sufficient to produce that effect.

We are technically still at war, because peace has not been negotiated finally or declared. But there is no longer the danger which always exists before surrender and armistice. Military necessity does not demand the same measures. The nation may be more secure now than at any time after peace is officially concluded. In these facts is one great difference from *Ex parte Quirin*, 317 U. S. 1. Punitive action taken now can be effective only for the next war, for purposes of military security. And enemy aliens, including belligerents, need the attenuated protections our system extends to them more now than before hostilities ceased or than they may after a treaty of peace is signed. Ample power there is to punish them or others for crimes, whether under the laws of war during its course or later during occupation. There can be no question of that. The only question is how it shall be done, consistently with universal constitutional commands or outside their restricting effects. In this sense I think the Constitution follows the flag.

The other thing to be mentioned in order to be put aside is that we have no question here of what the military might have done in a field of combat. There the maxim about the law becoming silent in the noise of arms applies. The purpose of battle is to kill. But it does not follow that this would justify killing by trial after capture or surrender, without compliance with laws or treaties made to apply in such cases, whether trial is before or after hostilities end.

I turn now to discuss some of the details of what has taken place. My basic difference is with the Court's view that provisions of the Articles of War and of treaties are not made applicable to this proceeding and with its ruling that, absent such applicable provisions, none of the things done so vitiated the trial and sentence as to deprive the commission of jurisdiction.

My brother MURPHY has discussed the charge with respect to the substance of the crime. With his conclusions in this respect I agree. My own primary concern will be with the constitution of the commission and other matters taking place in the course of the proceedings, relating chiefly to the denial of reasonable opportunity to prepare petitioner's defense and the sufficiency of the evidence, together with serious questions of admissibility, to prove an offense, all going as I think to the commission's jurisdiction.

Necessarily only a short sketch can be given concerning each matter. And it may be stated at the start that, although it was ruled in *Ex parte Quirin, supra,* that this Court had no function to review the evidence, it was not there or elsewhere determined that it could not ascertain whether conviction is founded upon evidence expressly excluded by Congress or treaty; nor does the Court purport to do so now.

II.

Invalidity of the Commission's Constitution.

The fountainhead of the commission's authority was General MacArthur's directive by which General Styer was ordered to and pursuant to which he did proceed with constituting the commission.[8] The directive was accompanied

[8] The line of authorization within the military hierarchy extended from the President, through the Joint Chiefs of Staff and General MacArthur, to General Styer, whose order of September 25th and others were made pursuant to and in conformity with General MacArthur's directive. The charge was prepared by the Judge Advocate General's Department of the Army. There is no

by elaborate and detailed rules and regulations prescribing the procedure and rules of evidence to be followed, of which for present purposes §16, set forth below,[9] is crucial.

Section 16, as will be noted, permits reception of documents, reports, affidavits, depositions, diaries, letters, copies of documents or other secondary evidence of their contents, hearsay, opinion evidence and conclusions, in fact of anything which in the commission's opinion "would be of assistance in proving or disproving the charge," without any of the usual modes of authentication.

A more complete abrogation of customary safeguards relating to the proof, whether in the usual rules of evidence or any reasonable substitute and whether for use in the trial of crime in the civil courts or military tribunals, hardly could have been made. So far as the admissibility and probative value of evidence was concerned, the directive made the commission a law unto itself.

---

dispute concerning these facts or that the directive was binding on General Styer and the commission, though it is argued his own authority as area commanding general was independently sufficient to sustain what was done.

[9] "16. Evidence.—a. The commission shall admit such evidence as in its opinion would be of assistance in proving or disproving the charge, or such as in the commission's opinion would have probative value in the mind of a reasonable man. In particular, and without limiting in any way the scope of the foregoing general rules, the following evidence may be admitted:

(1) Any document which appears to the commission to have been signed or issued officially by any officer, department, agency, or member of the armed forces of any government, without proof of the signature or of the issuance of the document.

(2) Any report which appears to the commission to have been signed or issued by the International Red Cross or a member thereof, or by a medical doctor or any medical service personnel, or by an investigator or intelligence officer, or by any other person whom the commission finds to have been acting in the course of his duty when making the report.

(3) Affidavits, depositions, or other statements taken by an officer detailed for that purpose by military authority.

(4) Any diary, letter or other document appearing to the commission to contain information relating to the charge.

(5) A copy of any document or other secondary evidence of its contents, if the commission believes that the original is not available or cannot be produced without undue delay. . . ."

It acted accordingly. As against insistent and persistent objection to the reception of all kinds of "evidence," oral, documentary and photographic, for nearly every kind of defect under any of the usual prevailing standards for admissibility and probative value, the commission not only consistently ruled against the defense, but repeatedly stated it was bound by the directive to receive the kinds of evidence it specified,[10] reprimanded counsel for continuing to make objection, declined to hear further objections, and in more than one instance during the course of the proceedings reversed its rulings favorable to the defense, where initially it had declined to receive what the prosecution offered. Every conceivable kind of statement, rumor, report, at first, second, third or further hand, written, printed or oral, and one "propaganda" film were allowed to come in, most of this relating to atrocities committed by troops under petitioner's command throughout the several thousand islands of the Philippine Archipelago during the period of active hostilities covered by the American forces' return to and recapture of the Philippines.[11]

The findings reflect the character of the proof and the charge. The statement quoted above[12] gives only a numerical idea of the instances in which ordinary safeguards in reception of written evidence were ignored. In addition to these 423 "exhibits," the findings state the commission "has heard 286 persons during the course of this trial, most of whom have given eye-witness accounts of what they endured or what they saw."

[10] In one instance the president of the commission said: "The rules and regulations which guide this Commission are binding upon the Commission and agencies provided to assist the Commission. . . . We have been authorized to receive and weigh such evidence as we can consider to have probative value, and further comments by the Defense on the right which we have to accept this evidence is decidedly out of order." But see note 19.

[11] Cf. text *infra* at note 19 concerning the prejudicial character of the evidence.

[12] Note 4.

But there is not a suggestion in the findings that petitioner personally participated in, was present at the occurrence of, or ordered any of these incidents, with the exception of the wholly inferential suggestion noted below. Nor is there any express finding that he knew of any one of the incidents in particular or of all taken together. The only inferential findings that he had knowledge, or that the commission so found, are in the statement that the "crimes *alleged to have been permitted* by the Accused in violation of the laws of war may be grouped into three categories" set out below,[13] in the further statement that "the Prosecution presented evidence to show that the crimes were so extensive and widespread, both as to time and area,[14] that *they must* either have been *wilfully permitted* by the Accused, *or secretly ordered* by" him; and in the conclusion of guilt and the sentence.[15] (Em-

[13] Namely, "(1) Starvation, execution or massacre without trial and maladministration generally of civilian internees and prisoners of war; (2) Torture, rape, murder and mass execution of very large numbers of residents of the Philippines, including women and children and members of religious orders, by starvation, beheading, bayoneting, clubbing, hanging, burning alive, and destruction by explosives; (3) Burning and demolition without adequate military necessity of large numbers of homes, places of business, places of religious worship, hospitals, public buildings, and educational institutions. In point of time, the offenses extended throughout the period the Accused was in command of Japanese troops in the Philippines. In point of area, the crimes extended throughout the Philippine Archipelago, although by far the most of the incredible acts occurred on Luzon."

[14] Cf. note 13.

[15] In addition the findings set forth that captured orders of subordinate officers gave proof that "they, at least," ordered acts "leading directly to" atrocities; that "the *proof offered* to the Commission *alleged* criminal *neglect* . . . as well as complete failure *by the higher echelons* of command *to detect* and prevent cruel and inhuman treatment accorded by local commanders and guards"; and that, although the "Defense established the difficulties faced by the Accused" with special reference among other things to the discipline and morale of his troops under the "swift and overpowering advance of American forces," and notwithstanding he had stoutly maintained his complete ignorance of the crimes, still he was an officer of long experience; his assignment was one of broad responsibility; it was his duty "*to discover* and control" crimes by his troops, if widespread, and therefore

"The Commission concludes: (1) That a series of atrocities and other high crimes have been committed by members of the Japanese armed forces under

phasis added.) Indeed the commission's ultimate findings[16] draw no express conclusion of knowledge, but state only two things: (1) the fact of widespread atrocities and crimes; (2) that petitioner "failed to provide effective control . . . as was required by the circumstances."

This vagueness, if not vacuity, in the findings runs throughout the proceedings, from the charge itself through the proof and the findings, to the conclusion. It affects the very gist of the offense, whether that was wilful, informed and intentional omission to restrain and control troops *known* by petitioner to be committing crimes or was only a negligent failure on his part *to discover* this and take whatever measures he then could to stop the conduct.

Although it is impossible to determine from what is before us whether petitioner in fact has been convicted of one or the other or of both these things,[17] the case has been presented

your command against people of the United States, their allies and dependencies throughout the Philippine Islands; that they were not sporadic in nature but in many cases were methodically supervised by Japanese officers and noncommissioned officers; (2) That during the period in question you failed to provide effective control of your troops as was required by the circumstances.

"Accordingly upon secret written ballot, two-thirds or more of the members concurring, the Commission finds you guilty as charged and sentences you to death by hanging." (Emphasis added.)

[16] See note 15.

[17] The charge, set forth at the end of this note, is consistent with either theory—or both—and thus ambiguous, as were the findings. See note 15. The only word implying knowledge was "permitting." If "wilfully" is essential to constitute a crime or charge of one, otherwise subject to the objection of "vagueness," cf. *Screws* v. *United States*, 325 U.S. 91, it would seem that "permitting" alone would hardly be sufficient to charge "wilful and intentional" action or omission; and, if taken to be sufficient to charge knowledge, it would follow necessarily that the charge itself was not drawn to state and was insufficient to support a finding of mere failure to detect or discover the criminal conduct of others.

At the most, "permitting" could charge knowledge only by inference or implication. And reasonably the word could be taken in the context of the charge to mean "allowing" or "not preventing," a meaning consistent with absence of knowledge and mere failure to discover. In capital cases such ambiguity is wholly out of place. The proof was equally ambiguous in the same respect, so far as we have been informed, and so, to repeat, were the

on the former basis and, unless as is noted below there is fatal duplicity, it must be taken that the crime charged and sought to be proved was only the failure, with knowledge, to perform the commander's function of control, although the Court's opinion nowhere expressly declares that knowledge was essential to guilt or necessary to be set forth in the charge.

It is in respect to this feature especially, quite apart from the reception of unverified rumor, report, etc., that perhaps the greatest prejudice arose from the admission of untrustworthy, unverified, unauthenticated evidence which could not be probed by cross-examination or other means of testing credibility, probative value or authenticity.

Counsel for the defense have informed us in the brief and at the argument that the sole proof of knowledge introduced at the trial was in the form of ex parte affidavits and depositions. Apart from what has been excerpted from the record in the applications and the briefs, and such portions of the record as I have been able to examine, it has been impossible for me fully to verify counsel's statement in this respect. But the Government has not disputed it; and it has maintained that we have no right to examine the record upon any question "of evidence." Accordingly, without concession to that view, the statement of counsel is taken for the fact. And in that state of things petitioner has been convicted of a crime in which knowledge is an essential element, with no proof

findings. The use of "wilfully," even qualified by a "must have," one time only in the findings hardly can supply the absence of that or an equivalent word or language in the charge or in the proof to support that essential element in the crime.

The charge was as follows: "Tomoyuki Yamashita, General Imperial Japanese Army, between 9 October 1944 and 2 September 1945, at Manila and at other places in the Philippine Islands, while commander of armed forces of Japan at war with the United States of America and its allies, unlawfully disregarded and failed to discharge his duty as commander to control the operations of the members of his command, permitting them to commit brutal atrocities and other high crimes against people of the United States and of its allies and dependencies, particularly the Philippines; and he, General Tomoyuki Yamashita, thereby violated the laws of war."

of knowledge other than what would be inadmissible in any other capital case or proceeding under our system, civil or military, and which furthermore Congress has expressly commanded shall not be received in such cases tried by military commissions and other military tribunals.[18]

Moreover counsel assert in the brief, and this also is not denied, that the sole proof made of certain of the specifications in the bills of particulars was by ex parte affidavits. It was in relation to this also vital phase of the proof that there occurred one of the commission's reversals of its earlier rulings in favor of the defense,[19] a fact in itself conclusive demonstration of the necessity to the prosecution's case of the prohibited type of evidence and of its prejudicial effects upon the defense.

These two basic elements in the proof, namely, proof of knowledge of the crimes and proof of the specifications in the bills, that is, of the atrocities themselves, constitute the

[18] Cf. text *infra* Part IV.

[19] On November 1, early in the trial, the president of the commission stated: "I think the Prosecution should consider the desirability of striking certain items. The Commission feels that there must be witnesses introduced on each of the specifications or items. *It has no objection to considering affidavits, but it is unwilling to form an opinion of a particular item based solely on an affidavit.* Therefore, until evidence is introduced, these particular exhibits are rejected." (Emphasis added.)

Later evidence of the excluded type was offered, to introduction of which the defense objected on various grounds including the prior ruling. At the prosecution's urging the commission withdrew to deliberate. Later it announced that "after further consideration, the Commission reverses that ruling [of November 1] and affirms its prerogative of receiving and considering affidavits or depositions, if it chooses to do so, for whatever probative value the Commission believes they may have, without regard to the presentation of some partially corroborative oral testimony." It then added: "The Commission *directs* the Prosecution again to introduce the affidavits or depositions then in question, and other documents of a similar nature which the Prosecution stated had been prepared for introduction." (Emphasis added.)

Thereafter this type of evidence was consistently received and again, by the undisputed statement of counsel, as the sole proof of many of the specifications of the bills, a procedure which they characterize correctly in my view as having "in effect, stripped the proceeding of all semblance of a trial and converted it into an ex parte investigation."

most important instances perhaps, if not the most flagrant,[20] of departure not only from the express command of Congress against receiving such proof but from the whole British-American tradition of the common law and the Constitution. Many others occurred, which there is neither time nor space to mention.[21]

Petitioner asserts, and there can be no reason to doubt, that by the use of all this forbidden evidence he was deprived of the right of cross-examination and other means to establish the credibility of the deponents or affiants, not to speak of the authors of reports, letters, documents and newspaper articles; of opportunity to determine whether the multitudinous crimes specified in the bills were committed in fact by troops under his command or by naval or air force troops not under his command at the time alleged; to ascertain whether the crimes attested were isolated acts of individual soldiers or were military acts committed by troop units acting under supervision of officers; and, finally, whether "in short, there was such a 'pattern' of" conduct as the prosecution alleged and its whole theory of the crime and the evidence required to be made out.

He points out in this connection that the commission based its decision on a finding as to the extent and number of the atrocities and that this of itself establishes the preju-

[20] This perhaps consisted in the showing of the so-called "propaganda" film, "Orders from Tokyo," portraying scenes of battle destruction in Manila, which counsel say "was not in itself seriously objectionable." Highly objectionable, inflammatory and prejudicial, however, was the accompanying sound track with comment that the film was "evidence which will convict," mentioning petitioner specifically by name.

[21] Innumerable instances of hearsay, once or several times removed, relating to all manner of incidents, rumors, reports, etc., were among these. Many instances, too, are shown of the use of opinion evidence and conclusions of guilt, including reports made after ex parte investigations by the War Crimes Branch of the Judge Advocate General's Department, which it was and is urged had the effect of "putting the prosecution on the witness stand" and of usurping the commission's function as judge of the law and the facts. It is said also that some of the reports were received as the sole proof of some of the specifications.

dicial effect of the affidavits, etc., and of the denial resulting from their reception of any means of probing the evidence they contained, including all opportunity for cross-examination. Yet it is said there is no sufficient showing of prejudice. The effect could not have been other than highly prejudicial. The matter is not one merely of "rules of evidence." It goes, as will appear more fully later, to the basic right of defense, including some fair opportunity to test probative value.

Insufficient as this recital is to give a fair impression of what was done, it is enough to show that this was no trial in the traditions of the common law and the Constitution. If the tribunal itself was not strange to them otherwise, it was in its forms and modes of procedure, in the character and substance of the evidence it received, in the denial of all means to the accused and his counsel for testing the evidence, in the brevity and ambiguity of its findings made upon such a mass of material and, as will appear, in the denial of any reasonable opportunity for preparation of the defense. Because this last deprivation not only is important in itself, but is closely related to the departures from all limitations upon the character of and modes of making the proof, it will be considered before turning to the important legal questions relating to whether all these violations of our traditions can be brushed aside as not forbidden by the valid Acts of Congress, treaties and the Constitution, in that order. If all these traditions can be so put away, then indeed will we have entered upon a new but foreboding era of law.

III.

Denial of Opportunity to Prepare Defense.

Petitioner surrendered September 3, 1945, and was interned as a prisoner of war in conformity with Article 9 of the Geneva Convention of July 27, 1929.[22] He was served with the charge on September 25 and put in confinement as

[22] Also with Paragraph 82 of the Rules of Land Warfare.

an accused war criminal. On October 8 he was arraigned and pleaded not guilty. On October 29 the trial began and it continued until December 7, when sentence was pronounced, exactly four years almost to the hour from the attack on Pearl Harbor.

On the day of arraignment, October 8, three weeks before the trial began, petitioner was served with a bill of particulars specifying 64 items setting forth a vast number of atrocities and crimes allegedly committed by troops under his command.[23] The six officers appointed as defense counsel thus had three weeks, it is true at the prosecution's suggestion a week longer than they sought at first, to investigate and prepare to meet all these items and the large number of incidents they embodied, many of which had occurred in distant islands of the archipelago. There is some question whether they then anticipated the full scope and character of the charge or the evidence they would have to meet. But, as will appear, they worked night and day at the task. Even so it would have been impossible to do thoroughly, had nothing more occurred.

But there was more. On the first day of the trial, October 29, the prosecution filed a supplemental bill of particulars, containing 59 more specifications of the same general character, involving perhaps as many incidents occurring over an equally wide area.[24] A copy had been given the de-

[23] Typical of the items are allegations that members of the armed forces of Japan under the command of the accused committed the acts "During the months of October, November and December 1944 [of] brutally mistreating and torturing numerous unarmed noncombatant civilians at the Japanese Military Police Headquarters located at Cortabitarte and Mabini Streets, Manila" and "On about 19 February 1945, in the Town of Cuenca, Batangas Province, brutally mistreating, massacring and killing Jose M. Laguo, Esteban Magsamdol, Jose Lanbo, Felisa Apuntar, Elfidio Lunar, Victoriana Ramo, and 978 other persons, all unarmed noncombatant civilians, pillaging and unnecessary [sic], deliberately and wantonly devastating, burning and destroying large areas of that town."

[24] The supplemental bill contains allegations similar to those set out in the original bill. See note 23. For example, it charged that members of the

fense three days earlier. One item, No. 89, charged that American soldiers, prisoners of war, had been tried and executed without notice having been given to the protecting power of the United States in accordance with the requirements of the Geneva Convention, which it is now argued, strangely, the United States was not required to observe as to petitioner's trial.[25]

But what is more important is that defense counsel, as they felt was their duty, at once moved for a continuance.[26] The application was denied. However the commission indicated that if, at the end of the prosecution's presentation concerning the original bill, counsel should "believe they require additional time . . . , the Commission will consider such a motion at that time," before taking up the items of the supplemental bill. Counsel again indicated, without other result, that time was desired at once "as much, if not more" to prepare for cross-examination "as the Prosecution's case goes in" as to prepare affirmative defense.

On the next day, October 30, the commission interrupted

---

armed forces of Japan under the command of the accused "during the period from 9 October 1944 to about 1 February 1945, at Cavite City, Imus, and elsewhere in Cavite Province," were permitted to commit the acts of "brutally mistreating, torturing, and killing or attempting to kill, without cause or trial, unarmed noncombatant civilians."

[25] See note 39 and text, Part V.

[26] In support of the motion counsel indicated surprise by saying that, though it was assumed two or three new specifications might be added, there had been no expectation of 59 "about entirely different persons and times." The statement continued:

"We have worked earnestly seven days a week in order to prepare the defense on 64 specifications. And when I say 'prepare the defense,' sir, I do not mean merely an affirmative defense, but to acquaint ourselves with the facts so that we could properly cross examine the Prosecution's witnesses.

". . . 'In advance of trial' means: Sufficient time to allow the Defense a chance to prepare its defense.

"We earnestly state that we must have this time in order to adequately prepare a defense. I might add, sir, we think that this is important to the Accused, but far more important than any rights of this Accused, we believe, is the proposition that this Commission should not deviate from a fundamental American concept of fairness . . ."

the prosecutor to say it would not then listen to testimony or discussion upon the supplemental bill. After colloquy it adhered to its prior ruling and, in response to inquiry from the prosecution, the defense indicated it would require two weeks before it could proceed on the supplemental bill. On November 1 the commission ruled it would not receive affidavits without corroboration by witnesses on any specification, a ruling reversed four days later.

On November 2, after the commission had received an affirmative answer to its inquiry whether the defense was prepared to proceed with an item in the supplemental bill which the prosecution proposed to prove, it announced: "Hereafter, then, unless there is no [sic] objection by the Defense, the Commission will assume that you are prepared to proceed with any items in the Supplemental Bill." On November 8, the question arose again upon the prosecution's inquiry as to when the defense would be ready to proceed on the supplemental bill, the prosecutor adding: "Frankly, sir, it took the War Crimes Commission some three months to investigate these matters and I cannot conceive of the Defense undertaking a similar investigation with any less period of time." Stating it realized "the tremendous task which we placed upon the Defense" and its "determination to give them the time they require," the commission again adhered to its ruling of October 29.

Four days later the commission announced it would grant a continuance "only for the most urgent and unavoidable reasons."[27]

On November 20, when the prosecution rested, senior de-

[27] The commission went on to question the need for all of the six officers representing the defense to be present during presentation of all the case, suggested one or two would be adequate and others "should be out of the courtroom" engaged in other matters and strongly suggested bringing in additional counsel in the midst of the trial, all to the end that "need to request a continuance may not arise."

fense counsel moved for a reasonable continuance, recalling the commission's indication that it would then consider such a motion and stating that since October 29 the defense had been "working day and night," with "no time whatsoever to prepare any affirmative defense," since counsel had been fully occupied trying "to keep up with that new Bill of Particulars."

The commission thereupon retired for deliberation and, on resuming its sessions shortly, denied the motion. Counsel then asked for "a short recess of a day." The commission suggested a recess until 1:30 in the afternoon. Counsel responded this would not suffice. The commission stated it felt "that the Defense should be prepared at least on its opening statement," to which senior counsel answered: "We haven't had time to do that, sir." The commission then recessed until 8:30 the following morning.

Further comment is hardly required. Obviously the burden placed upon the defense, in the short time allowed for preparation on the original bill, was not only "tremendous." In view of all the facts, it was an impossible one, even though the time allowed was a week longer than asked. But the grosser vice was later when the burden was more than doubled by service of the supplemental bill on the eve of trial, a procedure which, taken in connection with the consistent denials of continuance and the commission's later reversal of its rulings favorable to the defense, was wholly arbitrary, cutting off the last vestige of adequate chance to prepare defense and imposing a burden the most able counsel could not bear. This sort of thing has no place in our system of justice, civil or military. Without more, this wide departure from the most elementary principles of fairness vitiated the proceeding. When added to the other denials of fundamental right sketched above, it deprived the proceeding of any semblance of trial as we know that institution.

IV.

Applicability of the Articles of War.

The Court's opinion puts the proceeding and the petitioner, in so far as any rights relating to his trial and conviction are concerned, wholly outside the Articles of War. In view of what has taken place, I think the decision's necessary effect is also to place them entirely beyond limitation and protection, respectively, by the Constitution. I disagree as to both conclusions or effects.

The Court rules that Congress has not made Articles 25 and 38 applicable to this proceeding. I think it has made them applicable to this and all other military commissions or tribunals. If so, the commission not only lost all power to punish petitioner by what occurred in the proceedings. It never acquired jurisdiction to try him. For the directive by which it was constituted, in the provisions of § 16,[28] was squarely in conflict with Articles 25 and 38 of the Articles of War[29] and therefore was void.

[28] See note 9.

[29] Article 25 is as follows: "A duly authenticated deposition taken upon reasonable notice to the opposite party may be read in evidence before *any military court or commission in any case not capital,* or in any proceeding before a *court of inquiry or a military board, if* such deposition be taken when the witness resides, is found, or is about to go beyond the State, Territory, or district in which the court, commission, or board is ordered to sit, or beyond the distance of one hundred miles from the place of trial or hearing, or when it appears to the satisfaction of the court, commission, board, or appointing authority that the witness, by reason of age, sickness, bodily infirmity, imprisonment, or other reasonable cause, is unable to appear and testify in person at the place of trial or hearing: *Provided, That testimony by deposition may be adduced for the defense in capital cases.*" (Emphasis added.) 10 U.S.C. § 1496.

Article 38 reads: "The President may, by regulations, which he may modify from time to time, prescribe the procedure, *including modes of proof,* in cases before *courts-martial, courts of inquiry, military commissions, and other military tribunals,* which regulations shall insofar as he shall deem practicable, apply the rules of evidence generally recognized in the trial of criminal cases in the district courts of the United States: *Provided, That nothing contrary to or inconsistent with these articles shall be so prescribed: Provided further, That all rules made in pursuance of this article shall be laid before the Congress annually.*" (Emphasis added.) 10 U.S.C. § 1509.

Article 25 allows reading of depositions in evidence, under prescribed conditions, in the plainest terms "before *any* military court or commission *in any case not capital*," providing, however, that "testimony by deposition may be adduced *for the defense in capital* cases." (Emphasis added.) This language clearly and broadly covers every kind of military tribunal, whether "court" or "commission." It covers all capital cases. It makes no exception or distinction for any accused.

Article 38 authorizes the President by regulations to prescribe procedure, including modes of proof, even more all-inclusively if possible, "in cases before courts-martial, courts of inquiry, military commissions, and other military tribunals." Language could not be more broadly inclusive. No exceptions are mentioned or suggested, whether of tribunals or of accused persons. Every kind of military body for performing the function of trial is covered. That is clear from the face of the Article.

Article 38 moreover limits the President's power. He is so far as practicable to prescribe "the rules of evidence generally recognized in the trial of criminal cases in the district courts of the United States," a clear mandate that Congress intended all military trials to conform as closely as possible to our customary procedural and evidentiary protections, constitutional and statutory, for accused persons. But there are also two unqualified limitations, one "that nothing contrary to or inconsistent with *these* articles [specifically here Article 25] shall be so prescribed"; the other "that all rules made in pursuance of this article shall be laid before the Congress annually."

Notwithstanding these broad terms the Court, resting chiefly on Article 2, concludes the petitioner was not among the persons there declared to be subject to the Articles of War and therefore the commission which tries him is not subject to them. That Article does not cover prisoners of war or war criminals. Neither does it cover civilians in occupied territories, theatres of military operations or other places under military jurisdiction within or without the United States or territory subject to its sovereignty, whether they be neutrals or enemy aliens, even citizens of the United States, unless they are connected in the manner Article 2 prescribes with our armed forces, exclusive of the Navy.

The logic which excludes petitioner on the basis that prisoners of war are not mentioned in Article 2 would exclude all these. I strongly doubt the Court would go so far, if presented with a trial like this in such instances. Nor does it follow necessarily that, because some persons may not be mentioned in Article 2, they can be tried without regard to any of the limitations placed by any of the other Articles upon military tribunals.

Article 2 in defining persons "subject to the articles of war" was, I think, specifying those to whom the Articles in general were applicable. And there is no dispute that most of the Articles are not applicable to the petitioner. It does not follow, however, and Article 2 does not provide, that there may not be in the Articles specific provisions covering persons other than those specified in Article 2. Had it so provided, Article 2 would have been contradictory not only of Articles 25 and 38 but also of Article 15 among others.

In 1916, when the last general revision of the Articles of War took place,[30] for the first time certain of the Articles were specifically made applicable to military commissions. Until then they had applied only to courts-martial. There were two purposes, the first to give statutory recognition to

[30] Another revision of the Articles of War took place in 1920. At this time Article 15 was slightly amended.

In 1916 Article 15 was enacted to read: "The provisions of these articles conferring jurisdiction upon courts-martial shall not be construed as depriving military commissions, provost courts, or other military tribunals *of concurrent jurisdiction* in respect of offenders or offenses that by the law of war may be lawfully triable by such military commissions, provost courts, or other military tribunals." (Emphasis added.)

The 1920 amendment put in the words "by statute or" before the words "by the law of war" and omitted the word "lawfully."

the military commission without loss of prior jurisdiction and the second to give those tried before military commissions some of the more important protections afforded persons tried by courts-martial.

In order to effectuate the first purpose, the Army proposed Article 15.[31] To effectuate the second purpose, Articles 25

[31] Speaking at the Hearings before the Committee on Military Affairs, House of Representatives, 62d Cong., 2d Sess., printed as an Appendix to S. Rep. 229, 63d Cong., 2d Sess., General Crowder said:

"The next article, No. 15, is entirely new, and the reasons for its insertion in the code are these: In our War with Mexico two war courts were brought into existence by orders of Gen. Scott, viz, the military commission and the council of war. By the military commission Gen. Scott tried cases cognizable in time of peace by civil courts, and by the council of war he tried offenses against the laws of war. *The council of war did not survive the Mexican War period, and in our subsequent wars its jurisdiction has been taken over by the military commission*, which during the Civil War period tried more than 2,000 cases. While the military commission has not been formally authorized by statute, its jurisdiction as a war court has been upheld by the Supreme Court of the United States. It is an institution of the greatest importance in a period of war and should be preserved. In the new code *the jurisdiction of courts-martial has been somewhat amplified by the introduction of the phrase* 'Persons subject to military law.' *There will be more instances in the future than in the past when the jurisdiction of courts-martial will overlap that of the war courts*, and the question would arise whether Congress having vested jurisdiction by statute the common law of war *jurisdiction* was not ousted. I wish to make it *perfectly plain by the new article that in such cases the jurisdiction of the war court is concurrent*." S. Rep. No. 229, 63d Cong., 2d Sess., p. 53. (Emphasis added.)

And later, in 1916, speaking before the Subcommittee on Military Affairs of the Senate at their Hearings on S. 3191, a project for the revision of the Articles of War, 64th Cong., 1st Sess., printed as an Appendix to S. Rep. 130, 64th Cong., 1st Sess., General Crowder explained at greater length:

"Article 15 is new. We have included in article 2 as subject to military law a number of persons who are also subject to trial by military commission. A military commission is our comom-law war court. It has no statutory existence, though it is recognized by statute law. As long as the articles embraced them in the designation 'persons subject to military law,' and provided that they might be tried by court-martial, *I was afraid that, having made a special provision for their trial by court-martial, it might be held that the provision operated to exclude trials by military commission and other war courts; so this new article was introduced . . .*

"*It just saves to these war courts the jurisdiction they now have and makes it a concurrent jurisdiction with courts-martial, so that the military commander in the field* in time of war *will be at liberty to employ either form of* court that happens to be convenient. *Both classes of courts have the same* procedure. For the information of the committee and in explanation of these

and 38 and several others were proposed.[32] But as the Court now construes the Articles of War, they have no application to military commissions before which alleged offenders against the laws of war are tried. What the Court holds in effect is that there are two types of military commission, one to try offenses which might be cognizable by a court-martial,

---

war courts to which I have referred I insert here an explanation from Winthrop's Military Law and Precedents—

" 'The military commission—a war court—had its origin in G. O. 20, Headquarters of the Army at Tampico, February 19, 1847 (Gen. Scott). Its jurisdiction was confined mainly to criminal offenses of the class cognizable by civil courts in time of peace committed by inhabitants of the theater of hostilities. A further war court was originated by Gen. Scott at the same time, called "council of war," with jurisdiction to try the same classes of persons for violations of the laws of war, mainly guerrillas. These two jurisdictions were united in the later war court of the Civil War and Spanish War periods, for which the general designation of "military commission" was retained. The military commission was given statutory recognition in section 30, act of March 3, 1863, and in various other statutes of that period. The United States Supreme Court has acknowledged the validity of its judgments (Ex parte Vallandigham, 1 Wall., 243, and Coleman *v.* Tennessee, 97 U.S., 509). It tried more than 2,000 cases during the Civil War and reconstruction period. *Its composition, constitution, and procedure follows the analogy of courts-martial.* Another war court is the provost court, an inferior court with jurisdiction assimilated to that of justices of the peace and police courts; and other war courts variously designated "courts of conciliation," "arbitrators," "military tribunals," have been convened by military commanders in the exercise of the war power as occasion and necessity dictated.'

"Yet, as I have said, these war courts never have been formally authorized by statute.

"Senator COLT. They grew out of usage and necessity?

"Gen. CROWDER. Out of usage and necessity. I thought it was just as well, as inquiries would arise, to put this information in the record." S. Rep. No. 130, 64th Cong., 1st Sess. (1916) p. 40. (Emphasis added.)

Article 15 was also explained in the "Report of a committee on the proposed revision of the articles of war, pursuant to instructions of the Chief of Staff, March 10, 1915," included in Revision of the Articles of War, Comparative Prints, etc., 1904–1920, J. A. G. O., as follows:

"A number of articles . . . of the revision have the effect of giving courts-martial jurisdiction over certain offenders and offenses which, under the law of war or by statute, are also triable by military commissions, provost courts, etc. Article 15 is introduced for the purpose of making clear that in such cases a court-martial has only a concurrent jurisdiction with such war tribunals."

[32] Of course, Articles 25 and 38, at the same time that they gave protection to defendants before military commissions, also provided for the application by such tribunals of modern rules of procedure and evidence.

the other to try war crimes, and that Congress intended the Articles of War referring in terms to military commissions without exception to be applicable only to the first type.

This misconceives both the history of military commissions and the legislative history of the Articles of War. There is only one kind of military commission. It is true, as the history noted shows, that what is now called "the military commission" arose from two separate military courts instituted during the Mexican War. The first military court, called by General Scott a "military commission," was given jurisdiction in Mexico over criminal offenses of the class cognizable by civil courts in time of peace. The other military court, called a "council of war," was given jurisdiction over offenses against the laws of war. Winthrop, Military Law and Precedents (2d ed., reprinted 1920) *1298–1299. During the Civil War "the two jurisdictions of the earlier commission and council respectively ... [were] *united* in the ... war-court, for which the general designation of 'military commission' was retained as the preferable one." Winthrop, *supra*, at *1299. Since that time there has been only one type of military tribunal called the military commission, though it may exercise different kinds of jurisdiction,[33] according to the circumstances under which and purposes for which it is convened.

[33] Winthrop, speaking of military commissions at the time he was writing, 1896, says: "The offences cognizable by military commissions may thus be classed as follows: (1) Crimes and statutory offences cognizable by State or U.S. courts, and which would properly be tried by such courts if open and acting; (2) *Violations of the laws and usages of war* cognizable by military tribunals only; (3) Breaches of military orders or regulations for which offenders are not legally triable by court-martial under the Articles of war." (Emphasis added.) Winthrop, at *1309. And cf. Fairman, The Law of Martial Rule (2d ed. 1943): "Military commissions take cognizance of three categories of criminal cases: *offenses against the laws of war*, breaches of military regulations, and civil crimes which, where the ordinary courts have ceased to function, cannot be tried normally." (Emphasis added.) Fairman, 265–266. See also Davis, A Treatise on the Military Law of the United States (1915), 309–310.

The testimony of General Crowder is perhaps the most authoritative evidence of what was intended by the legislation, for he was its most active official sponsor, spending years in securing its adoption and revision. Articles 15, 25 and 38 particularly are traceable to his efforts. His concern to secure statutory recognition for military commissions was equalled by his concern that the statutory provisions giving this should not restrict their preexisting jurisdiction. He did not wish by securing additional jurisdiction, overlapping partially that of the court-martial, to surrender other. Hence Article 15. That Article had one purpose and one only. It was to make sure that the acquisition of partially concurrent jurisdiction with courts-martial should not cause loss of any other. And it was jurisdiction, not procedure, which was covered by other Articles, with which he and Congress were concerned in that Article. It discloses no purpose to deal in any way with procedure or to qualify Articles 25 and 38. And it is clear that General Crowder at all times regarded all military commissions as being governed by the identical procedure. In fact, so far as Articles 25 and 38 are concerned, this seems obvious for all types of military tribunals. The same would appear to be true of other Articles also, e. g., 24 (prohibiting compulsory self-incrimination), 26, 27, 32 (contempts), all except the last dealing with procedural matters.

Article 12 is especially significant. It empowers general courts-martial to try two classes of offenders: (1) "any person *subject to military law*," under the definition of Article 2, for any offense "made punishable by these articles"; (2) "and any other person who *by the law of war* is subject to trial *by military tribunals*," not covered by the terms of Article 2. (Emphasis added.)

Article 12 thus, in conformity with Article 15, gives the general court-martial concurrent jurisdiction of war crimes and war criminals with military commissions. Neither it nor any other Article states or indicates there are to be *two* kinds of general courts-martial for trying war crimes; yet this is the necessary result of the Court's decision, unless in the alternative that would be to imply that in exercising such jurisdiction there is only one kind of general court-martial, but there are two or more kinds of military commission, with wholly different procedures and with the result that "the commander in the field" will not be free to determine whether general court-martial or military commission shall be used as the circumstances may dictate, but must govern his choice by the kind of procedure he wishes to have employed.

The only reasonable and, I think, possible conclusion to draw from the Articles is that the Articles which are in terms applicable to military commissions are so uniformly and those applicable to both such commissions and to courts-martial when exercising jurisdiction over offenders against the laws of war likewise are uniformly applicable, and not diversely according to the person or offense being tried.

Not only the face of the Articles, but specific statements in General Crowder's testimony support this view. Thus in the portion quoted above[34] from his 1916 statement, after stating expressly the purpose of Article 15 to preserve unimpaired the military commission's jurisdiction, and to make it concurrent with that of courts-martial in so far as the two would overlap, "so that the *military commander in the field* in time of war will be at liberty to employ either form of court that happens to be convenient," he went on to say: "Both classes of courts have the same procedure," a statement so unequivocal as to leave no room for question. And his quotation from Winthrop supports his statement, namely: "Its [i. e., the military commission's] composition, consitution and procedure follow the analogy of courts-martial."

At no point in the testimony is there suggestion that there are two types of military commission, one bound by the pro-

[34] Note 31.

cedural provisions of the Articles, the other wholly free from their restraints or, as the Court strangely puts the matter, that there is only one kind of commission, but that it is bound or not bound by the Articles applicable in terms, depending upon who is being tried and for what offense; for that very difference makes the difference between one and two. The history and the discussion show conclusively that General Crowder wished to secure and Congress intended to give statutory recognition to all forms of military tribunals; to enable commanding officers in the field to use either court-martial or military commission as convenience might dictate, thus broadening to this extent the latter's jurisdiction and utility; but at the same time to preserve its full preexisting jurisdiction; and also to lay down identical provisions for governing or providing for the government of the procedure and rules of evidence of every type of military tribunal, wherever and however constituted.[35]

[35] In addition to the statements of General Crowder with relation to Article 15, set out in note 31 *supra*, see the following statements made with reference to Article 25, in 1912 at a hearing before the Committee on Military Affairs of the House: "We come now to article 25, which relates to the admissibility of depositions. . . . It will be noted further that *the application of the old article has been broadened to include military commissions, courts of inquiry, and military boards.*

"Mr. SWEET. Please explain what you mean by military commission.

"Gen. CROWDER. That is our common law of war court, and was referred to by me in a prior hearing. [The reference is to the discussion of Article 15.] This war court came into existence during the Mexican War, and was created by orders of Gen. Scott. It had jurisdiction to try all cases usually cognizable in time of peace by civil courts. Gen. Scott created another war court, called the 'council of war,' with jurisdiction to try offenses against the laws of war. The constitution, composition, and jurisdiction of these courts *have never been regulated by statute*. The council of war did not survive the Mexican War period, since which its jurisdiction has been taken over by the military commission. The military commission received express recognition in the reconstruction acts, and its *jurisdiction* has been affirmed and supported by all our courts. It was extensively employed during the Civil War period and also during the Spanish-American War. It is highly desirable that this important war court should be continued to be governed as heretofore, by the laws of war rather than by statute." S. Rep. No. 229, 63d Cong., 2d Sess., 59; cf. S. Rep. 130, 64th Cong., 1st Sess., 54–55. (Emphasis added.) See also Hearings before the Subcommittee of the Committee on Military Affairs of the

Finally, unless Congress was legislating with regard to all military commissions, Article 38, which gives the President the power to "prescribe the procedure, including modes of proof, in cases before courts-martial, courts of inquiry, military commissions, and other military tribunals," takes on a rather senseless meaning; for the President would have such power only with respect to those military commissions exercising concurrent jurisdiction with courts-martial.

All this seems so obvious, upon a mere reading of the Articles themselves and the legislative history, as not to require demonstration. And all this Congress knew, as that history shows. In the face of that showing I cannot accept the Court's highly strained construction, first, because I think it is in plain contradiction of the facts disclosed by the history of Articles 15, 25 and 38 as well as their language; and also because that construction defeats at least two of the ends General Crowder had in mind, namely, to secure statutory recognition for every form of military tribunal and to provide for them a basic uniform mode of procedure or method of providing for their procedure.

Accordingly, I think Articles 25 and 38 are applicable to this proceeding; that the provisions of the governing directive in § 16 are in direct conflict with those Articles; and for that reason the commission was invalidly constituted, was without jurisdiction, and its sentence is therefore void.

Senate on Establishment of Military Justice, 66th Cong., 1st Sess., 1182–1183.

Further evidence that procedural provisions of the Articles were intended to apply to all forms of military tribunal is given by Article 24, 10 U.S.C. § 1495, which provides against compulsory self-incrimination "before a military court, commission, court of inquiry, or board, or before an officer conducting an investigation." This article was drafted so that "The prohibition should reach all witnesses, *irrespective of the class of military tribunal* before which they appear . . ." (Emphasis added.) Comparative Print showing S. 3191 with the Present Articles of War and other Related Statutes, and Explanatory Notes, Printed for use of the Senate Committee on Military Affairs, 64th Cong., 1st Sess., 17, included in Revision of the Articles of War, Comparative Prints, Etc., 1904–1920, J. A. G. O.

V.

The Geneva Convention of 1929.

If the provisions of Articles 25 and 38 were not applicable to the proceeding by their own force as Acts of Congress, I think they would still be made applicable by virtue of the terms of the Geneva Convention of 1929, in particular Article 63. And in other respects, in my opinion, the petitioner's trial was not in accord with that treaty, namely, with Article 60.

The Court does not hold that the Geneva Convention is not binding upon the United States and no such contention has been made in this case.[36] It relies on other arguments to

[36] We are informed that Japan has not ratified the Geneva Convention. See discussion of Article 82 in the paragraphs below. We are also informed, however—and the record shows this at least as to Japan—that at the beginning of the war both the United States and Japan announced their intention to adhere to the provisions of that treaty. The force of that understanding continues, perhaps with greater reason if not effect, despite the end of hostilities. See note 40 and text.

Article 82 provides:

"The provisions of the present Convention must be respected by the High Contracting Parties under all circumstances.

"In case, in time of war, one of the belligerents is not a party to the Convention, its provisions shall nevertheless remain in force as between the belligerents who are parties thereto."

It is not clear whether the Article means that during a war, when one of the belligerents is not a party to the Convention, the provisions must nevertheless be applied by all the other belligerents to the prisoners of war not only of one another but also of the power that was not a party thereto or whether it means that they need not be applied to soldiers of the nonparticipating party who have been captured. If the latter meaning is accepted, the first paragraph would seem to contradict the second.

"Legislative history" here is of some, if little, aid. A suggested draft of a convention on war prisoners drawn up in advance of the Geneva meeting by the International Committee of the Red Cross (Actes de la Conférence Diplomatique de Genève, edited by Des Gouttes, pp. 21–34) provided in Article 92 that the provisions of the Convention "ne cesseront d'être obligatories qu'au cas où l'un des Etats belligérents participant à la Convention se trouve avoir à combattre les forces armées d'un autre Etat que n'y serait par partie et à l'égard de cet Etat seulement." See Rasmussen, Code des Prisonniers de Guerre (1931) 70. The fact that this suggested article was not included in the Geneva Convention would indicate that the nations in attendance were avoiding a decision on this problem. But I think it shows more,

show that Article 60, which provides that the protecting power shall be notified in advance of a judicial proceeding directed against a prisoner of war, and Article 63, which provides that a prisoner of war may be tried only by the same courts and according to the same procedure as in the case of persons belonging to the armed forces of the detaining power, are not properly invoked by the petitioner. Before considering the Court's view that these Articles are not applicable to this proceeding by their terms, it may be noted that on his surrender petitioner was interned in conformity with Article 9 of this Convention.

The chief argument is that Articles 60 and 63 have reference only to offenses committed by a prisoner of war while a prisoner of war and not to violations of the laws of war committed while a combatant. This conclusion is derived from the setting in which these Articles are placed. I do not agree that the context gives any support to this argument. The argument is in essence of the same type as the argument the Court employs to nullify the application of Articles 25 and 38 of the Articles of War by restricting their own broader coverage by reference to Article 2. For reasons set forth in the margin,[37] I think it equally invalid here.

---

that is, it manifests an intention not to foreclose a future holding that under the terms of the Convention a state is bound to apply the provisions to prisoners of war of nonparticipating states. And not to foreclose such a holding is to invite one. We should, in my opinion, so hold, for reasons of security to members of our own armed forces taken prisoner, if for no others.

Moreover, if this view is wrong and the Geneva Convention is not strictly binding upon the United States as a treaty, it is strong evidence of and should be held binding as representing what have become the civilized rules of international warfare. Yamashita is as much entitled to the benefit of such rules as to the benefit of a binding treaty which codifies them. See U.S. War Dept., Basic Field Manual, Rules of Land Warfare (1940), par. 5–*b*.

[37] Title III of the Convention, which comprises Articles 7 to 67, is called "Captivity." It contains § I, "Evacuation of Prisoners of War" (Articles 7–8); § II, "Prisoners-of-War Camps" (Articles 9–26); § III, "Labor of Prisoners of War" (Articles 27–34); § IV, "External Relations of Prisoners of War" (Articles 35–41); and § V, "Prisoners' Relations with the Authorities" (Ar-

Neither Article 60 nor Article 63 contains such a restriction of meaning as the Court reads into them.[38] In the ab-

ticles 42–67). Thus Title III regulates all the various incidents of a prisoner of war's life while in captivity.

Section V, with which we are immediately concerned, is divided into three chapters. Chapter 1 (Article 42) gives a prisoner of war the right to complain of his condition of captivity. Chapter 2 (Articles 43–44) gives prisoners of war the right to appoint agents to represent them. Chapter 3 is divided into three subsections and is termed "Penalties Applicable to Prisoners of War." Subsection 1 (Articles 45–53) contains various miscellaneous articles to be considered in detail later. Subsection 2 (Articles 54–59) contains provisions with respect to disciplinary punishments. And subsection 3 (Articles 60–67), which is termed "Judicial Suits," contains various provisions for protection of a prisoner's rights in judicial proceedings instituted against him.

Thus, subsection 3, which contains Articles 60 and 63, as opposed to subsection 2, of Chapter 3, is concerned not with mere problems of discipline, as is the latter, but with the more serious matters of trial leading to imprisonment or possible sentence of death; cf. Brereton, The Administration of Justice Among Prisoners of War by Military Courts (1935) 1 Proc. Australian & New Zealand Society of International Law, 143, 153. The Court, however, would have the distinction between subsection 2 and subsection 3 one between minor disciplinary action against a prisoner of war for acts committed while a prisoner and major judicial action against a prisoner of war for acts committed while a prisoner. This narrow view not only is highly strained, confusing the different situations and problems treated by the two subdivisions. It defeats the most important protections subsection 3 was intended to secure, for our own as well as for enemy captive military personnel.

At the most, there would be logic in the Court's construction if it could be said that all of Chapter 3 deals with acts committed while a prisoner of war.

[Footnote 37 continued on p. 319]

38 Article 60 pertinently is as follows: "At the opening of a judicial proceeding directed against a prisoner of war, the detaining Power shall advise the representative of the protecting Power thereof as soon as possible, and always before the date set for the opening of the trial.

"This advice shall contain the following information:

"a) Civil state and rank of prisoner;

"b) Place of sojourn or imprisonment;

"c) Specification of the [count] or counts of the indictment, giving the legal provisions applicable.

"If it is not possible to mention in that advice the court which will pass upon the matter, the date of opening the trial and the place where it will take place, this information must be furnished to the representative of the protecting Power later, as soon as possible, and at all events, at least three weeks before the opening of the trial."

Article 63 reads: "Sentence may be pronounced against a prisoner of war only by the same courts and according to the same procedure as in the case of persons belonging to the armed forces of the detaining Power."

sence of any such limitation, it would seem that they were intended to cover all judicial proceedings, whether instituted for crimes allegedly committed before capture or later. Policy supports this view. For such a construction is required for the security of our own soldiers, taken prisoner, as much as for that of prisoners we take. And the opposite one leaves prisoners of war open to any form of trial and punishment for offenses against the laws of war their captors may wish to use, while safeguarding them, to the extent of the treaty limitations, in cases of disciplinary offense. This, in many instances, would be to make the treaty strain at a gnat and swallow the camel.

The United States has complied with neither of these Articles. It did not notify the protecting power of Japan in advance of trial as Article 60 requires it to do, although the

---

[Footnote 37 continued from p. 318]

Of course, subsection 2 does, because of the very nature of its subject-matter. Disciplinary action will be taken by a captor power against prisoners of war only for acts committed by prisoners after capture.

But it is said that subsection 1 deals exclusively with acts committed by a prisoner of war after having become a prisoner, and this indicates subsection 3 is limited similarly. This ignores the fact that some of the articles in subsection 1 appear, on their face, to apply to all judicial proceedings for whatever purpose instituted. Article 46, for example, provides in part:

"Punishments other than those provided for the same acts for soldiers of the national armies may not be imposed upon prisoners of war by the military authorities and courts of the detaining Power."

This seems to refer to war crimes as well as to other offenses; for surely a country cannot punish soldiers of another army for offenses against the laws of war, when it would not punish its own soldiers for the same offenses. Similarly, Article 47 in subsection 1 appears to refer to war crimes as well as to crimes committed by a prisoner after his capture. It reads in part:

"Judicial proceedings against prisoners of war shall be conducted as rapidly as the circumstances permit; preventive imprisonment shall be limited as much as possible."

Thus, at the most, subsection 1 contains, in some of its articles, the same ambiguities and is open to the same problem that we are faced with in construing Articles 60 and 63. It cannot be said, therefore, that all of Chapter 3, and especially subsection 3, relate only to acts committed by prisoners of war after capture, for the meaning of subsection 3, in this argument, is related to the meaning of subsection 1; and subsection 1 is no more clearly restricted to punishments and proceedings in disciplinary matters than is subsection 3.

supplemental bill charges the same failure to petitioner in Item 89.[39] It is said that, although this may be true, the proceeding is not thereby invalidated. The argument is that our noncompliance merely gives Japan a right of indemnity against us and that Article 60 was not intended to give Yamashita any personal rights. I cannot agree. The treaties made by the United States are by the Constitution made the supreme law of the land. In the absence of something in the treaty indicating that its provisions were not intended to be enforced, upon breach, by more than subsequent indemnification, it is, as I conceive it, the duty of the courts of this country to insure the nation's compliance with such treaties, except in the case of political questions. This is especially true where the treaty has provisions—such as Article 60—for the protection of a man being tried for an offense the punishment for which is death; for to say that it was intended to provide for enforcement of such provisions solely by claim, after breach, of indemnity would be in many instances, especially those involving trial of nationals of a defeated nation by a conquering one, to deprive the Articles of all force. Executed men are not much aided by post-war claims for indemnity. I do not think the adhering powers' purpose was to provide only for such ineffective relief.

Finally, the Government has argued that Article 60 has no application after the actual cessation of hostilities, as there is no longer any need for an intervening power between the two belligerents. The premise is that Japan no longer needs Switzerland to intervene with the United States to protect the rights of Japanese nationals, since Japan is now in direct com-

[39] Item 89 charged the armed forces of Japan with subjecting to trial certain named and other prisoners of war "without prior notice to a representative of the protecting power, without opportunity to defend, and without counsel; denying opportunity to appeal from the sentence rendered; failing to notify the protecting power of the sentence pronounced; and executing a death sentence without communicating to the representative of the protecting power the nature and circumstances of the offense charged."

munication with this Government. This of course is in contradiction of the Government's theory, in other connections, that the war is not over and military necessity still requires use of all the power necessary for actual combat.

Furthermore the premise overlooks all the realities of the situation. Japan is a defeated power, having surrendered, if not unconditionally then under the most severe conditions. Her territory is occupied by American military forces. She is scarcely in a position to bargain with us or to assert her rights. Nor can her nationals. She no longer holds American prisoners of war.[40] Certainly, if there was the need of an independent neutral to protect her nationals during the war, there is more now. In my opinion the failure to give the notice required by Article 60 is only another instance of the commission's failure to observe the obligations of our law.

What is more important, there was no compliance with Article 63 of the same Convention. Yamashita was not tried "according to the same procedure as in the case of persons belonging to the armed forces of the detaining Power." Had one of our soldiers or officers been tried for alleged war crimes, he would have been entitled to the benefits of the Articles of War. I think that Yamashita was equally entitled to the same protection. In any event, he was entitled to their benefits under the provisions of Article 63 of the Geneva Convention. Those benefits he did not receive. Accordingly, his trial was in violation of the Convention.

VI.

The Fifth Amendment.

Wholly apart from the violation of the Articles of War and of the Geneva Convention, I am completely unable to accept or to understand the Court's ruling concerning the

[40] Nations adhere to international treaties regulating the conduct of war at least in part because of the fear of retaliation. Japan no longer has the means of retaliating.

applicability of the due process clause of the Fifth Amendment to this case. Not heretofore has it been held that any human being is beyond its universally protecting spread in the guaranty of a fair trial in the most fundamental sense. That door is dangerous to open. I will have no part in opening it. For once it is ajar, even for enemy belligerents, it can be pushed back wider for others, perhaps ultimately for all.

The Court does not declare expressly that petitioner as an enemy belligerent has no constitutional rights, a ruling I could understand but not accept. Neither does it affirm that he has some, if but little, constitutional protection. Nor does the Court defend what was done. I think the effect of what it does is in substance to deny him all such safeguards. And this is the great issue in the cause.

For it is exactly here we enter wholly untrodden ground. The safe signposts to the rear are not in the sum of protections surrounding jury trials or any other proceeding known to our law. Nor is the essence of the Fifth Amendment's elementary protection comprehended in any single one of our time-honored specific constitutional safeguards in trial, though there are some without which the words "fair trial" and all they connote become a mockery.

Apart from a tribunal concerned that the law as applied shall be an instrument of justice, albeit stern in measure to the guilt established, the heart of the security lies in two things. One is that conviction shall not rest in any essential part upon unchecked rumor, report, or the results of the prosecution's ex parte investigations, but shall stand on proven fact; the other, correlative, lies in a fair chance to defend. This embraces at the least the rights to know with reasonable clarity in advance of the trial the exact nature of the offense with which one is to be charged; to have reasonable time for preparing to meet the charge and to have the aid of counsel in doing so, as also in the trial itself; and if, during its course, one is taken by surprise, through the injection of new charges or reversal of rulings which brings forth new masses of evidence, then to have further reasonable time for meeting the unexpected shift.

So far as I know, it has not yet been held that any tribunal in our system, of whatever character, is free to receive such evidence "as *in its opinion* would be *of assistance* in proving or disproving the charge," or, again as in its opinion, "would have probative value in the mind of a reasonable man"; and, having received what in its unlimited discretion it regards as sufficient, is also free to determine what weight may be given to the evidence received without restraint.[41]

When to this fatal defect in the directive, however innocently made, are added the broad departures from the fundamentals of fair play in the proof and in the right to defend which occurred throughout the proceeding, there can be no accommodation with the due process of law which the Fifth Amendment demands.

All this the Court puts to one side with the short assertion that no question of due process under the Fifth Amendment or jurisdiction reviewable here is presented. I do not think this meets the issue, standing alone or in conjunction with the suggestion which follows that the Court gives no intimation one way or the other concerning what Fifth Amendment due process might require in other situations.

It may be appropriate to add here that, although without doubt the directive was drawn in good faith in the belief that it would expedite the trial and that enemy belligerents in

[41] There can be no limit either to the admissibility or the use of evidence if the only test to be applied concerns probative value and the only test of probative value, as the directive commanded and the commission followed out, lies "in the Commission's opinion," whether that be concerning the assistance the "evidence" tendered would give in proving or disproving the charge or as it might think would "have value in the mind of a reasonable man." Nor is it enough to establish the semblance of a constitutional right that the commission declares, in receiving the evidence, that it comes in as having only such probative value, if any, as the commission decides to award it and this is accepted as conclusive.

petitioner's position were not entitled to more, that state of mind and purpose cannot cure the nullification of basic constitutional standards which has taken place.

It is not necessary to recapitulate. The difference between the Court's view of this proceeding and my own comes down in the end to the view, on the one hand, that there is no law restrictive upon these proceedings other than whatever rules and regulations may be prescribed for their government by the executive authority or the military and, on the other hand, that the provisions of the Articles of War, of the Geneva Convention and the Fifth Amendment apply.

I cannot accept the view that anywhere in our system resides or lurks a power so unrestrained to deal with any human being through any process of trial. What military agencies or authorities may do with our enemies in battle or invasion, apart from proceedings in the nature of trial and some semblance of judicial action, is beside the point. Nor has any human being heretofore been held to be wholly beyond elementary procedural protection by the Fifth Amendment. I cannot consent to even implied departure from that great absolute.

It was a great patriot who said:

"He that would make his own liberty secure must guard even his enemy from oppression; for if he violates this duty he establishes a precedent that will reach to himself."[42]

Mr. Justice Murphy joins in this opinion.

[42] 2 The Complete Writings of Thomas Paine (edited by Foner, 1945) 588.